"*The Essential Gay Mystics* is a much-needed antidote to the vilification and persecution of gay people that is today spreading like a medieval plague. It is an unusually sensitive selection of poetry and mystical writings by gay men and women that brings to life the works of well-known poets in a way that has never been fully appreciated. It also offers us the gift of less well-known poets and mystics with the same evocative sense of what poetry and life are about."

Riane Eisler, author of *The Chalice and the Blade,*
Sacred Pleasure, and *The Partnership Way*

"A brilliant and beautiful collection. . . . Andrew Harvey has pulled together some of the most passionate and touching works in all of mystical literature, and as it happens, the authors are all gay. But the words speak for themselves: that is, the Divine directly speaks through the words in this volume, words that flowed through gay hearts and gay minds and gay love, but words which speak profoundly, eloquently, gorgeously, to the same Divine in all of us. A mystic is not one who sees God as an object, but one who is immersed in God as an atmosphere, and the works collected here are a radiant testament to that all-encompassing condition. Harvey has given us a cornucopia of mystical wisdom, tender as tears and gentle as fog, but also passionately ablaze with the relentless fire of the very Divine."

Ken Wilber, author of *A Brief History of Everything*

"The Essential Gay Mystics is an illuminating anthology whose great value lies in the double revelation that many of the world's most renowned mystics have been lovers of the same sex, and that the mystical impulse has inspired the works of a goodly number of the homoerotically inclined luminaries of the literary canon. I am especially delighted by Harvey's inclusion of lesser-known mystical writers like Lewis Thompson and Hildegard Elsberg, and by his sensitive and highly informative introductions to the writers."

Randy P. Conner, co-author of *Cassell's Encyclopedia of Queer Myth, Symbol, and Spirit*

"Once again Andrew Harvey has given us a treasure. This will be a classic and indispensable for readers in both religion and gay history. Finally we can see how the courage of homosexuality and the courage of vision are intertwined."

Susan Griffin, author of *A Chorus of Stones*

THE ESSENTIAL GAY MYSTICS

THE
ESSENTIAL
GAY MYSTICS

EDITED AND WITH
AN INTRODUCTION BY

ANDREW HARVEY

HarperSanFrancisco
An Imprint of HarperCollins*Publishers*

Permissions begin on p. 289 and are considered a continuation of the copyright page.

HarperSanFrancisco and the author, in association with The Basic Foundation, a not-for-profit
organization whose primary mission is reforestation, will facilitate the planting of two trees
for every one tree used in the manufacture of this book.

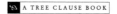 A TREE CLAUSE BOOK

HarperCollins Web Site: http://www.harpercollins.com
HarperCollins®, ♣®, HarperSanFrancisco™, and A TREE CLAUSE BOOK®
are trademarks of HarperCollins Publishers Inc.

Design by Ralph L. Fowler
Set in Adobe Garamond

Library of Congress Cataloging-in-Publication Data
The essential gay mystics / edited and with an introduction by Andrew Harvey.
Includes bibliographical references.
ISBN 0–06–251379–6 (cloth)
ISBN 0–06–251524–1 (pbk.)
1. Mysticism. 2. Gays—Religious life. I. Harvey, Andrew.
BL625.E76 1997
291.4'22'08663—dc21 96–52873

97 98 99 00 01 ❖RRDH 10 9 8 7 6 5 4 3 2 1

ACKNOWLEDGMENTS

My deepest thanks to:

Maria Todisco, whose spiritual and intellectual passion, dedication, and acumen made her the ideal assistant throughout the creation of this book. Without her superb work, the selection would have been less rich and the labor of realizing this anthology far less joyful.

Kevin Bentley, excellent editor, for his patience and skill.

Leila and Henry Luce III for their unconditional love, support, and hospitality.

Mollie Corcoran, matchless friend, whose warm and lucid loyalty illumines my life.

Kathy Granby, whose heart is a sun of tolerance and wild joy.

CONTENTS

THE ESSENTIAL GAY MYSTICS

INTRODUCTION

What is a mystic? The most beautiful short definition I have ever heard was given me by an old woman friend in Paris: "A mystic is someone who has a direct and naked perception of Godhead, beyond dogma, beyond ideas, beyond any possible formulation in words of any kind." Throughout history, men and women of all sexualities and cultures have had this "direct and naked perception of Godhead" and have been transformed by its rapture and challenge. Almost always they have chosen to interpret this perception in terms of the existing religious and cultural symbols of their time; the perception itself, however, remains timeless and essentially beyond all formal expression, born as it is from a wordless conversation between the human God and Heart, life and its Source, that is more intense and intimate than any other relationship.

In her masterpiece, *Mysticism*, Evelyn Underhill writes, "Mysticism offers us the history, as old as civilization, of a race of adventurers who have carried to its term the process of a deliberate and active return to the divine fount of things. They have surrendered themselves to the life-movement of the universe, hence have lived an intenser life than other beings can even know. . . . Therefore they witness to all that our latent spiritual consciousness, which shows itself in the 'hunger for the absolute,' can be made to mean to us if we develop it, and have in this respect an unique importance for the race."

There has never been a more important time for taking completely seriously the evidence and testimony of this "race of adventurers." Without a belief in, and the radical cultivation of, mystical consciousness and the insights into the interconnectedness of all reality in sacred joy and sacred love it alone can bring, we will not be able to develop the necessary awareness to help us solve the terrible problems that threaten our lives and the very life of the planet.

In the great chorus of witnesses to the transforming power of direct relationship with the "divine fount of things," a surprisingly large number have been gay. Surprising, because the rhetoric of nearly all the world's major religions would have you believe that spiritual insight and achievement are incompatible with homosexuality. Homophobia has stained all the Semitic religions; Mohammed fulminates against it in the Koran; the Jewish sages who composed the Pentateuch condemn it; the record of Christianity from Paul onward, despite some degree of early tolerance, has been one of overwhelming ignorance, cruelty, and persecution. Nor have Hinduism and Buddhism been exempt from this rejection of a sizable portion of the human race; many Hindu sages, both ancient and modern, have been vociferous in their condemnation of same-sex relations. In his recent *The Way to Freedom*, the Dalai Lama writes, lamentably, that "sexual misconduct . . . is a sexual act performed with an unsuitable person . . . [for men, this] also includes other males." Nor is the New Age, for all its slogans of universal love and compassion, free of homophobia. Many contemporary "masters" of every stripe are frank about their rejection of homosexuals. I myself have experienced this prejudice in agonizing and humiliating ways, and I have talked to scores of other disillusioned gay seekers from many different churches, religions, and ashrams who have discovered that the definition of universal love mouthed by their guru or priest does not include homosexuals. To those acquainted with the facts of contemporary homophobia in all its forms, and with both the blatant and the subtle ways in which religions of all kinds perpetuate it, there can be little surprise in learning that, according to Amnesty International, homosexuality is punishable by death in over forty countries, in many cases with the full sanction of religious law.

It is as a loving protest against this obscene and tragic state of affairs that I conceived of this anthology of gay mystics. I wanted everyone—most of all my gay brothers and sisters—to be fully aware that whatever the mullahs and gurus and archbishops and pseudoavatars might say, there is no record of the Divine itself in any way excluding homosexuals from the direct contact with its love, which is offered freely and forever to every sentient being.

Delving into the truth of homosexual history, one begins to understand that homophobia is a purely human and relatively recent cultural construct, and it has no basis in divine ordination. In earlier times, up until the Roman era, contemporary cultural historians such as Riane Eisler and Randy Conner make clear in their calmly groundbreaking work, reverence for the Sacred Feminine and the Divine Mother led to a reverence for all forms of life and love. Many shamans were and are homosexual; many of the worshipers of the Goddess under her various names and in her various cults all over the world—from the Mediterranean to the Near East to the Celtic parts of northern Europe—openly avowed their homosexuality and were accepted and even specially revered as priests, oracles, healers, and diviners. Homosexuals, far from being rejected, were seen as sacred—people who, by virtue of a mysterious fusion of feminine and masculine traits, participated with particular intensity in the life of the Source. The Source of Godhead is, after all, both masculine and feminine, and exists in a unity that includes but transcends both. The homosexual was thought to mirror this unity and its enigmatic fertility and power in a special way. The tribe or culture gave to him or her specific duties that were highly important and sacred, acknowledging this intimacy with divine truth and the clairvoyant help it could bring to the whole society. This wise and spacious understanding of what some cultural historians and sociologists have called the third and fourth sexes continues, however fragmentarily, in the Native American traditions in which the berdache or gay, cross-dressing shaman (known in different tribes by different names) holds an honored, essential place in the life of the tribe.

Many ancient cultures, especially those devoted to celebrating the Mother, recognized and honored the holiness of diversity. The homosexual was seen not as a figure excluded from ordinary cultural life and the embrace of the sacred but as holy as anyone else, and with a special access to sacred understanding by virtue of falling outside the "normal" categories. What we are beginning to learn about the early homosexual priests of Astarte, about the Roman "Galli" (gender-variant priests who served and worshiped the Roman mother goddess, Cybele), about the sexual lives of the early shamanic tribes of Neolithic Europe and Siberia, and about the different North American native traditions makes it clear that in past times humanity was far less divided against itself than it is now, and people were able, by worshiping the unity of all life and so the holiness of all that lives, to realize both the value *and* the potential sacred function of the homosexual in society.

The continued resistance to this information in political, academic, and religious circles of all kinds can only mean that allowing for and accepting the holiness of the homosexual choice and personality would effect a revolutionary change in existing conditions. Allowing the wisdom of the third and fourth sexes to be fully vocal in our culture would dissolve the false, rigid categorization of "male" and "female," and the male-centered, male-dominated, competitive, exploitative, war-and-power obsessed mentality that it keeps alive. The return of the Sacred Feminine that is everywhere trying to occur is, in part, a return of the *uncanny*, of those insights and aspects of ourselves that have been banished from our awareness for too long, repressed or demonized. The Mother is preparing a revolution of consciousness for the whole human race, but this revolution will be possible only when we invite the wisdom of the feminine, with its instinctual understanding of the sacredness of all life and of all true love, back into our hearts and minds in its full radical splendor.

In mystical terms, what is being prepared for humankind—if we are brave enough to embrace the challenge—is our *birth* into a wholly new unified cosmic consciousness, what many mystics call *divine childhood*: that state of naked and elemental freedom beyond all barriers, dogmas, and conventions, the final reward of long years of prayer, discipline, and ordeal in the crucible of mystical transformation. Many mystics also believe—as I do—that this birth into divine childhood under the direct inner guidance of the Father-Mother is the one remaining hope for humanity. Unless this transformation takes place on a vast, politically and economically radical scale, the race will not survive.

The main mystical traditions also agree that this birth of a new being can only take place through a long, arduous, and increasingly conscious inner marriage of the masculine and feminine within each one of us, male or female. Only such an inner marriage can give birth to the sacred, androgynous, free child of the Source that is potential in each of us. Homophobia drastically blocks this revolution of the sacred androgyne by breeding fear, self-hatred, and repression in everyone toward his or her own complex mixture of masculine and feminine traits and prevents the fully conscious and empowering fusion of different energies from taking place. Only the being who can fearlessly embrace all inner facets of his or her self—all the innner possibilities and paradoxes—who can see and know all kinds of love as being one with the love that guides and rules all things, can achieve union with the unity of God, and so be born again into the fullness of divine reality.

Such a being is free, under and in God, and this freedom and the radical energy for change to which it gives birth, the all-embracing understanding of relations in the world it engenders, profoundly threatens all forms of patriarchal power, including the power of all the churches and religious leaders and gurus. This, I believe, is the deepest reason why homophobia is still so prevalent. Many, many powers do not want this birth into sacred androgyny to take place, the birth of a self-empowered, free humanity beyond barriers and conventions. Healing the fear of sex and sexual relations threatens absolutely the domination of those whose power depends on sexual fear and rigid distinctions between the sexes.

The best weapon in this war of minds and hearts is accurate information. The testimonies of the homosexual mystics I have collected here speak far louder than any rhetoric could of the extraordinary achievements throughout history of the homosexual mystical genius. It is my hope that this anthology will offer alternative—and divine—images of what gay relationships can be. Plato's testimony to the same-sex beloved as a door to revelation; Sadi's and Attar's knowledge of the same-sex lover as being potentially a *shahid*—a witness to divine beauty; Walt Whitman's and Elsa Gidlow's fearless mystical celebration of holy sexuality as direct initiation into divine being; Edward Carpenter's beautiful argument for homosexuality's essential healing place in the creation of a new worldwide sacred democracy; all of these visions and ideals can inspire the gay seeker to go beyond the limiting and negative self-images this culture propagates—can encourage him or her to see his or her powers of love in their highest perspective. It is also my hope that this anthology will offer to heterosexuals not provocation as to who was or wasn't a same-sex lover but a vision of the noble wisdom that homosexual seeking, both in and beyond relationship, has to offer everyone, and the contribution it has made and continues to make toward healing the heart-wounds of humanity.

In collecting all of these mystical gay voices together—some of these writings are published here for the first time—I have not wanted to limit or overdefine their testimony. As you would expect, gay people have taken many different mystical paths. You will find here austere as well as flamboyant lovers of God. Some are hungry for sacred silence and radiant absence, like Pesssoa or Kobo Daishi or Christina Rossetti, while others, like Sappho or Sophia Parnok or Esenin, embrace all the suffering glory of reality. You will find here every aspect of the soul's relationship to its beloved. I have, however, emphasized one particular strand in the gay contribution to mystical understanding, because I believe it to be of fundamental importance for the future: the tantric vision of reality. This is the vision that rejects the old separations between heaven and earth, body and spirit, heart and mind, instead seeing and knowing reality as one constantly explosive dance of divine energy, love, and bliss, interconnected in all of its events and particulars.

You can see traces of this marvelous, liberating vision in Plato, in what remains to us of the works of the Greek poets and dramatists, and especially in Sappho. You can hear strains of its ecstatic music in the praise of beauty in the Persian tradition. But its full truth, challenge, and transforming power enter the human imagination with most complete force in the work of Walt Whitman. He is the pivotal figure of gay mystical history; his work gives total expression to a Mother-vision of humanity healed within and without and released from all forms of authority and power hunger into a full and normal human divinity. His eloquence and direct gnostic passion make Whitman, I believe, the equal of Dante, a heart brother of Rumi, and a pioneer more prescient and modern than either.

Whitman's vision—born out of a series of overwhelming mystical experiences in his thirties and out of his own abandonment of sexual fear and shame and consequent discovery of the body's inherent holiness—calls for an end to all patriarchal distinctions between the sacred and the profane. Initiated directly as he was into the Source of love, Whitman saw and felt and knew that body, soul, heart, and mind are not separate but one living, divine being, that humanity and nature are interfused at every level in the heart of truth and love, and that the energy of true and deep sexual love is one with that energy that is birthing all the universes. Whitman also saw and felt and knew that allowing such a vast vision to penetrate all levels of one's being brings forth an almost infinite capacity for divine joy and compassionate action. He saw that this joy and its action were the sweetest secrets of every human identity, *and* key to the flowering of a wholly new humanity, released from all fears and confining powers into the democratic plenitude planned from eternity in the mind of God.

As Edward Carpenter, Whitman's brave English disciple, wrote, "We are arriving at one of the most fruitful and important turning-points in the history of the race. The Self is entering into relation with the body. For, that the individual should conceive and know himself, not as a toy and chance-product of his own bodily heredity, but as identified and continuous with the Eternal Self of which his body is a manifestation, is indeed to begin a new life and to enter a hitherto undreamed world of possibilities." Carpenter's whole work makes clear, as Whitman's had done before him, that "entering this undreamed world of possibilities" means making a rubble of all old divisions and certainties, and makes possible an alchemical, tantric transformation at every level of the being; the gates between "soul" and "body," which the patriarchal and homophobic religions keep closed, are flung wide open so the soul's pure fire can penetrate and illuminate and transfigure the body, and the body can taste and live resurrection and freedom in time and on the earth. Neither Whitman nor Carpenter underestimated the cost and difficulty of such a transformation. As Carpenter wrote, "Whilst [this transformation is] the greatest and most wonderful, it is also the most difficult in Man's evolution for him to effect. It may roughly be said that the whole of the civilisation-period in Man's history is the preparation for it."

We are living in the time of this greatest, most wonderful, most difficult transformation, and as all seekers, gay and straight, try to heal the wounds that patriarchal religions and mystical transmission systems have inflicted on us all in the name of God, the fearless, ecstatic witness of gay visionaries such as Whitman and Carpenter and successors like D. H. Lawrence, Elsa Gidlow, and Audre Lorde will increasingly be seen as crucial. Many modern seekers—I am one of them—now believe that one of the most important aspects of this difficult transformation will be a return on a global scale to the practice of tantric sexuality. When two beings, of whatever sexes, are in harmony on every level—mental, emotional, spiritual, and physical—and living in tenderness, respect, fidelity, and rigorous honesty with each other, their lovemaking becomes an experience and an invocation of divine passion and divine energy; both are initiated mutually and simultaneously into the dance of the universe in the ground of ordinary life. Slowly, if they persist in meeting the sometimes extreme demands of such a relationship, a transformation of great, intense beauty takes place in all of their senses, faculties, powers, and creative energies. They become two parts of a single irreducibly powerful and empowered sacred unit, guided by each other and by the Divine that manifests continually in and around them—in dreams and visions, in sacred lights that illumine their lovemaking, in revelations their intimacy continually brings to birth. Whitman knew and lived such tantric relationship, knew its radical power, and knew too how it could be the base of the true sacred democracy of the Mother—because its very nature frees it from external authority and the need for any outside mediation, because it fuses divine and human things together in an experience of continuing, explosive, sacred joy. It is this radical tantric path of relationship that the Mother is now opening up to the whole human race as a way of progressing into self-empowerment and as a way of making ordinary life divine and ending the deformations of patriarchal power. A humanity that has been sexually healed and released into full human divinity will not want to destroy nature or exploit the poor. In the new world that this understanding can make possible, gay visionaries will be passionate and informed guides.

Listen to Whitman:

O we can wait no longer
We too take ship O soul,
Joyous we too launch out on trackless seas,
Fearless for unknown shores on waves of ecstasy to sail,
Amid the wafting winds (thou pressing me to thee, I thee to me,
    O soul)
Caroling free, singing our song of God.

POSTSCRIPT

There is an obvious difficulty one encounters in assembling an anthology such as this: whom can one reasonably "claim" as lovers of their own sex? Social constructionism maintains that terms such as "gay" and "gayness" are imaginary and recent—social constructs. This argument is buttressed by an extremely narrow definition of "gay." As Randy Conner wryly put it in the introduction to his pioneering work *Blossom of Bone: Reclaiming the Connection Between Homoeroticism and the Sacred*, constructionists insist that "gay" basically refers to an individual (often male, traditionally masculine, and middle class) who, living in the West in the late twentieth century, self-consciously *chooses* to identify himself as one who engages in homosexual behavior and participates in a related urban, subcultural lifestyle. As Conner makes clear, such a narrow view entails denying many things: that there was, for example, any cultural or historical interaction at all between gender-variant people in the ancient or pre-modern world.

How can such a claim stand up to the implications of modern cross-cultural research? Moreover, the constructionists' insistence that concepts are dependent on language, and that terms precede ideas, is highly questionable. While defining an activity or way of life might make for a greater degree of self-awareness (and social pride and legal protection), this does not mean that the activity and conscious identity did not occur before in many different settings.

Conner and others have gone a long way toward showing that many of the world's peoples have held that homoerotic inclination and gender variance are traits bestowed before birth by a divine power or powers. As Conner says, "Many peoples have believed gender variance and homoerotic inclination to be essential qualities and not culturally constructed behaviors—whether we like it or not. In spite of various forces of obscuration, awareness of the linking between male gender variance, homoeroticism, and sacred role or function has repeatedly surfaced across cultures and epochs. Those embodying the domain, while dwelling in the shadows, the wings, or the spaces between the texts, have not been entirely erased."

A great body of cultural and historical evidence suggests that not only has same-sex desire always existed (and been known to exist), but that in many cultures those who followed its inspiration were seen as connected in particular and luminous ways to the sacred. Such evidence leads us—or should lead us—to expand our vision of what gayness has been and could be. It is this larger human continuity and tradition that I have chosen to celebrate here.

Another difficulty I have had to confront was the dearth of *identifiable* lesbian mystical literature. This does not, of course, indicate a lack of lesbian mystics; rather, it shows that they suffered the same fate as so many other women—oppression and silencing. I am convinced that many of the most distinguished women Christian mystics of the thirteenth and fourteenth centuries may well have been wholly or partly lesbian, but there is little evidence to warrant including, as I longed to do, either a Mechthild of Magdeburg or a Hildegard of Bingen. I have tried to right this imbalance by beginning with a great lesbian voice, that of Sappho, and ending with four great modern lesbian mystics: Marguerite Yourcenar, Elsa Gidlow, Audre Lorde, and Hildegard Elsberg. Because of space limitations, I have limited this anthology to deceased writers; I might easily have included contemporary lesbian seekers such as Susan Griffin, Judy Grahn, and Dorothy

Walters, among many others, whose work I honor and from whom I have learned.

Yet another difficulty I have had to face is the thick silence surrounding the probable homosexuality of many mystics writing within conventional religious structures. How many of the great Christian monks of all Christian denominations must have been homosexual, and how little—even given the efforts of historians such as John Boswell—we will ever know about them. The same silence confronts us in the other major traditions. Fear, embarrassment, and the tendency, especially in the Asiatic traditions, to idealize the Master of either sex as a sexless being beyond desire have obscured, probably forever, the power of many gay voices.

I have chosen to include in this anthology some artists and writers (Oscar Wilde, Jean Cocteau, and Colette, for instance) who would not normally be thought of as mystics. This was partly because I realized—like all explorers of gay history—that many gay people in all cultures, repelled by the homophobia of the existing religions, have diverted their religious passions into art. Also, as a poet and novelist myself, I am aware of how so-called secular art can be everywhere informed by spiritual truth and insight and can be one of the most effective vehicles for its secret propagation. Colette was once described to me by a well-read Japanese Zen abbot as "the greatest Zen writer of the century," and Claudel, in a wild but moving moment of enthusiasm, called Rimbaud "the greatest mystic seer of France, greater than any of the official mystics of the Church." It is also my belief that our current definitions of the word *mystic* are too specialized, elitist, and narrow; everyone is potentially a mystic, given the right training, dedication, and environment. The mystical truth is the truth of every being. When we look at the last two hundred years of the prevailing materialistic culture, we often find the greatest mystical insights in the work of artists of all kinds, rather than in the dreary lucubrations of theologians or the repetitive formulas of those mystics who stick too close to the conventions of their own tradition.

Bringing together *The Essential Gay Mystics* has been one of the richest joys of my life. I can remember myself as a young gay man hungering for images of gayness more noble and inspiring than those I was given by either straight or contemporary gay culture—images that would transcend the stereotypes of tortured aesthete, queen, leather-boy, or promiscuous sexual rebel. Slowly, in the course of long, often bewildering and painful personal seeking, I discovered them both in my own inner consciousness and in the writings of the people whose work I am honored to present here. I feel them now as living and invigorating companions on my journey into entire self-acceptance and fully divine human awareness and compassion. May these marvelous *adventurers* and their wisdom come to live with—and in—you now.

CHAPTER ONE

SANCTUARY OF LOVE

THE GREEK TRADITIONS

SAPPHO

Sappho (ca. 610–580 B.C.) is the earliest known woman writer in the central Western tradition. The Greeks called her simply "the poetess," the female counterpart of Homer, and compatriots admired her so deeply that her portrait graced the coins of her native Lesbos (from which the word *lesbian* is derived). To lesbians around the world, Sappho is the archetypal ideal and spiritual mother. Her work radiates a vision of the sacredness of love, a belief that the divine revels in our passion for joy and beauty and manifests itself in and through it.

Leave Crete,
Aphrodite,
and come to this
sacred place
encircled by apple trees,
fragrant with offered smoke.

Here, cold springs
sing softly
amid the branches;
the ground is shady with roses;
from trembling young leaves,
a deep drowsiness pours.

In the meadow,
horses are cropping
the wildflowers of spring,
scented fennel
blows on the breeze.

In this place, Lady of Cyprus, pour
the nectar that honors you
into our cups,
gold, and raised up for drinking.

I confess

I love that
which caresses
me. I believe

Love has his
share in the
Sun's brilliance
and virtue

To an army wife, in Sardis:

Some say a cavalry corps,
some infantry, some, again,
will maintain that the swift oars

of our fleet are the finest
sight on dark earth; but I say
that whatever one loves, is.

This is easily proved: did
not Helen—she who had scanned
the flower of the world's manhood—

choose as first among men one
who laid Troy's honor in ruin?
Warped to his will, forgetting

love due her own blood, her own
child, she wandered far with him.
So Anactoria, although you

being far away forget us,
the dear sound of your footstep
and light glancing in your eyes

would move me more than glitter
of Lydian horse or armored
tread of mainland infantry.

PRAYER TO MY LADY OF PAPHOS

Dapple-throned Aphrodite,
eternal daughter of God,
snare-knitter! Don't, I beg you,

cow my heart with grief! Come,
as once when you heard my far-
off cry and, listening, stepped

from your father's house to your
gold car, to yoke the pair whose
beautiful thick-feathered wings

oaring down mid-air from heaven
carried you to light swiftly
on dark earth; then, blissful one,

smiling your immortal smile
you asked, What ailed me now that
made me call you again? What

was it that my distracted
heart most wanted? "Whom has
Persuasion to bring round now

"to your love? Who, Sappho, is
unfair to you? For, let her
run, she will soon run after;

"if she won't accept gifts, she
will one day give them; and if

she won't love you—she soon will
"love, although unwillingly . . . "
If ever—come now! Relieve
this intolerable pain!

What my heart most hopes will
happen, make happen; you yourself join forces on my side!

PINDAR

Pindar (ca. 510–430 B.C.) is considered, with Sappho, to be the greatest of
Greek lyric poets. His work was so revered it is said that when Alexander
the Great razed Thebes, Pindar's hometown, he left only the poet's house
standing. His surviving odes all praise the physical and moral beauty of
athletes who were winners of the Olympic and other Panhellenic games
and are suffused by the light of what Goethe called "the noble sublimity
of the true and holy lover."

Wide is the strength of wealth
when mixed with stainless virtue
and, granted of destiny, mortal man leads it home,
most dear companion.
Arkesilas, God's destiny is on you;
from the towering stairs

of your renowned life
you approach it in glory
by Kastor's favor, of the golden chariot,
who, after storm of winter, makes
your hearth shine in the blessed quiet.

Even power granted of God
is carried the better for wisdom.
You walk in righteousness, and great prosperity is unceasing about
    you,
twice over: since you are king
of great cities,
for this high privilege
is a shining heritage in your house,
which matches your own temper;
and blessed are you even now, in that,
winning from the famed Pythiad success with horses, your prayer's
    end,
you are given this festal choir of men,
delight of Apollo; whereby, forget not,
as you are sung at Kyrene's sweet garden of Aphrodite,
to ascribe all cause to God
and love Karrhotos beyond all companions. . . .

From Pythia 5

Listen! It is the field of Aphrodite
with the fluttering eyes or the Graces
we labor now. We approach the templed
centerstone of the thunderous earth.
There stands built for the glory of Emmenos' children
and Akragas of the river, and for Xenokrates,
a treasure house of song
for victory at Pytho in Apollo's
glen, with its burden of gold.

Neither rain driven from afar on the storm,
nor the merciless armies

of the crying cloud, no wind shall sweep it, caught
and stricken with the blown debris into the corners
of the sea. The front shines in the clear air,
Thrasyboulos, on your father announcing
for you and yours the pride
of a chariot victory in the folds of Krisa—
a tale to run on the lips of men.

You, keeping Victory erect beside your right hand,
bring home the meaning
of the things men say once on the mountain Chiron,
Philyra's son, urged on strong Peleiades
left in his care: *First of all gods, honor*
the deep-voiced lord of the lightning and thunderstroke,
Zeus Kronides;
next, through all their destiny never deprive
your parents of such reverence even as this . . .

Of men living now, Thrasyboulos
comes beyond others to the mark in his father's eyes,
and visits his father's brother with fame complete.
He carries wealth with discretion.
The blossom of youth he gathers is nothing violent,
but wise in the devious ways of the Muses.
To you Poseidon, shaker of the earth, lord
of the mastering of horses, he comes, with mind to please you.
Also his heart, that is gentle
in the mixing of friends,
passes for sweetness the riddled work of the bees.

   From Pythia 6

EMPEDOCLES

Empedocles (ca. 495–435 B.C.) was one of the most brilliant and original
of the pre-Socratic Greek thinkers. Philosopher, mystic, magician, and
open lover of beautiful young men (one of whose names, Pausanias, has

come down to us), Empedocles believed, like some Hindu mystics, that the universe arises perpetually out of a wild, complex "dance" of opposites. Born into a rich family in Acragas, Sicily, Empedocles is said to have taken his mystic search so seriously that he died by jumping into the crater of Mount Etna to become one with the gods.

LOVE AND STRIFE

I will tell a twofold story.
At one time they grew to be one alone from being many,
and at another they grew apart again to be many from being one.
Double is the generation of mortal things, double their passing away:
one is born and destroyed by the congregation of everything,
the other is nurtured and flies apart as they grow apart again.
And these never cease their continual change,
now coming together by Love all into one,
now again all being carried apart by the hatred of Strife.
Thus insofar as they have learned to become one from many
and again become many as the one grows apart,
to that extent they come into being and have no lasting life;
but insofar as they never cease their continual change,
to that extent they exist forever, unmoving in a circle.
But come, hear my words; for learning enlarges the mind.
As I said before when I revealed the limits of my words,
I will tell a twofold story.
At one time they grew to be one alone from being many,
and at another they grew apart again to be many from being one—
fire and water and earth and the endless height of air,
and cursed Strife apart from them, balanced in every way,
and Love among them, equal in length and breadth.
Her you must regard with your mind: do not sit staring with your eyes.
She is thought to be innate also in the limbs of mortals,
by whom they think thoughts of love and perform deeds of union,
calling her Joy by name and Aphrodite,
whom no one has seen whirling among them—
no mortal man. Listen to the course of my argument, which does not
deceive:

these are all equal and of the same age,
but they hold different offices and each has its own character;
and in turn they come to power as time revolves.
And in addition to them nothing comes into being or ceases.
For if they were continually being destroyed they would no longer
  exist.
And what could increase this universe? and whence might it come?
And where indeed might it perish, since nothing is empty of them?
But these themselves exist, and passing through one another
they become different at different times—and are ever and always
  the same.

AESCHYLUS

Aeschylus (525–456 B.C.) is generally considered to be the father of Greek tragedy. One of the greatest losses to world gay literature is that of his play *Myrmidons*, which dealt with the passion of Achilles and Patroclus. Fragments of this lost masterpiece survive in the writings of Antaeus, a second-century A.D. Alexandrian; in one, Achilles mourns his dead lover, speaking of their "many kisses" and the "holy union of their thighs." In his other great plays, *Seven Against Thebes, The Suppliant Maidens, Prometheus Bound,* and *The Theban Trilogy,* Aeschylus presents us with his dark and passionate mystic vision of the power of fate and the inscrutability, sometimes even cruelty, of divine law. In *Prometheus Bound* (excerpted here), Aeschylus seems to be imagining a new divine humanity, released from the terrors of slavery to the old gods into its own authentic truth.

PROMETHEUS:
Bright light, swift-winged winds, springs of the rivers, numberless
laughter of the sea's waves
earth, mother of all,
and the all-seeing circle of the sun:
I call upon you to see what I, a God, suffer

at the hands of Gods—
see with what kind of torture
worn down I shall wrestle ten thousand
years of time—
such is the despiteful bond that the Prince
has devised against me, the new Prince
of the Blessed Ones. Oh woe is me!
I groan for the present sorrow,
I groan for the sorrow to come, I groan
questioning when there shall come a time
when He shall ordain a limit to my sufferings.
What am I saying? I have known all before,
all that shall be, and clearly known; to me,
nothing that hurts shall come with a new face.
So must I bear, as lightly as I can,
the destiny that fate has given me;
for I know well against necessity,
against its strength, no one can fight and win. . . .

Yet shall this Zeus, for all his pride of heart,
be humble yet: such is the match he plans,
a marriage that shall drive him from his power
and from his throne, out of the sight of all.
So shall at last the final consummation
be brought about of Father Kronos' curse
which he, driven from his ancient throne, invoked
against the son deposing him: no one
of all the Gods save I alone can tell
a way to escape this mischief: I alone
know it and how. So let him confidently
sit on his throne and trust his heavenly thunder
and brandish in his hand his fiery bolt.
Nothing shall all of this avail against
a fall intolerable, a dishonored end.
So strong a wrestler Zeus is now equipping
against himself, a monster hard to fight.
This enemy shall find a plan to best

the thunderbolt, a thunderclap to best
the thunderclap of Zeus: and he shall shiver
Poseidon's trident, curse of sea and land.
So, in his crashing fall shall Zeus discover
how different are rule and slavery.

From Prometheus Bound

SOPHOCLES

Sophocles was born at Colonus, just outside Athens, in 496 B.C. and lived ninety years. He is known to have loved many young men and to have written a *Niobe* (now lost), which was also known as the *Paiderastria* ("Love of Youths"). His long life spanned the rise and fall of the Athenian empire; he was a friend of Pericles and held several public offices. One of the greatest of all the world's dramatists, he wrote over a hundred plays and won the first prize in the drama contests at Athens twenty-four times. Even the darkest of his plays, *Oedipus the King* and *Antigone,* are pervaded by a religious serenity and a fundamental mysterious faith in the holiness of the human experience.

[CHORUS:]
Numberless wonders
terrible wonders walk the world but none match for man—
that great wonder crossing the heaving gray sea,
driven on by the blasts of winter
on through breakers crashing left and right,
holds his steady course
and the oldest of the gods he wears away—
the Earth, the immortal, the inexhaustible—
as his plows go back and forth, year in, year out
with the breed of stallions turning up the furrows.

And the blithe, light-headed race of birds he snares,
the tribes of savage beasts, the life that swarms the depths—

with one fling of his nets
woven and coiled tight, he takes them all,
man the skilled, the brilliant!
He conquers all, taming with his techniques
the prey that roams the cliffs and wild lairs,
training the stallion, clamping the yoke across
his shaggy neck, and the tireless mountain bull.

And speech and thought, quick as the wind
and the mood and mind for law that rules the city—
all these he has taught himself
and shelter from the arrows of the frost
when there's rough lodging under the cold clear sky
and the shafts of lashing rain—
ready, resourceful man!
Never without resources
never an impasse as he marches on the future—
only Death, from Death alone he will find no rescue
but from desperate plagues he has plotted his escapes.

Man the master, ingenious past all measure
past all dreams, the skills within his grasp—
he forges on, now to destruction
now again to greatness. When he weaves in
the laws of the land, and the justice of the gods
that binds his oaths together
he and his city rise high—
but the city casts out
that man who weds himself to inhumanity
thanks to reckless daring. Never share my hearth
never think my thoughts, whoever does such things.

    From Antigone

[CHORUS:]
Wisdom is by far the greatest part of joy,
and reverence toward the gods must be safeguarded.
The mighty words of the proud are paid in full

with mighty blows of fate, and at long last
those blows will teach us wisdom.

From Antigone

THE DEATH OF OEDIPUS

MESSENGER:
My countrymen,
the quickest way to tell you is this:
Oedipus is gone.
But what took place—it's not short in the telling,
not short in all that really happened there . . .

You know how he left this spot, of course,
you saw him go. No friend to lead the way,
he led us all himself.

Now, when he reached
the steep descent, the threshold rooted deep
in the earth by the great brazen steps, he stopped . . .
pausing at one of the many branching paths there,
near the bowl scooped out in the smooth stone
where the pact sealed by Theseus and Perithous
is cut in stone forever. He took his stand midway
between that bowl and the Rock of Thoricus,
the hollow wild-pear and the marble tomb,
and sat him down and loosed his filthy rags.
Then he called for his daughters, commanded them
to bring water from some running spring, water
to bathe himself and pour the last libations.
And they climbed the gentle rise, just in sight,
the Hill of Demeter, goddess of new green life,
and soon returned with what their father ordered,
bathed him in holy water, decked his body out
in shining linen, the custom for the dead.

But when he was content that all was done,
and of all he wanted, nothing more was needed,
nothing left to do—all at once

Zeus of the Underworld thundered from the depths,
and the young girls shuddered in horror at the sound,
they fell at their father's knees, choked with tears,
they couldn't stop, beating their breasts, wailing,
endless . . . but when he heard their sharp piercing cry,
he flung his arms around them both and said, "My children,
this is the day that ends your father's life.
All that I was on earth is gone:
no longer will you bear the heavy burden
of caring for your father. It was hard, I know,
my children, but one word alone repays you
for the labor of your lives—love, my children.
You had love from me as from no other man alive,
and now you must live without me all your days to come."

It was unbearable. Locked in each other's arms
they heaved and sobbed, all three as one.
But when they'd made an end of grief
and the long wail rose up no more,
a deep silence fell . . . and suddenly,
a voice, someone crying out to him, startling,
terrifying, the hair on our heads bristled—
it was calling for him, over and over,
echoing all around us now—it was some god!
"You, you there, Oedipus—what are we waiting for?
You hold us back too long! We must move on, move on!"

Then, knowing it was the god that called him on,
he asked for Theseus, and when our king came up
beside him, Oedipus spoke out, "Oh dear friend,
give my children the binding pledge of your right hand,
and children, give him yours. And swear that you
will never forsake them, not if you can help it—
you will do all within your power, your kindness,
all that is best for them—now and always."

And Theseus, noble man, not giving way to grief,
swore to carry out the wishes of his friend.
And soon as he made that pledge, Oedipus

reached out at once with his blind hands,
feeling for his children, saying, "Oh my children,
now you must be brave, noble in spirit,
you must leave this place behind,
and never ask to see what law forbids
or hear the secret voices none may hear.
Now go—quickly. Only the appointed one,
Theseus, let him stand beside me:
he must see this mystery,
he must witness what will happen now."

That was the last we heard him say, all of us
clustering there, and as we followed the daughters
sobbing, streaming ears . . . moving away we turned
in a moment, looked back, and Oedipus—
we couldn't see the man—he was gone—nowhere!
And the king, alone, shielding his eyes,
both hands spread out against his face as if—
some terrible wonder flashed before his eyes and he,
he could not bear to look. And then, quickly,
we see him bow and kiss the ground and stretch
his arms to the skies, salute the gods of Olympus
and the powers of the Earth in one great prayer,
binding both together.

From Oedipus at Colonus

EURIPIDES

Euripides (484–406 B.C.) was born in Athens into a distinguished family.
He seems, however, to have avoided all public duties to devote himself to
the practice of drama. With Sophocles and Aeschylus, he is the greatest of
the ancient Greek dramatists. Like his two predecessors, he was homosexual and wrote at least one gay play, *Chryssipus* (now lost). At the end of
his life, Euripides became the lover of Agathon, one of the other great
contemporary playwrights. In his *Erotics,* Plutarch describes this love af-

fair between two of the greatest poets of their age as the archetype, the noblest and most creative example, of masculine same-sex love. Euripides' greatest plays—*Medea, Helen, The Bacchae*—all show a complex, riddling, and sometimes dark view of divine power and presence, and stress the necessity and difficulty of living in humble holiness of heart.

[CHORUS:]
O for long nights of worship, gay
With the pale gleam of dancing feet,
With head tossed high to the dewy air—
Pleasure mysterious and sweet!
O for the joy of a fawn at play
In the fragrant meadow's green delight,
Who has leapt out free from the woven snare,
Away from the terror of chase and flight,
And the huntsman's shout, and the straining pack,
And skims the sand by the river's brim
With the speed of wind in each aching limb,
To the blessed lonely forest where
The soil's unmarked by a human track,
And leaves hang thick and the shades are dim.

[Refrain:]
What prayer should we call wise?
What gift of Heaven should man
Count a more noble prize,
A prayer more prudent, than
To stretch a conquering arm
Over the fallen crest
Of those who wished us harm?
And what is noble every heart loves best.

[Antistrophe:]
Slow, yet unfailing, move the Powers
Of heaven with the moving hours.
When mind runs mad, dishonors God,
And worships self and senseless pride,

Then Law eternal wields the rod.
Still Heaven hunts down the impious man,
Though divine subtlety may hide
Time's creeping foot. No mortal ought
To challenge Time—to overbear
Custom in act, or age in thought.
All men, at little cost, may share
The blessing of a pious creed;
Truths more than mortal, which began
In the beginning, and belong
To very nature—these indeed
Reign in our world, are fixed and strong . . .

Blest is the man who cheats the stormy sea
And safely moors beside the sheltering quay;
So, blest is he who triumphs over trial.
One man, by various means, in wealth or strength
Outdoes his neighbor; hope in a thousand hearts
Colors a thousand different dreams; at length
Some find a dear fulfillment, some denial.
But this I say,
That he who best
Enjoys each passing day
Is truly blest. . . .

[CHORUS:]
See! With contempt of right, with a reckless rage
To combat your and your mother's mysteries, Bacchus,
With maniac fury out Pentheus goes, stark mad,
For a trial of strength against your invincible arm!
His proud purposes death shall discipline.
He who unquestioning gives the gods their due,
And knows that his days are as dust, shall live untouched.
I have no wish to grudge the wise their wisdom;
But the joys I seek are greater, outshine all others,
And lead our life to goodness and loveliness:
The joy of the holy heart

That night and day is bent to honor the gods
And disown all custom that breaks the bounds of right . . .

From The Bacchae

PLATO

▼

Plato (ca. 428–348 B.C.) came from a rich and powerful family; he had a
wide acquaintance with the prominent men of his time, traveled extensively abroad, and at the age of forty founded the Academy and directed
its affairs until his death. It is impossible to exaggerate the influence of his
thought on the history of Western philosophy and mystical thought.
Socrates was Plato's master, his spiritual hero, and in his writings the
mouthpiece through which he expressed many of his major ideas. Ironic
and uncompromising, Socrates was also the first avowedly homosexual
"mystic"; he infuriated the respectable and was put to death, after a
rigged trial, by being forced to drink hemlock. Plato was himself homosexual and in his greatest and most influential work developed a mystical
vision of male love as leading to an epiphany of the Absolute.

SOCRATES' DEFENSE

Suppose, then, that you acquit me, and pay no attention to Anytus,
who has said that either I should not have appeared before this court
at all, or, since I have appeared here, I must be put to death, because
if I once escaped your sons would all immediately become utterly de-
moralized by putting the teaching of Socrates into practice. Suppose
that, in view of this, you said to me, Socrates, on this occasion we shall
disregard Anytus and acquit you, but only on one condition, that you
give up spending your time on this quest and stop philosophizing. If
we catch you going on in the same way, you shall be put to death.

Well, supposing, as I said, that you should offer to acquit me on
these terms, I should reply, Gentlemen, I am your very grateful and
devoted servant, but I owe a greater obedience to God than to you,
and so long as I draw breath and have my faculties, I shall never stop

practicing philosophy and exhorting you and elucidating the truth for everyone that I meet. I shall go on saying, in my usual way, My very good friend, you are an Athenian and belong to a city which is the greatest and most famous in the world for its wisdom and strength. Are you not ashamed that you give your attention to acquiring as much money as possible, and similarly with reputation and honor, and give no attention or thought to truth and understanding and the perfection of your soul?

And if any of you disputes this and professes to care about these things, I shall not at once let him go or leave him. No, I shall question him and examine him and test him; and if it appears that in spite of his profession he has made no real progress toward goodness, I shall reprove him for neglecting what is of supreme importance, and giving his attention to trivialities. I shall do this to everyone that I meet, young or old, foreigner or fellow citizen, but especially to you, my fellow citizens, inasmuch as you are closer to me in kinship. This, I do assure you, is what my God commands, and it is my belief that no greater good has ever befallen you in this city than my service to my God. For I spend all my time going about trying to persuade you, young and old, to make your first and chief concern not for your bodies nor for your possessions, but for the highest welfare of your souls, proclaiming as I go, Wealth does not bring goodness, but goodness brings wealth and every other blessing, both to the individual and to the state.

From the Apology

THE GREAT BLESSING

I know not . . . any greater blessing to a young man beginning life than a virtuous lover, or to the lover than a beloved youth. For the principle which ought to be the guide of men who nobly live—that principle, I say, neither kindred, nor honor, nor wealth, nor any other motive is able to implant so well as love. Of what am I speaking? Of the sense of honor and dishonor, without which neither states nor individuals ever do any good or great work. And I say that a lover who is detected in doing any dishonorable act, or submitting, through cowardice, when any dishonor is done to him by another, will be more pained at being detected by his beloved than at being seen by his father, or by his companions, or by any one else. The beloved, too, when he is seen in any disgraceful situation, has the same feeling about his lover. And if there were only some way of contriving that a state or an army should be made up of lovers and their loves, they would be the very best governors of their own city, abstaining from all dishonor; and emulating one another in honor; and when fighting at one another's side, although a mere handful, they would overcome the world. For what lover would not choose rather to be seen by all mankind than by his beloved, either when abandoning his post, or throwing away his arms? He would be ready to die a thousand deaths rather than endure this. Or who would desert his beloved or fail him in the hour of danger? The veriest coward would become an inspired hero, equal to the bravest, at such a time; love would inspire him. That courage which, as Homer says, the god breathes into the soul of heroes, love of his own nature inspires into the lover. . . .

In a like manner the followers of Apollo and of every other god, walking in the ways of their god, seek a love who is to be like their god, and when they have found him, they themselves imitate their god, and persuade their love to do the same, and bring him into harmony with the form and ways of the god as far as they can; for they have no feelings of envy or jealousy toward their beloved, but they do their utmost to create in him the greatest likeness of themselves and the god whom they honor. Thus fair and blissful to the beloved when he is taken, is the desire of the inspired lover, and the initiation of which I speak into the mysteries of true love, if their purpose is effected.

From the Phaedrus

ARISTOPHANES' SPEECH

Well then, Eryximachus, Aristophanes began, I propose, as you suggested, to take quite a different line from you and Pausanias. I am convinced that mankind has never had any conception of the power of Love, for if we had known him as he really is, surely we should have raised the mightiest temples and altars, and offered the most splendid sacrifices, in his honor, and not—as in fact we do—have utterly neglected him. Yet he of all the gods has the best title to our service, for he, more than all the rest, is the friend of man; he is our great ally, and it is he that cures us of those ills whose relief opens the way to man's highest happiness. And so, gentlemen, I will do my best to acquaint you with the power of Love, and you in your turn shall pass the lesson on.

First of all I must explain the real nature of man, and the change which it has undergone—for in the beginning we were nothing like we are now. For one thing, the race was divided into three; that is to say, besides the two sexes, male and female, which we have at present, there was a third which partook of the nature of both, and for which we still have a name, though the creature itself is forgotten. For though "hermaphrodite" is only used nowadays as a term of contempt, there really was a man-woman in those days, a being which was half male and half female.

And secondly, gentlemen, each of these beings was globular in shape, with rounded back and sides, four arms and four legs, and two faces, both the same, on a cylindrical neck, and one head, with one face one side and one the other, and four ears, and two lots of privates, and all the other parts to match. They walked erect, as we do ourselves, backward or forward, whichever they pleased, but when they broke into a run they simply stuck their legs straight out and went whirling round and round like a clown turning cartwheels. And since they had eight legs, if you count their arms as well, you can imagine that they went bowling along at a pretty good speed.

The three sexes, I may say, arose as follows. The males were descended from the Sun, the females from the Earth, and the hermaphrodites from the Moon, which partakes of either sex, and they were round and they *went* round, because they took after their parents. And such, gentlemen, were their strength and energy, and such their arrogance, that they actually tried—like Ephialtes and Otus in Homer—to scale the heights of heaven and set upon the gods.

At this Zeus took counsel with the other gods as to what was to be done. They found themselves in rather an awkward position; they didn't want to blast them out of existence with thunderbolts as they did the giants, because that would be saying good-by to all their offerings and devotions, but at the same time they couldn't let them get altogether out of hand. At last, however, after racking his brains, Zeus offered a solution.

I think I can see my way, he said, to put an end to this disturbance by weakening these people without destroying them. What I propose to do is to cut them all in half, thus killing two birds with one stone, for each one will be only half as strong, and there'll be twice as many of them, which will suit us very nicely. They can walk about, upright, on their two legs, and if, said Zeus, I have any more trouble with them, I shall split them up again, and they'll have to hop about on one.

So saying, he cut them all in half just as you or I might chop up sorb apples for pickling, or slice an egg with a hair. And as each half was ready he told Apollo to turn its face, with the half-neck that was left, toward the side that was cut away—thinking that the sight of such a gash might frighten it into keeping quiet—and then to heal the whole thing up. So Apollo turned their faces back to front, and, pulling in the skin all the way round, he stretched it over what we now call the belly—like those bags you pull together with a string—and tied up the one remaining opening so as to form what we call the navel. As for the creases that were left, he smoothed most of them away, finishing off the chest with the sort of tool a cobbler uses to smooth down the leather on the last, but he left a few puckers round about the belly and the navel, to remind us of what we suffered long ago.

Now, when the work of bisection was complete it left each half with a desperate yearning for the other, and they ran together and flung their arms around each other's necks, and asked for nothing better than to be rolled into one. So much so, that they began to die of hunger and general inertia, for neither would do anything without the other. And whenever one half was left alone by the death of its mate, it wandered about questioning and clasping in the hope of finding a spare half-woman—or a whole woman, as we should call her nowadays—or half a man. And so the race was dying out.

Fortunately, however, Zeus felt so sorry for them that he devised another scheme. He moved their privates round to the front, for of course they had originally been on the outside—which was now the back—and they had begotten and conceived not upon each other, but, like the grasshoppers, upon the earth. So now, as I say, he moved their members round to the front and made them propagate among themselves, the male begetting upon the female—the idea being that if, in all these clippings and claspings, a man should chance upon a woman, conception would take place and the race would be continued, while if man should conjugate with man, he might at least obtain such satisfaction as would allow him to turn his attention and his energies to the everyday affairs of his life. So you see, gentlemen, how far back we could trace our innate love for one another, and how this love is always trying to reintegrate our former nature, to make two into one, and to bridge the gulf between one human being and another.

And so, gentlemen, we are all like pieces of the coins that children break in half for keepsakes—making two out of one, like the flatfish—and each of us is forever seeking the half that will tally with himself. The man who is a slice of the hermaphrodite sex, as it was called, will naturally be attracted by women—the adulterer, for instance—and women who run after men are of similar descent—as, for instance, the unfaithful wife. But the woman who is a slice of the original female is attracted by women rather than by men—in fact she is a Lesbian—while men who are slices of the male are followers of the male, and show their masculinity throughout their boyhood by the way they make friends with men, and the delight they take in lying beside them and being taken in their arms. And these are the most hopeful of the nation's youth, for theirs is the most virile constitution.

I know there are some people who call them shameless, but they are wrong. It is not immodesty that leads them to such pleasures, but daring, fortitude, and masculinity—the very virtues that they recognize and welcome in their lovers—which is proved by the fact that in after years they are the only men who show any real manliness in public life. And so, when they themselves have come to manhood, their love in turn is lavished upon boys. They have no natural inclination to marry and beget children. Indeed, they only do so in deference to the usage of society, for they would just as soon renounce marriage altogether and spend their lives with one another.

Such a man, then, gentlemen, is of an amorous disposition, and gives his love to boys, always clinging to his like. And so, when this boy lover—or any lover, for that matter—is fortunate enough to meet his other half, they are both so intoxicated with affection, with friendship, and with love, that they cannot bear to let each other out of sight for a single instant. It is such reunions as these that impel men to spend their lives together, although they may be hard put to it to say what they really want with one another, and indeed, the purely sexual pleasures of their friendship could hardly account for the huge delight they take in one another's company. The fact is that both their souls are longing for a something else—a something to which they can neither of them put a name, and which they can only give an inkling of in cryptic sayings and prophetic riddles.

From the Symposium

THE SOUL AS CHARIOTEER

Each soul is divided into three parts, two being like steeds and the third like a charioteer. . . . Now of the steeds, so we declare one is good and the other is not, but we have not described the excellence of the one nor the badness of the other, and that is what must now be done. He that is on the more honorable side is upright and clean-limbed, carrying his neck high, with something of a hooked nose; in color he is white, with black eyes; a lover of glory, but with temperance and modesty; one that consorts with genuine renown, and needs no whip, being driven by the word of command alone. The other is crooked of frame, a massive jumble of a creature, with thick short neck, snub nose, black skin, and gray eyes; hot-blooded, consorting with wantonness and vainglory; shaggy of ear, deaf, and hard to control with whip and goad.

Now when the driver beholds the person of the beloved, and causes a sensation of warmth to suffuse the whole soul, he begins to experience a tickling or prickling of desire, and the obedient steed, constrained now as always by modesty, refrains from leaping upon the beloved. But his fellow, heeding no more the driver's goad or whip, leaps and dashes on, sorely troubling his companion and his driver, and forcing them to approach the loved one and remind him of the delights of love's commerce. For a while they struggle, indignant that he should force them to a monstrous and forbidden act, but at last, finding no end to their evil plight, they yield and agree to do his bidding. And so he draws them on, and now they are quite close and behold the spectacle of the beloved flashing upon them.

At that sight the driver's memory goes back to that form of beauty, and he sees her once again enthroned by the side of temperance upon her holy seat; then in awe and reverence he falls upon his back, and therewith is compelled to pull the reins so violently that he brings both steeds down on their haunches, the good one willing and unresistant, but the wanton sore against his will. Now that they are a little way off, the good horse in shame and horror drenches the whole soul with sweat, while the other, contriving to recover his wind after the pain of the bit and his fall, bursts into angry abuse, railing at the charioteer and his yokefellow as cowardly treacherous deserters. Once again he tries to force them to advance, and when they beg him to delay awhile he grudgingly consents.

But when the time appointed is come, and they feign to have forgotten, he reminds them of it—struggling and neighing and pulling until he compels them a second time to approach the beloved and renew their offer—and when they have come close, with head down and tail stretched out he takes the bit between his teeth and shamelessly plunges on. But the driver, with resentment even stronger than before, like a racer recoiling from the starting rope, jerks back the bit in the mouth of the wanton horse with an even stronger pull, bespatters his railing tongue and his jaws with blood, and forcing him down on legs and haunches delivers him over to anguish.

And so it happens time and again, until the evil steed casts off his wantonness; humbled in the end, he obeys the counsel of his driver, and when he sees the fair beloved is like to die of fear. Wherefore at long last the soul of the lover follows after the beloved with reverence and awe.

From the Phaedrus

THE FINAL REVELATION: THE HEAVENLY LADDER

DIOTIMA: "Well now, my dear Socrates, I have no doubt that even you might be initiated into these, the more elementary mysteries of

Love. But I don't know whether you could apprehend the final revelation, for so far, you know, we are only at the bottom of the true scale of perfection.

"Never mind," Diotima went on, "I will do all I can to help you understand, and you must strain every nerve to follow what I'm saying.

"Well then," she began, "the candidate for this initiation cannot, if his efforts are to be rewarded, begin too early to devote himself to the beauties of the body. First of all, if his preceptor instructs him as he should, he will fall in love with the beauty of one individual body, so that his passion may give life to noble discourse. Next he must consider how nearly related the beauty of any one body is to the beauty of any other, when he will see that if he is to devote himself to loveliness of form it will be absurd to deny that the beauty of each and every body is the same. Having reached this point, he must set himself to be the lover of every lovely body, and bring his passion for the one into due proportion by deeming it of little or of no importance.

"Next he must grasp that the beauties of the body are as nothing to the beauties of the soul, so that wherever he meets with spiritual loveliness, even in the husk of an unlovely body, he will find it beautiful enough to fall in love with and to cherish—and beautiful enough to quicken in his heart a longing for such discourse as tends toward the building of a noble nature. And from this he will be led to contemplate the beauty of laws and institutions. And when he discovers how nearly every kind of beauty is akin to every other, he will conclude that the beauty of the body is not, after all, of so great moment.

"And next, his attention should be diverted from institutions to the sciences, so that he may know the beauty of every kind of knowledge. And thus, by scanning beauty's wide horizon, he will be saved from a slavish and illiberal devotion to the individual loveliness of a single body, a single man, or a single institution. And, turning his eyes toward the open sea of beauty, he will find in such contemplation the seed of the most fruitful discourse and the loftiest thought, and reap a golden harvest of philosophy, until, confirmed and strengthened, he will come upon one single form of knowledge, the knowledge of the beauty I am about to speak of.

"And here," she said, "you must follow me as closely as you can.

"Whoever has been initiated so far in the mysteries of Love and has viewed all these aspects of the beautiful in due succession is at last drawing near the final revelation. And now, Socrates, there bursts upon him that wondrous vision which is the very soul of the beauty he has toiled so long for. It is an everlasting loveliness which neither comes nor goes, which neither flowers nor fades, for such beauty is the same on every hand, the same then as now, here as there, this way as that way, the same to every worshiper as it is to every other.

"Nor will his vision of the beautiful take the form of a face, or of hands, or of anything that is of the flesh. It will be neither words, nor knowledge, not a something that exists in something else, such as a living creature, or the earth, or the heavens, or anything that is—but subsisting of itself and by itself in an eternal oneness, while every lovely thing partakes of it in such sort that, however much the parts may wax and wane, it will be neither more nor less, but still the same inviolable whole.

"And so, when his prescribed devotion to boyish beauties has carried our candidate so far that the universal beauty dawns upon his inward sight, he is almost within reach of the final revelation. And this is the way, the only way, he must approach, or be led toward, the sanctuary of Love.

"Starting from individual beauties, the quest for the universal beauty must find him ever mounting the heavenly ladder, stepping from rung to rung—that is, from one to two, and from two to every lovely body, from bodily beauty to the beauty of institutions, from institutions to learning, and from learning in general to the special lore that pertains to nothing but the beautiful itself—until at last he comes to know what beauty is. . . .

"And remember," she said, "that it is only when he discerns beauty itself through what makes it visible that a man will be quickened with the true, and not the seeming, virtue or it is virtue's self that quickens him, not virtue's semblance. And when he has brought forth and reared this perfect virtue, he shall be called the friend of god, and if ever it is given to man to put on immortality, it shall be given to him."

From the Symposium

Theocritus (ca. third century B.C.) lived and wrote in Alexandria during the height of the Hellenistic age. His poems reflect the internationalism of his time; they are set all over the Mediterranean as well as in Alexandria itself. His idylls became extremely famous throughout the classical world and were the model for many homosexual poems in all the various European languages up until the nineteenth century. Behind their deceptively airy and graceful "pastoral" settings lies a religious vision of the truth of love between men, of that love that Achilles and Patroclus, "those men of gold," knew and realized; it is this vision (and the drama of its frequent betrayal) that gives his work its depth.

IDYLL XII

Art come, dear youth? two days and nights away!
(Who burn with love, grow aged in a day.)
As much as apples sweet the damson crude
Excel; the blooming spring the winter rude;
In fleece the sheep her lamb; the maiden in sweetness
The thrice-wed dame; the fawn the calf in fleetness;
The nightingale in song all feathered kind—
So much thy longed-for presence cheers my mind.
To thee I hasten, as to shady beech,
The traveler, when from the heaven's reach
The sun fierce blazes. May our love be strong,
To all hereafter times the theme of song!
"Two men each other loved to that degree,
That either friend did in the other see
A dearer than himself. They lived of old
Both golden natures in an age of gold."

O father Zeus! ageless immortals all!
Two hundred ages hence may one recall,
Down-coming to the irremeable river,
This to my mind, and this good news deliver:
"E'en now from east to west, from north to south,

Your mutual friendship lives in every mouth."
This, as they please, th' Olympians will decide:
Of thee, by blooming virtue beautified,
My glowing song shall only truth disclose;
With falsehood's pustules I'll not shame my nose.
If thou dost sometime grieve me, sweet the pleasure
Of reconcilement, joy in double measure
To find thou never didst intend the pain,
And feel myself from all doubt free again.

And ye Megarians, at Nisaea dwelling,
Expert at rowing, mariners excelling,
Be happy ever! for with honors due
Th' Athenian Diocles, to friendship true
Ye celebrate. With the first blush of spring
The youth surround his tomb: there who shall bring
The sweetest kiss, whose lip is purest found,
Back to his mother goes with garlands crowned.
Nice touch the arbiter must have indeed,
And must, methinks, the blue-eyed Ganymede
Invoke with many prayers—a mouth to own
True to the touch of lips, as Lydian stone
To proof of gold—which test will instant show
The pure or base, as money changers know.

IDYLL XXIX

They say, dear boy, that wine and truth agree;
And, being in wine, I'll tell the truth to thee—
Yes, all that works in secret in my soul.
'Tis this: thou dost not love me with thy whole
Untampered heart. I know; for half my time
Is spent in gazing on thy beauty's prime;
The other half is nought. When thou art good,
My days are like the gods'; but when the mood
Tormenting takes thee, 'tis my night of woe.
How were it right to vex a lover so?

Take my advice, my lad, thine elder friend,
'Twill make thee glad and grateful in the end:
In one tree build one nest, so no grim snake
May creep upon thee. For today thou'lt make
Thy home on one branch, and tomorrow changing
Wilt seek another, to what's new still ranging;
And should a stranger praise your handsome face,
Him more than three-year-proven friend you'll grace,
While him who loved you first you'll treat as cold
As some acquaintanceship of three days old.
Thou fliest high, methinks, in love and pride;
But I would say: keep ever at thy side
A mate that is thine equal; doing so,
The townsfolk shall speak well of thee alway,
And love shall never visit thee with woe—
Love that so easily men's hearts can flay,
And mine has conquered that was erst of steel.
Nay, by thy gracious lips I make appeal:
Remember thou wert younger a year agone
And we grow grey and wrinkled, all, or e'er
We can escape our doom; of mortals none
His youth retakes again, for azure wings
Are on her shoulders, and we sons of care
Are all too slow to catch such flying things.

Mindful of this, be gentle, is my prayer,
And love me, guileless, ev'n as I love thee;
So when thou hast a beard, such friends as were
Achilles and Patroclus we may be.

CHAPTER TWO

PAN OUR ART
APPROVES

THE ROMAN TRADITIONS

VERGIL

Vergil (70–19 B.C) was born near Mantua, in the north of Italy, where his parents owned a farm. When civil war broke out in 49 B.C. he retired to Naples for most of the rest of his life. The *Eclogues*—which he modeled partly on the idylls of Theocritus and in which he freely and tenderly expresses his homosexuality—was completed in 37 B.C.; the *Georgics*—his visionary "pastoral" epic—was finished in 30 B.C.; the remaining years of his creative life were spent toiling on the *Aeneid,* an epic poem that deals with the story of Aeneas, prince of Troy and founder, after innumerable ordeals, of the Roman Empire. The poem was left unfinished at his death in Brindisi in 19 B.C.

During the medieval period, Vergil was credited in Christian thought with prophetic and healing powers; he was, for example, Dante's guide through the spiritual and psychological labyrinth of the *Divine Comedy.* Those who read Vergil find themselves in the presence of one of the most refined religious intellects of humankind, radiant with compassion, love of the divine beauty of nature, and awe at the complexity and power of fate and divine order.

ECLOGUE II

Young Corydon (hard Fate) an humble swain
Alexis loved, the joy of all the plain,
He loved, but could not hope for love again.
Yet every day through groves he walked alone,
And vainly told the hills and woods his moan.
"Cruel Alexis! Can't my verses move!
Hast thou not pity? Must I die for love?
Just now the flocks pursue the shades and cool,
And every lizard creeps into his hole.
Brown Thestylis the weary reapers seeks,
And brings their meat, their onions and their leeks:
And whilst I trace thy steps in every tree
And every bush, poor insects sigh with me.
And had it not been better to have borne
The peevish Amaryllis' frowns and scorn,
Or else Menalcas', than this deep despair?
Though he was black, and thou art lovely fair!
Ah charming beauty! 'tis a fading grace,
Trust not too much, sweet youth, to that fair face:
Things are not always used that please the sight,
We gather black berries when we scorn the white.
Thou dost despise me, thou dost scorn my flame,
Yet dost not know me, nor how rich I am:
A thousand tender lambs, a thousand kine,
A thousand goats I feed, and all are mine:
My dairy's full, and my large herd affords,
Summer and winter, cream and milk and curds.
I pipe as well as when through Theban plains
Amphion fed his flocks, or charmed the swains;
Nor is my face so mean: I lately stood
And viewed my figure in the quiet flood,
And think myself, though it were judged by you,

As fair as Daphnis, if that glass be true.
Oh that with me the humble plains would please,
The quiet fields and lowly cottages!
Oh that with me you'd live and hunt the hare,
Or drive the kids, or spread the following snare!
Then you and I would sing like Pan in shady groves,
Pan taught us pipes and Pan our art approves:
Pan both the sheep and harmless shepherd loves.
Nor must you think the pipe too mean for you,
To learn to pipe, what won't Amyntas do:
I have a pipe, well-seasoned, brown and try'd,
Which good Dametas left me when he died.
He said, here, take it, for a legacy,
Thou art my second, it belongs to thee,
He said, and dull Amyntas envied me.
Besides, I found two wanton kids at play
In yonder vale, and those I brought away,
Young sportive creatures, and of spotted hue,
Which suckle twice a day, I keep for you.
These Thestylis hath begged, and begged in vain,
But now they're hers, since you my gifts disdain.
Come, lovely boy, the nymphs their baskets fill,
With poppy, violet and daffodil,
The rose, and thousand other fragrant flowers,
To please thy senses in thy softest hours.
These Nais gathers to delight my boy;
Come dear Alexis, be no longer coy.
I'll seek for chestnuts too in every grove,
Such as my Amaryllis used to love.
The glossy plums and juicy pears I'll bring,
Delightful all, and many a pretty thing.
The laurel and the neighboring myrtle tree,
Confus'dly planted 'cause they both agree,
And prove more sweet, shall send their boughs to thee.
Ah Corydon! Thou art a foolish swain
And coy Alexis doth thy gifts disdain,
Or if gifts could prevail, if gifts could woo,
Iolas can present him more than you.

What doth the madman mean? He idly brings
Storms on his flowers and boars into his springs.
Ah, whom dost thou avoid? Whom fly? The gods
And charming Paris too, have lived in woods.
Let Pallas, she whose art first raised a town,
Live there, let us delight in woods alone.
The boar, the wolf, the wolf the kid pursues,
The kid her thyme, as fast as t'others do's,
Alexis Corydon, and him alone.
Each hath his game, and each pursues his own.
Look how the wearied ox brings home the plow,
The sun declines, and shades are doubled now:
And yet my passion nor my cares remove,
Love burns me still, what flame so fierce as love!
Ah, Corydon, what fury's this of thine!
On yonder elm there hangs thy half-pruned vine:
Come, rather mind thy useful work, prepare,
Thy harvest baskets and make those thy care.
Come, mind thy plow, and thou shalt quickly find
Another, if Alexis prove unkind."

Translated by Thomas Creech

How lucky, if they know their happiness,
Are farmers, more than lucky, they for whom,
Far from the clash of arms, the earth herself,
Most fair in dealing, freely lavishes
An easy livelihood. What if no palace
With arrogant portal out of every cranny
Belches a mighty tide of morning callers
And no one gapes at doors inlaid so proudly
With varied tortoiseshell, cloth trickled with gold
And rare Corinthian bronzes? What if wool
Is white, not tainted with Assyrian poison,
And honest olive oil not spoilt with cassia?
Yet peace they have and a life of innocence
Rich in variety; they have for leisure
Their ample acres, caverns, living lakes,

Cool Tempes; cattle low, and sleep is soft
Under a tree. Coverts of game are there
And glades, a breed of youth inured to labor
And undemanding, worship of the gods
And reverence for the old. Departing Justice
Left among these her latest earthly footprints.
For my own part my chiefest prayer would be:
May the sweet Muses, whose acolyte I am,
Smitten with boundless love, accept my service,
Teach me to know the paths of the stars in heaven,
The eclipses of the sun and the moon's travails,
The cause of earthquakes, what it is that forces
Deep seas to swell and burst their barriers
And then sink back again, why winter suns
Hasten so fast to plunge themselves in the ocean
Or what it is that slows the lingering nights.
But if some chill in the blood about the heart
Bars me from mastering these sides of nature,
Then will I pray that I may find fulfillment
In the country and the streams that water valleys,
Love rivers and woods, unglamorous . . .
Blessed is he whose mind had power to probe
The causes of things and trample underfoot
All terrors and inexorable fate
And the clamor of devouring Acheron;
But happy too is he who knows the gods
Of the countryside, knows Pan and old Silvanus
And the sister Nymphs. Neither the people's gift,
The fasces, nor the purple robes of kings,
Nor treacherous feuds of brother against brother
Disturb him, not the Danube plotting raids
Of Dacian tribesmen, nor the affairs of Rome
And crumbling kingdoms, nor the grievous sight
Of poor to pity and of rich to envy.

From the Georgics, *Book II*
Translated by L. P. Wilkinson

While in these terms he prayed and pressed the altar,
Breaking in, the Sibyl said:
                              "Offspring
Of gods by blood, Trojan Anchises' son,
The way downward is easy from Avernus.
Black Dis's door stands open night and day.
But to retrace your steps to heaven's air,
There is the trouble, there is the toil. A few
Whom a benign Jupiter has loved or whom
Fiery heroism has borne to heaven,
Sons of gods, could do it. All midway
Are forests, then Cocytus, thick and black,
Winds through the gloom. But if you feel such love,
And such desire to cross the Stygian water
Twice, to view the night of Tartarus twice—
If this mad effort's to your liking, then
Consider what you must accomplish first.
A tree's deep shade conceals a bough whose leaves
And pliant twigs are all of gold, a thing
Sacred to Juno of the lower world.
The whole grove shelters it, and thickest shade
In dusky valleys shuts it in. And yet
No one may enter hidden depths
Below the earth unless he picks this bough,
The tree's fruit, with its foliage of gold.
Proserpina decreed this bough, as due her,
Should be given into her own fair hands
When torn away. In place of it a second
Grows up without fail, all gold as well,
Flowering with metallic leaves again.
So lift your eyes and search, and once you find it
Pull away the bough. It will come willingly,
Easily, if you are called by fate.
If not, with all your strength you cannot conquer it,
Cannot lop it off with a sword's edge. . . .

Aeneas wondered, studying the unmeasured forest,
And fell to prayer:
                    "If only the golden bough
Might shine for us in such a wilderness!
As all the prophetess foretold was true—
Misenus, in your case only too true."
The words were barely uttered when two doves
In casual flight out of the upper air
Came down before the man's eyes to alight
On the green grass, and the great hero knew
These birds to be his mother's. Joyously
He prayed:
            "O be my guides, if there's a way.
Wing on, into that woodland where the bough,
The priceless bough, shadows the fertile ground.
My divine mother, do not fail your son
In a baffling time."
                    Then he stood still to see
What signs the doves might give, or where their flight
Might lead him. And they fed, and then flew on,
Each time as far as one who came behind
Could keep in view. Then when they reached the gorge
Of sulphurous Avernus, first borne upward
Through the lucent air, they glided down
To their desired rest, the two-hued tree
Where glitter of gold filtered between green boughs.
Like mistletoe that in the woods in winter
Thrives with yellowish berries and new leaves—
A parasite on the trunk it twines around—
So bright amid the dark green ilex shone
The golden leafage, rustling in light wind.
Aeneas at once briskly took hold of it
And, though it clung, greedily broke it off,
Then carried it to the Sibyl's cave. . .

From the Aeneid, Book VI

Aeneas advancing toward him on the grass,
Anchises stretched out both his hands in eagerness
As tears wetted his cheeks. He said in welcome:

"Have you at last come, has that loyalty
Your father counted on conquered the journey?
Am I to see your face, my son, and hear
Our voices in communion as before?. . .

             Aeneas said:
                    "Your ghost,
Your sad ghost, father, often before my mind,
Impelled me to the threshold of this place.
My ships ride anchored in the Tuscan sea.
But let me have your hand, let me embrace you,
Do not draw back."
               At this his tears brimmed over
And down his cheeks. And there he tried three times
To throw his arms around his father's neck,
Three times the shade untouched slipped through his hands,
Weightless as wind and fugitive as dream.
Aeneas now saw at the valley's end
A grove standing apart, with stems and boughs
Of woodland rustling, and the stream of Lethe
Running past those peaceful glades. Around it
Souls of a thousand nations filled the air,
As bees in meadows at the height of summer
Hover and home on flowers and thickly swarm
On snow-white lilies, and the countryside
Is loud with humming. At the sudden vision
Shivering, at a loss, Aeneas asked
What river flowed there and what men were those
In such a throng along the riverside.
His father Anchises told him:
                      "Souls for whom
A second body is in store: their drink

Is water of Lethe, and it frees from care
In long forgetfulness. For all this time
I have so much desired to show you these
And tell you of them face to face—to take
The roster of my children's children here,
So you may feel with me more happiness
At finding Italy."

                    "Must we imagine,
Father, there are souls that go from here
Aloft to upper heaven, and once more
Return to bodies' dead weight? The poor souls,
How can they crave our daylight so?"

                                    "My son,
I'll tell you, not to leave you mystified,"
Anchises said, and took each point in order:

"First, then, the sky and lands and sheets of water,
The bright moon's globe, the Titan sun and stars,
Are fed within by Spirit, and a Mind
Infused through all the members of the world
Makes one great living body of the mass.
From Spirit come the races of man and beast,
The life of birds, odd creatures the deep sea
Contains beneath her sparkling surfaces,
And fiery energy from a heavenly source
Belongs to the generative seeds of these,
So far as they are not poisoned or clogged
By earthiness and deathliness of flesh.
This makes them fear and crave, rejoice and grieve.
Imprisoned in the darkness of the body
They cannot clearly see heaven's air; in fact
Even when life departs on the last day
Not all the scourges of the body pass
From the poor souls, not all distress of life.
Inevitably, many malformations,
Growing together in mysterious ways,
Become inveterate. Therefore they undergo

The discipline of punishments and pay
In penance for old sins; some hang full length
To the empty winds, for some the stain of wrong
Is washed by floods or burned away by fire.
We suffer each his own shade. We are sent
Through wide Elysium, where a few abide
In happy lands, till the long day, the round
Of Time fulfilled, has worn our stains away,
Leaving the soul's heaven-sent perception clear,
The fire from heaven pure. These other souls,
When they have turned Time's wheel a thousand years,
The god calls in a crowd to Lethe stream,
That there unmemoried they may see again
The heavens and wish re-entry into bodies."
Anchises paused. He drew both son and Sibyl
Into the middle of the murmuring throng,
Then picked out a green mound from which to view
The souls as they came forward, one by one.

From the Aeneid, *Book VI*

HORACE

▼

Horace (65–8 B.C.) was born the son of a freed slave of Venusia in south-eastern Italy. His father, though once a slave, made enough money as an auctioneer to send his son to a well-known school in Rome and then to the university in Athens. While in Greece, Horace joined Brutus's army and remained with it until its defeat at Philippi in 42 B.C. Years of vicissitude followed until he was "rescued" by Maecenas, a rich art lover who was to become his patron and give him a farm near the Tiber, some miles east of Rome, where he enjoyed the leisure in which he created most of his greatest work.

Horace was unself-consciously bisexual; his odes celebrate the charms of men as well as women. It is easy to praise Horace for his brilliance, wit, and *savoir vivre;* what is harder to see, perhaps, is how profound and religious, in the widest sense, Horace's vision of the brevity of time and so of the holiness of authentic pleasure is, and how sincere his praise, in a brutally precarious world, of the sacred healing powers of friendship and art.

INTERMISSA, VENUS (THEN IS IT WAR AGAIN, VENUS . . .)

Then is it war again, Venus,
after so long a truce? Mercy, mercy, please.
I am not as I was in the reign
of my dear Cinara. Desist, fierce mother

of pretty Cupids;
do not bend my inflexible five decades
to your tender command; go away—
attend to the fluent prayers of younger men.

Carousal would be
more timely in Paulus Maximus' house:
take your silver swans to him
if you seek a suitable life to inflame.

Both highborn and handsome,
not silent on behalf of the anxious defendant,
this youth has a hundred arts
to advance your standards far and wide:

and when he has mocked
and surpassed some rival's lavish gifts,
Paulus will erect your statue
under citrus beams by the Alban lake.

There you shall snuff
much incense; and a choir concerted with lyres
and Berecyntian flutes,
and recorders too, shall strive to attract you:

there twice a day youths
and tender girls praising your godhead
shall pace with gleaming feet
in the triple step of the Salian dance.

But me—neither woman, boy,
nor credulous hope of sharing souls,
nor contests in wine,
nor garlands about my hair, can move me now.

Then why, my Ligurinus, why
these unaccustomed tears on my cheeks
Why does my eloquent tongue
ineptly fall silent among the words?

Each night in my dreams
I hold you captive, or else pursue
your obdurate flight
across the Field of Mars, through swirling water.

KEEP AN EQUABLE MIND

Dellius, all must die: be sure to retain
an equable mind in vexation
avoiding also intemperate joy
at advantages gained,

whether you lead a life of gloom
or relax stretched out on some sequestered
lawn throughout the holy days
and rejoice in classic Falernian wine.

Why do the pines and silvery poplars
share their hospitable shade?
Why does runaway water
tremble in winding streams?

With us, for us. Command all perfumes, wines
and the too brief spell of the rose
while affairs and times
and the Fates' black thread allow:

then good-bye freehold woodlands, home
and the manor the yellow Tiber washed
and the spoils piled up to the heights,
which your heir shall get.

Rich man born from ancient Inachus
or poor man, it makes no odds, from the lowest
race under sky you shall fall
Orcus's victim, who pities none.

All are thus compelled;
early or late the urn is shaken;
fate will out; a little boat
will take us to eternal exile.

SEE HOW SORACTE STANDS DEEP

See how Soracte stands deep
in dazzling snow and the trees cannot bear
their loads and bitter frosts
have paralyzed the streams.

Unfreeze, heap plentiful logs
on the hearth and produce
your four-year Sabine, Thaliarchus,
a fine and generous wine.

Commit all else to the Gods:
once they have quelled the melee
of wind and churning water, cypress
and mountain ash will be still.

Avoid speculation
about the future; count as credit the days
chance deals; youth should not spurn
the dance or sweet desire;

this is your green time, not your white
and morose. In field or piazza,
now is the proper season for
trading soft whispers in the dark;

the telltale complaisant laugh
of a girl in some secret nook;
the pledge removed from an arm
of a helpfully helpless finger.

"Galli" were the gender-variant, usually mendicant, "priests" of the Roman mother goddess, Cybele. Diviners, healers, astrologers, rainmakers, talisman creators, and magicians, they were known in Greece as *metragyrtes,* "wandering beggar priests of the Mother." They dressed extravagantly in feminine and sacred garments, were known to have same-sex erotic rituals, and had a long "reign" from the third millennium B.C. to the third and fourth centuries A.D., when a scandalized Christian church enlisted the power of Rome to suppress them.

A great deal of their symbolic power derived from the fact that they were ritually castrated. Some scholars think they underwent castration because they wanted to imitate the mother goddess and a woman's being as much as possible; some maintain it was to imitate the death-by-castration and subsequent apotheosis of Cybele's male consort, Attis. Whatever the reason, their castration set them apart—to be living radical symbols, perhaps, of the principle of sacrificial death and spiritual resurrection.

Only a few names of Galli have come down to us and a handful of spells and poems. No anthology of gay mystics could be complete without a gesture of recognition to their long tradition of passionate and radical "witness" to the creativity of breaking all barriers and dissolving all genders in the name of the Mother's all-embracing love.

> Thou art powerful, of the Gods Thou art
> The queen and also the goddess.
> Thee, Goddess, and Thy power I now invoke,
> Thou canst easily grant me all that I ask,
> And in exchange I will give Thee, Goddess,
> sincere thanks.
>
> *Anonymous*

> I, the priest of Rhea, long-haired
> castrato, Tmolian dancer, whose
> high shriek is famed for carrying power,
> now, at last, rest from my throes
> and give the Great Dark Mother on

the banks of the Sangarius all:
my tambourines, my bone-linked scourge,
my brazen cymbals, and a curl
of my long heavy perfumed hair
in dedication, Holy Rhea.

Erucius

CHAPTER THREE

I CAME UP WITH THEM
NATIVE TRADITIONS

This section is dedicated to the celebration of the wise and spacious vision of homosexuality and its sacred function as understood and practiced by Native American tribes. In many tribes, homosexuality in both sexes was accepted as a fact of nature and the homosexual *berdache* (derived by early white settlers from a Persian word meaning "kept boy" or "male prostitute") accorded a wide-ranging array of sacred and practical powers and given great respect. Many berdaches cross-dressed and so inhabited, with social approval, a region "between" the sexes. By all indications, the berdache role was an ancient one, and the respect given to it may well echo an ancient tolerance of variety in human nature that patriarchal cultures have lost. Certain ethnologists believe that some form of berdache practices, such as cross-dressing and homosexual relations by shamans, existed among the ancient Siberians who began migrating from Asia to North America thirty thousand years ago.

In many tribes, berdaches played an integral role in the life of the people. They were the ones who gave sacred names, who cut down the Sun Dance pole in the central sacred rituals, who foretold future events. They were famous for their bead and quill work, hide-tanning abilities, and extravagant fancy dress (not all berdaches dressed in women's clothes; it depended on their vision). They were considered good luck to take along on a war party or horse-stealing raid. Many were married as second or third wives to warriors; some became the wives of chiefs. Often, berdaches would live together in a group of teepees on the outer edge of the camp, where they would exercise their many roles as doctors, storytellers, matchmakers, and leading scalp dancers. Different names were given to the berdache by different tribes. The Sauk and Fox tribes called the berdache *i-coo-coa;* the Ojibway (Chippewa) named him *agokwa;* the Cheyenne called him *hee-man-eh;* and the Sioux, *winkte.*

Many gay activists and mystics today look to the Native American tradition of berdaches as a sign of what the sacred role of homosexuals within a healthy culture might be.

WE'WA

We'wa (1849–96), an important and influential member of the Zuni tribe, played a key role in its modern history. Stories of We'wa are still told, with humor and reverence. In her report on the Zuni (1904), Matilda Coxe Stevenson described We'wa "as the strongest character and most intelligent of the Zuni tribe." We'wa was a skilled weaver and potter, versed in all forms of sacred and secular lore; he played a vital part—though dressed in female clothes—in all important male religious activities; he managed the large household of his adopted family and was one of the first Zuni to earn money, washing clothes for whites and selling his weaving and pottery. In 1886 We'wa spent six months in Washington, where he was hailed by Washington society as a "Zuni princess," met President Grover Cleveland, and demonstrated weaving at the Smithsonian. When he died in 1896, a whole sane and beautiful tradition seemed to die with him. Now that tradition is being reclaimed by gay seekers everywhere.

We'wa was a remarkable woman, a fine blanket and sash maker, an excellent cook, an adept in all the work of her sex, and yet strange to say, she was a man. There never has been, as yet, any satisfactory explanation given, as far as I know, of the peculiar custom followed by the Pueblos of having one or two men in each tribe, who forswear their manhood and who dress as, act like, and seemingly live the life of, women. We'wa was one of these. . . .

She seldom sang at her grinding, but at a word from her, I have heard as many as a half hundred voices all raised at once in one wonderful unison of melody, from all parts of the pueblo as the women ground their corn and sang simultaneously. . . .

We'wa was the attendant at a certain shrine, and was quite a noted character. As will be seen from her picture she was of masculine build and had far more of the man in her character than the woman. Yet she excelled all other of the Zuni women in the exercise of her skill in blanket and pottery making. Her blanketry was noted far and wide, and her pottery fetched twice the price of that of any other maker. . . .

She was perhaps the tallest person in Zuni; certainly the strongest, both mentally and physically. . . . She had a good memory, not only for the lore of her people, but for all that she heard of the outside world. . . . She possessed an indomitable will and an insatiable thirst for knowledge. Her likes and dislikes were intense. Though severe she was considered just. . . . Owing to her bright mind and excellent memory, she was called upon by her own clan and also by the clans of her foster mother and father when a long prayer had to be repeated or a grace was to be offered over a feast. In fact she was the chief personage on many occasions.

George Wharton James

WE'WA AND THE ROCKS

We'wa was an accomplished potter who shared the deeply religious attitude of Zuni women toward this art. During one of their return visits to Zuni, the Stevensons accompanied We'wa when he collected clay on Corn Mountain. We'wa followed religious protocols all along the way:

On passing a stone heap she picked up a small stone in her left hand, and spitting upon it, carried the hand around her head and threw the stone over one shoulder upon the stone heap in order that her strength might not go from her when carrying the heavy load down the mesa. She then visited the shrine at the base of the Mother Rock and tearing off a bit of her blanket deposited it in one of the tiny pits in the rock as an offering to the Mother Rock. When she drew near to the clay bed she indicated to Mr. Stevenson that he must remain behind, as men never approached the spot. Proceeding a short distance the party reached a point where We'wa requested the writer to remain perfectly quiet and not talk, saying: "Should we talk, my pottery would crack in the baking, and unless I pray constantly the clay will not appear to me." She applied the hoe vigorously to the hard soil, all the while murmuring prayers to Mother Earth.

Matilda Coxe Stevenson

THE DEATH OF WE'WA

When a week or more had passed after the close of the great autumn ceremonial of the Sha'lako, and the many guests had departed, the writer dropped in at sunset to the spacious room in the house of We'wa's foster father, the late Jose Palle. We'wa was found crouching on the ledge by the fireplace. That a great change had come over her was at once apparent. Death evidently was rapidly approaching. She had done her last work. Only a few days before, this strong-minded, generous-hearted creature had labored to make ready for the reception of her gods; now she was preparing to go to her beloved Ko'thluwala'wa [Sacred Lake]. When the writer asked, "Why do you not lie down?" We'wa replied: "I cannot breathe if I lie down; I think my heart break." The writer at once sent to her camp for a comfortable chair, and fixed it at a suitable angle for the invalid, who was most grateful for the attention. There was little to be done for the sufferer. She knew that she was soon to die and begged the writer not to leave her.

From the moment her family realized that We'wa was in a serious condition they remained with her, ever ready to be of assistance. The family consisted of the aged foster mother, a foster brother, two foster sisters with their husbands and children, and an own brother with his wife and children. The writer never before observed such attention as every member of the family showed her. The little children ceased their play and stood in silence close to their mothers, occasionally toddling across the floor to beg We'wa to speak. She smiled upon them and whispered, "I cannot talk." The foster brother was as devoted as the one related by blood. . . .

The foster brother, with streaming eyes, prepared *te'likinawe* [prayer sticks] for the dying, the theurgist having said that her moments on earth were few. We'wa asked the writer to come close and in a feeble voice she said, in English: "Mother, I am going to the other world. I will tell the gods of you and Captain Stevenson. I will tell them of Captain Carlisle, the great seed priest, and his wife, whom I love. They are my friends. Tell them good-by. Tell President Cleveland, my friend, good-by. Mother, love all my people; protect them; they are your children; you are their mother." These sentences were spoken with many breaks. The family seemed somewhat grieved that We'wa's last words should be given to the writer, but she understood that the thoughts of the dying were with and for her own people. A good-by was said to the others, and she asked for more light.

It is the custom for a member of the family to hold the prayer plumes near the mouth of the dying and repeat the prayer, but this practice was not observed in We'wa's case. She requested the writer to raise the back of the chair, and when this was done she asked if her prayer plumes had been made. Her foster brother answered "Yes," whereupon she requested him to bring them. The family suppressed their sobs that the dying might not be made sad. The brother offered to hold the plumes and say the prayers, but We'wa feebly extended her hand for them, and clasping the prayer plumes between her hands made a great effort to speak. She said but a few words and then sank back in her chair. Again the brother offered to hold the plumes and pray, but once more she refused. Her face was radiant in the belief that she was going to her gods. She leaned forward with the plumes tightly clasped, and as the setting sun lighted up the western windows, darkness and desolation entered the hearts of the mourners, for We'wa was dead.

Matilda Coxe Stevenson

Hasteen Klah (1867–1937) was one of the most famous Navajo medicine men and artists of all time. He was also a berdache, or *nadle.*

Klah began his training in Navajo ceremonial practice early in life. Because he was a *nadle,* he also learned to weave—normally women's work. He traveled extensively in the white world, demonstrating Navajo arts at world's fairs in Chicago in 1893 and 1933. Like the Zuni We'wa, Klah also met an American president—Franklin D. Roosevelt.

Klah formed close friendships with several white people interested in Navajo culture—in particular, Frances Newcomb, wife of a nearby trader, and Mary Cabot Wheelwright, a wealthy Bostonian. According to Wheelwright,

> I grew to respect and love him for his real goodness, generosity—and holiness, for there is no other word for it. He never had married, having spent twenty-five years studying not only the ceremonies he gave, but all the medicine lore of the tribe. . . . When I knew him he never kept anything for himself. It was hard to see him almost in rags at his ceremonies, but what was given him he seldom kept, passing it on to someone who needed it. . . . Our civilization and miracles he took simply without much wonder, as his mind was occupied with his religion and helping his people. . . . Everything was the outward form of the spirit world that was very real to him (Wheelwright, in Klah 1942:11–13).

NAVAJO CREATION MYTH

Beginning of the World Song

Creating the World
Creating the Mountain Gods
Creating mountain rain and creating beads and jewelry
Creating *Sahanahray Bekayhozhon*
Creating Mountain Man
Creating Little Rain on the Mountain

Creating jewelry and beads
Creating the holy spirit
Creating little rain spirit
Creating *Sahanahray Bekayhozhon*
Creating the Spirit of Creation
Creating the Spirit of Corn Pollen
Creating *Sahanahray Bekayhozhon.*

The song is repeated three times, substituting for "creating":

Second verse: The beginning of the world, *I knew about it before.*
Third verse: The beginning of the world, *I am thinking about it.*
Fourth verse: The beginning of the world, *I am talking about it.*

   As related by Hasteen Klah to Mary C. Wheelwright

NAVAJO CEREMONIAL SONGS

Second Song of the Flood

They are running from the water, I came up with it
   When my spiritual power was strong, I came up with it
   When it was holy, I came up with it
They start moving from the water, I came up with it
   When my spiritual power was strong, I came up with it
   When it was holy, I came up with it
The rocks which extend upward, I came up with them
   When my spiritual power was strong, I came up with them
   When it was holy, I came up with them
The mountains which extend upward, I came up with them
   When my spiritual power was strong, I came up with them
   When it was holy, I came up with them
The waters which extend upward, I came up with them
   When my spiritual power was strong, I came up with them
   When it was holy, I came up with them
The clouds which extend upward, I came up with them
   When my spiritual power was strong, I came up with them
   When it was holy, I came up with them

The mists which extend upward, I came up with them
   When my spiritual power was strong, I came up with them
   When it was holy, I came up with them
They arrived at the sky, I came up with them
   When my spiritual power was strong, I came up with them
   When it was holy, I came up with them
They came through the sky, I came up with them
   When my spiritual power was strong, I came up with them
   When it was holy, I came up with them
They came up to it, I came up with them
   When my spiritual power was strong, I came up with them
   When it was holy, I came up with them
They are camping in it, I came up with them
   When my spiritual power was strong, I came up with them
   When it was holy, I came up with them
They are moving away from each other, I came up with them
   When my spiritual power was strong, I came up with them
   When it was holy, I came up with them.

Song of Creating People

*Hozhoni, hozhoni, hozhoni**
Hozhoni, hozhoni, hozhoni.
The Earth, its life am I, *hozhoni, hozhoni*
The Earth, its feet are my feet, *hozhoni, hozhoni.*
The Earth, its legs are my legs, *hozhoni, hozhoni.*
The Earth, its body is my body, *hozhoni, hozhoni*
The Earth, its thoughts are my thoughts, *hozhoni, hozhoni*
The Earth, its speech is my speech, *hozhoni, hozhoni*
The Earth, its down-feathers are my down-feathers, *hozhoni, hozhoni.*

The sky, its life am I, *hozhoni, hozhoni*—
The mountains, their life am I—
Rain-mountain, its life am I—
Changing-Woman, her life am I—

*Hozhoni means harmony.

The Sun, its life am I—
Talking God, his life am I—
House God, his life am I—
White corn, its life am I—
Yellow corn, its life am I—
Corn-pollen, its life am I—
The corn-beetle, its life am I—

Hozhoni, hozhoni, hozhoni
Hozhoni, hozhoni, hozhoni.

    From the Hail Chant

Song of the Earth

The Earth is beautiful
The Earth is beautiful
The Earth is beautiful.

Below the East, the Earth, its face toward East,
    the top of its head is beautiful
The soles of its feet, they are beautiful
Its feet, they are beautiful
Its legs, they are beautiful
Its body, it is beautiful
Its chest, it is beautiful
Its breast, it is beautiful
Its head-feather, it is beautiful
The Earth is beautiful.
Below the West, the Sky, it is beautiful, its face toward West,
    the top of its head is beautiful—
Below the East, the dawn, its face toward East,
    the top of its head is beautiful—
Below the West, the afterglow of sundown, its face toward West,
    the top of its head is beautiful—
Below the East, White Corn, its face toward East,
    the top of its head is beautiful—
Below the South, Blue Corn, its face toward South,
    the top of its head is beautiful—

Below the West, Yellow Corn, its face toward West,
the top of its head is beautiful—
Below the North, Varicolored Corn, its face toward North,
the top of its head is beautiful—
Below the East, *Sahanahray*, its face toward East,
the top of its head is beautiful—
Below the West, *Bekayhozhon*, its face toward West,
the top of its head is beautiful—
Below the East, corn-pollen, its face toward East,
the top of its head is beautiful—
Below the West, the corn-beetle, its face toward West,
the top of its head is beautiful—

The Earth is beautiful.

From the Blessing Chant

MAURICE KENNY

Maurice Kenny (b. 1929, Mohawk) is a pioneer of the revival of berdache
or *winkte* consciousness (*winkte* is the Sioux word for male homosexual).
The "contemporary" period of lesbian and gay Native writing began in
1976 with the publication by Gay Sunshine of Maurice Kenny's key essay
"Tinselled Bucks: An Historical Study of Indian Homosexuality." Kenny's
fine essay cites a wide range of ethnographic and literary references to two-
spirit and male homosexuality in traditional times and ends with an opti-
mistic prediction of their restoration. Collections of his poems include
The Mama Poems (1984), for which he received an American book award.

WINKTE

*He told me that if nature puts a burden on a man by making him
different, it also gives him a power.*
                    —*John (Fire) Lame Deer, Sioux Medicine Man*

We are special to the Sioux!
They gave us respect for strange powers

Of looking into the sun, the night.
They paid us with horses not derision.

To the Cheyenne we were no curiosity!
We were friends or wives of brave warriors
Who hunted for our cooking pots
Who protected our tipis from Pawnee.

We went to the mountain for our puberty vision.
No horse or lance or thunderbird
Crossed the dreaming eye which would have sent us
Into war or the hunter's lonely woods.
To some song floated on mountain air.
To others colors and design appeared on clouds.
To a few words fell from the eagle's wing,
And they took to the medicine tent,
And in their holiness made power
For the people of the Cheyenne Nation.
There was space for us in the village.

The Crow and Ponca offered deerskin
When the decision to avoid the warpath was made,
And we were accepted into the fur robes
Of a young warrior, and lay by his flesh
And knew his mouth and warm groin:
Or we married (a second wife) to the chief.
And if we fulfilled our duties, he smiled
And gave us his grandchildren to care for.

We were special to the Sioux, Cheyenne, Ponca
And the Crow who valued our worth and did not spit
Names at our lifted skirts nor kicked our nakedness.
We had power with the people!

And if we cared to carry the lance, or dance
Over enemy scalps and take buffalo
Then that, too, was good for the Nation,
And contrary to our stand we walked backwards.

CHAPTER FOUR

OPEN WIDE THE
DOOR OF HEAVEN

TRADITIONS OF THE FAR EAST

QU YUAN

Qu Yuan is thought of as China's first major poet. He was a homosexual cross-dressing shaman-priest and poet of extraordinary range and power. Among his works are the epic *Li Sao* ("Encountering Sorrow"), the *Tain Wen* ("Heavenly Questions"), and many mystical songs. He was born about 340 B.C. in the kingdom of Ch'u; astrologers predicted he would become a healer and poet. The people of Ch'u were of Mongolian origin and had practiced shamanism and Goddess worship for a long time; Qu Yuan himself studied healing and clairvoyance with a shamaness. Although the ancient shamanic tradition with its tolerance of cross-dressing, same-sex eroticism, and vision of the sacred dynamic unity of all life was under attack, even in Ch'u, from the prevailing Confucianism of the time, its vigor, richness, and flamboyant merging of different worlds and dimensions live on in Qu Yuan's poetry.

The first excerpt here is from Qu Yuan's *Li Sao*, in which he expresses his anguish at being rejected by King Huai, the ruler he worked for and was in love with. The second two excerpts come from his *Songs* and show Qu Yuan "using" poetry as a way of invoking the living divine presence of different "shamanic" deities.

Scion of the high lord Gao Yang,
Bo Yong was my father's name.
When She Ti pointed to the first month of the year,
On the day I passed from the womb.
My father, seeing the aspect of my nativity,
Took omens to give me an auspicious name.
The name he gave me was True Exemplar;
The title he gave me was Divine Balance.

Having from birth this inward beauty,
I added to it fair outward adornment:
I dressed in selinea and shady angelica,
And twined autumn orchids to make a garland.
Swiftly I sped as in fearful pursuit,
Afraid Time would race on and leave me behind.
In the morning I gathered the angelica on the mountains;
In the evening I plucked the sedges of the islets.

The days and months hurried on, never delaying;
Springs and autumns sped by in endless alternation:
And I thought how the trees and flowers were fading and falling,
And feared that my Fairest's beauty would fade too.
"Gather the flower of youth and cast out the impure!
Why will you not change the error of your ways?
I have harnessed brave coursers for you to gallop forth with:
Come, let me go before and show you the way!

"The three kings of old were most pure and perfect:
Then indeed fragrant flowers had their proper place.
They brought together pepper and cinnamon;
All the most prized blossoms were woven in their garlands.
Glorious and great were those two, Yao and Shun,
Because they had kept their feet on the right path.

And how great was the folly of Jie and Zhou,
Who hastened by crooked paths, and so came to grief.

"The fools enjoy their careless pleasure,
But their way is dark and leads to danger.
I have no fear for the peril of my own person,
But only lest the chariot of my lord should be dashed.
I hurried about your chariot in attendance,
Leading you in the tracks of the kings of old."
But the Fragrant One refused to examine my true feelings:
He lent ear instead to slander, and raged against me.

How well I know that loyalty brings disaster;
Yet I will endure: I cannot give it up.
I called on the ninefold heaven to be my witness,
And all for the sake of the Fair One, and no other.
There was once a time when he spoke with me in frankness;
But then he repented and was of another mind.
I do not care, on my own count, about this divorcement,
But it grieves me to find the Fair One so inconstant . . .

Yet, though cast off, I would wear my orchid girdle;
I would pluck some angelicas to add to its beauty;
For this it is that my heart takes most delight in,
And though I died nine times, I should not regret it.
What I regret is the Fair One's waywardness,
That never stops to ask what is in men's minds.
All your ladies were jealous of my delicate beauty;
In their spiteful chattering they said I was a wanton.

Eagles do not flock like birds of lesser species;
So it has ever been since the olden time.
How can the round and square ever fit together?
How can different ways of life ever be reconciled?
Yet humbling one's spirit and curbing one's pride,
Bearing blame humbly and enduring insults,
But keeping pure and spotless and dying in righteousness:
Such conduct was greatly prized by the wise men of old.

From Encountering Sorrow

The Child of God, descending the northern bank,
Turns on me her eyes that are dark with longing.
Gently the wind of autumn whispers;
On the waves of the Dong-ting lake the leaves are falling.

Over the white sedge I gaze out wildly;
For a tryst is made to meet my love this evening.
But why should the birds gather in the duckweed?
And what are the nets doing in the treetops?
The Yuan has its angelicas, the Li has its orchids:
And I think of my lady, but dare not tell it,
As with trembling heart I gaze on the distance
Over the swiftly moving waters.

What are the deer doing in the courtyard?
Or the water-dragons outside the waters?
In the morning I drive my steeds by the river;
In the evening I cross to the western shore.
I can hear my beloved calling to me:
I will ride aloft and race beside her.
I will build her a house within the water
Roofed all over with lotus leaves;

With walls of iris, of purple shells in the chamber;
Perfumed pepper shall make the hall.
With beams of cassia, orchid rafters,
Lily-tree lintel, a bower of peonies,
With woven fig-leaves for the hangings
And melilotus to make a screen;
Weights of white jade to hold the mats with,
Stone-orchids strewn to make the floor sweet:
A room of lotus thatched with the white flag
Shall all be bound up with stalks of asarum.

A thousand sweet flowers shall fill the courtyard,
And rarest perfumes shall fill the gates.
In hosts from their home on Doubting Mountain
Like clouds in number the spirits come thronging.

I'll throw my thumb-ring into the river,
Leave my girdle-gem in the bay of the Li.
Sweet pollia I've plucked in the little islet
To send to my faraway Beloved.
Oh, rarely, rarely the time is given!
I wish I could play here a little longer.

From Songs

THE GREATER MASTER OF FATE

Open wide the door of heaven!
On a black cloud I ride in splendor,
Bidding the whirlwind drive before me,
Causing the rainstorm to lay the dust.

In sweeping circles my lord is descending:
"Let me follow you over the Kong-sang mountain!
See, the teeming peoples of the Nine Lands:
The span of their lives is in your hand!"

Flying aloft, he soars serenely,
Riding the pure vapor, guiding yin and yang.
Speedily, lord, I will go with you,
Conducting High God to the height of heaven.

My cloud-coat hangs in billowing folds;
My jade girdle-pendants dangle low:
A yin and a yang, a yin and a yang:
None of the common folk know what I am doing.

I have plucked the glistening flower of the Holy Hemp
To give to one who lives far away.
Old age already has crept upon me:
I am no longer near him, fast growing a stranger.

He drives his dragon chariot with thunder of wheels;
High up he rides, careering heavenwards.
But I stand where I am, twisting a spray of cassia:
The longing for him pains my heart.

It pains my heart, but what can I do?
If we could only stay as we were, unchanging!
But all man's life is fated;
Its meeting and partings not his to arrange.

From Songs

KUKAI (KOBO DAISHI)

Kukai (774–835) is commonly known as Kobo Daishi, an honorific title that was given to him by the Heian court of his time. *Kobo* means "spreading widely the Buddhist teachings" and *daishi* "a great teacher." The exalted title of *daishi* was conferred on other eminent Buddhist masters, but as the popular Japanese saying goes, "*Kobo* stole the title of *daishi*." Kukai is one of the most respected and popular masters of Japan. In addition to the common legend that, as the inventor of the *kana* syllabary, he was the founder of Japanese culture, he is remembered as the founder of Shingon, or Esoteric Buddhism, in Japan, the founder of the monastic center on Mount Koya, the originator of the pilgrimage circuit of eighty-eight temples on Shikoku, a builder of lakes, a wandering saint who undertook severe ascetic ordeals, and a master calligrapher. His homosexuality was always well known and accepted, as one part of the creative love-nature of an extraordinary religious genius.

At fifteen I began my studies [of Chinese classics] under the guidance of Ato Otari, the teacher of a prince and an uncle on my mother's side. At eighteen I entered the college in the capital and studied diligently. Meanwhile a Buddhist monk showed me a scripture called the *Kokuzo gumonji no ho*. In that work it is stated that if one recites the mantra one million times according to the proper method, one will be able to memorize passages and understand the meaning of any scripture. Believing what the Buddha says to be true, I recited the mantra incessantly, as if I were rubbing one piece of wood against another to make fire, all the while earnestly hoping to achieve this result. I climbed up Mount Tairyu in Awa Province and meditated at Cape Muroto in Tosa. The valley reverberated to the sound of my voice as I recited, and the planet Venus appeared in the sky.

From that time on, I despised fame and wealth and longed for a life in the midst of nature. Whenever I saw articles of luxury—light furs, well-fed horses, swift vehicles—I felt sad, knowing that, being transient as lightning, they too would fade away. Whenever I saw a cripple or a beggar, I lamented and wondered what had caused him to spend his days in such a miserable state. Seeing these piteous conditions encouraged me to renounce the world. Can anyone now break my determination? No, just as there is no one who can stop the wind.

From the Preface to Sango Shiki
("Indications of the Goals of the Three Teachings")

The light of the sun and moon breaks through darkness,
And the three teachings illumine ignorance.
Nature and desire vary from person to person,
Treatment differs with each physician.
Human duties were preached by Confucius;
On learning them one becomes a high government official.
Lao Tzu taught the creation by yin and yang;
On receiving his instructions one can observe the world from the
    tower of a Taoist temple.
Most significant and profound is the teaching of the ultimate path of
    Mahayana.
It teaches the salvation of oneself and of others;
It does not exclude even animals or birds.
The flowers in the spring fall beneath the branches;
Dew in autumn vanishes before the withered grass.
Flowing water can never be stopped;
Whirling winds howl constantly.
The world of senses is a sea in which one well may drown;
Eternity, Bliss, the Self, and Purity are the summits on which we
    ultimately belong.
I know the fetters that bind me in the triple world;
Why should I not give up the thought of serving the court?

The sea of Mind is forever tranquil
Without even a single ripple;

Stirred by the storm of discriminations,
Billows rage to and fro.

Men in the street are deluded;
They are fascinated by phantomlike men and women.
Heretics are crazed;
They adhere to the grand tower of mirage.

They do not know
That heaven and hell are fabricated by their own minds.
Do they come to realize
That "mind-only" will free them from their tragedies?

Be that as it may,
By practicing the Six Paramitas for three aeons,
By practicing the fifty-two stages for enlightenment,
They will uncover One Mind.

When they become pure-hearted,
Cutting off their emotional and mental obstacles,
They will find their own Treasury—
Enlightenment, or Nirvana.

Now they are fully endowed with
The Three Excellent Qualities and the Four Attributes.
Unaware of their own possessions,
How long have they groped after them elsewhere!

That which is beyond speech and conception
Pervades the entire universe;
Alas, not knowing this,
A son drifts like duckweed in the water of samsara.

ZEAMI

Zeami (1363–1443), the founder of the Japanese theatrical form called No,
is the greatest artist of the Muromachi period. Building on the insights
and experiences of his father, Kan'ami, Zeami was able through his own

skills and innate genius to transform what had been essentially country entertainment with powerful ritual overtones into a marvelous total theatrical experience. In No, mime, dance, poetry, and song are fused in such a way that the limitations of each separate art are transcended and audiences experience the full shock of a profound spiritual art form. Zeami was openly homosexual and famous for his beauty as a young man, although he also married.

Zeami's theoretical writing on No is contained in twenty-three treatises, of which the most celebrated is the *Kadensho* (excerpted here). One of the authoritative books on the spiritual and mystical inner nature of art and one of the supreme works of Japanese literature, the *Kadensho* shows throughout the author's search for a truth in which art and spirit are one.

THE ACTOR AS VESSEL OF THE UNIVERSE

In the *Analects* it is written, "Zi Gong inquired of the Master saying, 'What am I?' The master replied, 'Thou art a vessel.'. . . 'What manner of vessel?' 'A chalice for ancestral offerings.'". . .

Now then, in terms of our art, this vessel is actually the master who has attained to the myriad pieces from the Two Arts and the Three Modes, that is to say, a vessel of diverse accomplishment. It consists in the artistic power whereby one contains within one's being the full diversity of styles and techniques. When the visual and aural attainments from the Two Arts and the Three Modes are made manifest, extending throughout one's acting for inexhaustible artistic effect, this is the vessel of diverse accomplishment.

If you understand this in terms of Substance and Nothingness, Substance is the visible phenomenon, nothingness is the vessel. That which manifests Substance is Nothingness. For example, crystal is itself colorless and patternless, but from it come fire and water. How is it that things of such diametrically opposed natures as fire and water can both be born of colorless emptiness?

There is a poem that reads:

Sakuragi wa   Take a cherry tree,
Kudakite mireba   Break it apart and you will find

Hana mo nashi	No blossoms.
Hana koso haru no	Blossoms come to bloom
Sora ni sakikere	Out of the empty springtime sky.

The seeds and flowers of the myriad pieces in the performing arts are born of the mind pervading the performer's artistic powers. Just as crystal gives birth to fire and water out of the air, and a cherry tree bears blossoms and fruit out of its colorlessness, so also does the accomplished master create the phenomenal manifestations of his art out of the intentional content of his mind, and as such, he is indeed a vessel.

Many are the graces of nature that embellish this auspicious and life-stretching art. The universe is the vessel that gives birth to all things, from the seasonal changes of flower and leaf, the snow and moon, mountains and seas, plants and trees, the sentient and nonsentient. In taking these many things as the affective materials of our art, our aim is to make the mind a vessel of the universe, establish that vessel of mind securely in the vast and formless emptiness, and attain the miraculous flower of attainment in the art.

ON HANA: THE SPIRIT OR "FLOWER" OF NO DRAMA

Now how shall we understand this *hana* of No in these secret instructions? First of all, you must understand the reason why they have used the symbol of flowers for *hana*. As every kind of plant and flower blooms at its proper time in the four seasons, people think it is beautiful because they feel its blooming as something fresh and rare. In the art of No the point at which the audience feels this freshness and rarity will be the interesting part to them. So the "*hana*," the "interesting part," and the "rarity" are one and the same thing. No flower can remain in bloom for ever. It gives pleasure to the eye because its bloom has been so long awaited. In the art of No it is the same, and a *shite* (principal actor) must know first of all that *hana* is a thing which is constantly changing. To change its style, not always keeping to the same one, will make the audience more interested. But in doing so, there is a method. Even if I recommend that he employs a rare style, I do not mean that he should use an eccentric or abnormal one which will not be acceptable to most people. After mastering everything that

I have mentioned in the Ages of Training, he must perform, as the occasion requires, various kinds of plays, which he has practiced and learned during his training. We appreciate the freshness and beauty of flowers when they appear in their due season. It is the same in the art of No, and after studying earnestly every kind of play, with severe practice and exercise, he should perform a play which is suitable to the taste of the audience at that time. It is just like the blooming of flowers in their season. A flower is just like the one that bloomed last year. In No, a *shite* will appear in a play which he has not acted for many years, during which interval he has rounded out his repertory with all kinds of dramas, and it will seem new and fresh to an audience which has not seen him do it for such a long time. Furthermore, the taste of the audience varies, and as they have different tastes in music, dancing, action, and *monomane* (the imitation of things), a *shite* is not a real master unless he can perform acceptably to each kind of taste. So the *shite* who has mastered all the kinds of plays is like one who has the seeds of all kinds of flowers throughout the year, from the plum blossom of early spring to the chrysanthemum of autumn. He is able to offer any kind of flower, according to the taste of the audience, the occasion, and the season. . . . Without severe training of various kinds one cannot acquire the real *hana*. *Hana* cannot exist by itself. *Hana* means to understand how to give the impression of freshness and novelty, as a result of many exercises. This is what I mean by "*Hana* is spirit, and the seed is technique."

Even familiar music and action, if performed by a real master, can be extremely interesting. It will never be interesting if an immature actor does them, because he can only do it the way he has been taught. The real master always penetrates to the spirit of the music, even when it is familiar. This spirit of the music is *hana*. Among real masters, a great master who has attained the secret of No can distinguish the supreme *hana* from ordinary *hana*.

ON ACTING AN OLD MAN IN NO

An accomplished actor approaches the role of an old man with the same intent as an old amateur decking himself out to dance and perform. . . . Being an old man to begin with, he has no need to imitate an old man, but instead concentrates all his efforts on the particular role he is playing. . . .

The secret in playing an old man, the way to seem old and still bring your performance to full dramatic flowering is as follows. First of all, don't set your mind on the decrepitude of age. It's generally the case that the dances of No—both elegant and vigorous—are done in time to music; the actor moves his feet, extends and draws back his arms, and performs the appropriate actions in accordance with the beat. But when an old man is dancing, he moves his feet and extends and draws back his arms just a little late, catching the beat slightly behind the *taiko* (large drum) and song and the cadences of the *tsuzumi* (small drum). He does everything just as if he were young, but unavoidably he falls slightly off beat. . . . [His performance] is like blossoms on an ancient tree. . . .

The representation of an old man is [one of] the ultimate accomplishments of our art. Since this is a mode in which your level of achievement is immediately apparent to the viewer, it is of the utmost importance. Indeed, many relatively good actors have never mastered the mode. But then, it's really a mistake in critical judgment to assume that someone is accomplished just because he can mimic the actions of an old woodcutter or salt maker. The figure of an old man in formal or informal court dress—*that* can only be done fittingly by an accomplished actor. Without years of practice and lofty achievements, you cannot perform the role suitably. . . . Most important of all is the dance of an old man. Your problem is how to look old and yet retain the dramatic flower—it's just like blossoms on an ancient tree.

THE HIGHEST LEVEL

The music of virtuosic transcendence [*rangyoku*] is of the highest level. Once you have exhausted your training in the myriad pieces and attained complete proficiency, you mix the positive and negative in the same sound and sing with a voice like, yet unlike, all others. In poetic theory, among the ten styles, in speaking of the strong rank, they mention "the demon-quelling style"; it must be of the same sort of level. This is the transcendent return and is the musical level of singing with complete fruition.

Basho (1644–94) is the pen name of Matsuo Munefusa, the greatest Japanese poet. Bisexual, like many of his contemporaries, he was born in Iga-ueno, near Kyoto. He spent his youth as "intimate companion" to the son of the local lord, and with him he studied the writing of seventeen-syllable verse (haiku). Eventually he became a recluse and lived on the outskirts of Edo in a hut. He continued to travel extensively, however; his masterpiece, *Narrow Road to the Interior*, is an account of a journey he made in 1689 into the deep country north and west of Edo. His work—both in prose and verse—is everywhere penetrated by the fierce precision and compassion of Zen.

Few poets in any language convey, as Basho does, the mystical power and presence of the ordinary. He wrote: "What is important is to keep mind high in the world of true understanding, then, returning to daily experience, seek therein the true and the beautiful. No matter what the activity of the moment, we must never forget it has a bearing on everlasting self, our poetry."

In this poor body, composed of one hundred bones and nine openings, is something called spirit, a flimsy curtain swept this way and that by the slightest breeze. It is spirit, such as it is, which led me to poetry, at first little more than a pastime, then the full business of my life. There have been times when my spirit, so dejected, almost gave up the quest; other times when it was proud, triumphant. So it has been from the very start, never finding peace with itself, always doubting the worth of what it makes. . . . All who achieve greatness in art— Saigyo in traditional poetry, Sogi in linked verse, Sesshu in painting, Rikyu in the tea ceremony—possess one thing in common: they are one with nature.

The master said, "Learn about a pine tree from a pine tree, and about a bamboo stalk from a bamboo stalk." What he meant was that the poet should detach his mind from self . . . and enter into the object, sharing its delicate life and its feelings. Whereupon a poem forms itself. Description of the object is not enough: unless a poem contains feelings which have come from the object, the object and the poet's self will be separate things.

His disciple Doho on Basho

Plunging hoofs stir
Futami sand—divine white
horse greets New Year.

Spring night,
cherry—
blossom dawn.

Wearing straw cloaks,
with spring
saints greet each other.

Spring rain—
under trees
a crystal stream.

Monks' feet clomping
through icy dark,
drawing sweet water.

Spring moon—
flower face
in mist.

Sparrows in eaves,
mice in ceiling—
celestial music.

Old pond,
leap—splash—
a frog.

Awaiting snow,
poets in their cups
see lightning flash.

Dozing on horseback,
smoke from tea-fires
drifts to the moon.

Buddha's death-day—
old hands
clicking rosaries.

Year's end, all
corners of this
floating world, swept.

Autumn—even
birds and clouds
look old.

Dew-drops—
how better wash away
world's dust?

Tomb, bend
to autumn wind—
my sobbing.

Summer grasses,
all that remains
of soldiers' dreams.

Sick on a journey—
over parched fields
dreams wander on.

The months and days are wayfarers of a hundred generations, and
the years that come and go are also travelers. Those who float all their
lives on a boat or reach their old age leading a horse by the bit make
travel out of each day and inhabit travel. Many in the past also died
while traveling. In which year it was I do not recall, but I, too, began
to be lured by the wind like a fragmentary cloud and have since been
unable to resist wanderlust, roaming out to the seashores. Last fall,
I swept aside old cobwebs in my dilapidated hut in Fukagawa, and
soon the year came to a close; as spring began and haze rose in the
sky, I longed to walk beyond Shirakawa Barrier and, possessed and
deranged by the distracting deity and enticed by the guardian deity
of the road, I was unable to concentrate on anything. In the end I
mended the rips in my pants, replaced hat strings, and, the moment
I gave a moxa treatment to my kneecaps, I thought of the moon over
Matsushima. I gave my living quarters to someone and moved into
Sampu's villa:

> *Kusa no to mo sumi-kawaru yo zo hina no ie*
> In my grass hut the residents change: now a dolls' house

I left the first eight links hung on a post of my hut.
. . . .
On the first day of the fourth month, we paid our respects to
The Mountain. In ancient times the name of this mountain used to
be written to read *Futurasan* (Mount Two Disasters), but when the
Great Teacher Kukai founded the temple, he changed it to *Nikko*
(Sunlight). He must have foreseen the future a thousand years ahead:
today the light from this place illuminates the entire heaven, its

beneficence fills the whole land, and the easeful home for all four classes of people is peaceful. Awestruck, I was barely able to take up my brush:

> *Ara toto aoba wakaba no hi no hikari*
> Look, so holy: green leaves young leaves in the light of the sun

... The Ojima shore, connected to the mainland, is an isle jutting out into the sea. There are things like the site where Zen Master Ungo's detached residence used to be and his Zen meditation rock. I also saw under pine trees a smattering of people who had renounced this world quietly living in a grass hut from which smoke rose from a fire of gleanings and pine cones. I did not know who they were, but I stopped by, feeling close to them. The moon shining on the sea gave a view different from that of daytime. We went back to the bay shore and sought an inn. It had a second floor with an open window, and as we lay in the midst of wind and cloud, I felt mysteriously exhilarated.

· ·

In the domain of Yamagata is a mountain temple called Ryushaku-ji. Founded by the Great Teacher Jikaku, it is a particularly pure, tranquil place. Because people urged us to take a look at it, we turned back from Obanazawa, the distance between them about seven *li*. The sun was not down yet. After reserving lodging at the visitors' quarters at the foot we climbed to the temple on the mountaintop. The mountain was made of rocks piled upon boulders, the pines and cypresses were aged, and with the soil and stones old and smooth with moss and the doors of the lesser halls upon the rocks all closed, we heard not a sound. As we went around the cliff, crawled up the rocks, and paid respects to the Buddhist sanctum, the splendid scenery was so hushed and silent that we could only feel our hearts grow clear.

> *Shizukasa ya iwa ni shimiiru semi no koe*
> Quietness: seeping into the rocks, the cicada's voice

From Narrow Road to the Interior

CHAPTER FIVE

LOVE IS THE DIAMOND

THE PERSIAN SUFI TRADITIONS

ATTAR

Farid ud-Din Attar was born during the twelfth century in Nishapur in northeast Iran. His date of birth is variously given between 1120 and 1157; the earlier date is more likely. His early life was spent in wandering from one educational establishment to another in Egypt, Syria, Arabia, Turkestan, and India. After his wanderings, he settled down in his hometown and bought a pharmacy, and it was there that he wrote the great masterpieces that made him the favorite mystical poet of many of the Sufi masters, including Rumi. Later in his life he was, it seems, arraigned on charges of heresy; the charges were upheld and Attar was banished and his property looted. However, he returned to Nishapur before his death, which was shortly before 1220.

His chief works are *The Book of the Divine*, *The Book of Affliction*, and *The Book of Secrets*. In his masterpiece, *The Conference of the Birds* (excerpted below), homosexual love is frequently praised for its intensity and passion, and the homosexual's ability to give up all respectability in the name of love is represented as mirroring the necessity of abandoning all restrictions and social shibboleths in the search for God. Throughout his work homosexual and heterosexual love are treated with equal reverence and both are seen as forms of initiation into divine life.

A STORY OF MAHMOUD AND AYAZ

Shah Mahmoud called Ayaz to him and gave
His crown and throne to this bewitching slave,
Then said: "You are the sovereign of these lands;
I place my mighty army in your hands—
I wish for you unrivaled majesty,
That you enslave the very sky and sea."
But when the soldiers heard of this, their eyes
Grew black with envy they could not disguise.
"What emperor in all the world," they said,
"Has heaped such honors on a servile head?"
Though even as they murmured Ayaz wept
That what the king decreed he must accept;
The courtiers said to him: "You are insane
To change from slave to king and then complain!"
But Ayaz answered them: "O, rather say
My king desires me to be far away,
To lead the army and be occupied
In almost any place but by his side.
What he commands I'll do, but in my heart
We shall not—for one instant—live apart;
And what have I to do with majesty?
To see my king is realm enough for me."
If you would be a pilgrim of the Truth,
Learn how to worship from this lovely youth.
Day follows night—you argue and protest
And cannot pass the first stage of our quest;
Each night you chatter as the hours pass by
And send Orion down the dawning sky,
And still you linger—though another day
Has broken, you're no further on your way.
From highest heaven they came to welcome you,
And you made lame excuses and withdrew!

Alas! You're not the man for this; your thoughts
See hell's despair and heaven's wondrous courts—
Forget these two, and glory's radiant light
Will stage by stage emerge from darkest night;
The pilgrim does not long for paradise—
Keep back your heart; He only will suffice.

AYAZ'S SICKNESS

Ayaz, afflicted with the Evil Eye,
Fell ill. For safety he was forced to lie
Sequestered from the court, in loneliness.
The king (who loved him) heard of his distress
And called a servant. "Tell Ayaz," he said,
"What tears of sympathy I daily shed.
Tell him that I endure his suffering,
And hardly comprehend I am the king;
My soul is with him (though my flesh is here)
And guards his bed solicitous with fear;
Ayaz, what could this Evil Eye not do,
If it destroys such loveliness as you!"
The king was silent; then again he spoke:
"Go quickly as a fire, return like smoke;
Stop nowhere, but outrun the brilliant flash
That lights the world before the thunder's crash.
Go now; if you so much as pause for breath
My anger will pursue you after death."
The servant scuttled off, consumed with dread,
And like the wind arrived at Ayaz' bed—
There sat his sovereign, by the patient's head!
Aghast, the servant trembled for his life
And pictured in his mind the blood-smeared knife.
"My king," he said, "I swear, I swear indeed,
That I have hurried here with utmost speed—
Although I see you here I cannot see
How in the world you have preceded me;
Believe my innocence, and if I lie

I am a heathen and deserve to die."
His sovereign answered him: "You could not know
The hidden ways by which we lovers go;
I cannot bear my life without his face,
And every minute I am in this place.
The passing world outside is unaware
Of mysteries Ayaz and Mahmoud share;
In public I ask after him, although
Behind the veil of secrecy I know
Whatever news my messengers could give;
I hide my secret and in secret live."

THE VALLEY OF LOVE

Love's valley is the next, and here desire
Will plunge the pilgrim into seas of fire,
Until his very being is enflamed
And those whom fire reflects turn back ashamed.
The lover is a man who flares and burns,
Whose face is fevered, who in frenzy yearns,
Who knows no prudence, who will gladly send
A hundred worlds toward their blazing end,
Who knows of neither faith nor blasphemy,
Who has no time for doubt or certainty,
To whom both good and evil are the same,
And who is neither, but a living flame. . . .

Love led a lord through paths of misery.
He left his splendid house and family
And acted like a drunkard to be near
The boy he loved, who lived by selling beer—
He sold his house and slaves and all he had
To get the means to buy beer from this lad.
When everything was gone and he grew poor
His love grew stronger, more and then yet more—
Though food was given him by passers-by,
His endless hunger made him long to die
(Each morsel that he had would disappear,

Not to be eaten but exchanged for beer,
And he was happy to endure the pain,
Knowing that soon he could buy beer again).
When someone asked: "What is this love?" he cried:
"It is to sell the world and all its pride—
A hundred times—to buy one drop of beer."
Such acts denote true love, and it is clear
That those who cannot match this devotee
Have no acquaintance with love's misery.

A watchman fell in love—the poor man kept
Love's vigil day and night and never slept.
A friend reproved this lover. "Sleep!" he cried,
"Sleep for one moment!" But the man replied:
"I am a lover and a watchman; how
Could I know sleep and break this double vow?
How can a watchman sleep? Especially
A wretched watchman who's in love like me?
My earthly duties and my love unite
To ward off sleep throughout the longest night.
There's no sleep in me—can I ask a friend
For sleep? It's not a substance you can lend!
Each night love puts his watchman to the test,
Watching to see the watchman has no rest,
Beating a drum as if to wake the dead,
Or slapping me about the face and head—
And if I slept a moment, sleepless love
Would raise a tumult to the skies above."
His friend said: "But you never even blink;
All night you burn and cannot sleep a wink!"
He answered him: "A watchman never sleeps;
He knows no water but the tears he weeps—
A watchman's duty is to stay awake,
And lovers parch with thirst for passion's sake;
Since lovers' eyes are filled with flowing tears
Sweet sleep is driven out and disappears—
A lover and a watchman should agree,
Since neither sleeps through all eternity.

Love helps the watchman's vigilance; its pain
Will banish slumber from his fevered brain."
Shun sleep if you would be this sentinel
(Though if your vigil is mere talk, sleep well!).
Pace the heart's streets; thieves lurk in ambush there,
Waiting for you to waver in your care. . . .

Abbasseh told a wandering scholar once:
"The man who's kindled by love's radiance
Will give birth to a woman; when love's fire
Quickens within a woman this desire,
She gives birth to a man; is it denied
That Adam bore a woman from his side,
That Mary bore a man? Until this light
Shines out, such truths are hidden from your sight;
But when its glory comes you will receive
Blessings far greater than you can conceive.
Count this as wealth; here is the faith you need.
But if the world's base glory is your creed,
Your soul is lost—seek the wealth insight gives;
In insight our eternal kingdom lives.
Whoever drinks the mystics' wine is king
Of all the world can show, of everything—
Its realms are specks of his authority,
The heavens but a ship on his wide sea;
If all the sultans of the world could know
That shoreless sea, its mighty ebb and flow,
They'd sit and mourn their wretched impotence
With eyes ashamed to meet each other's glance.

SADI

Musharrif ud-Din Sadi, the great Persian mystical poet, was born in Shiraz
sometime before 1189. His hagiographers tell us that after his twelfth year
he spent thirty years studying and then thirty more years in travels that

took him all over the Middle East and even to India (he is said to have made the pilgrimage to Mecca no less than fourteen times). His wanderings over, he settled in Shiraz, where he wrote the masterpieces that made him famous all over the East as "the Nightingale of a Thousand Songs."

His main work, the *Gulestan,* "The Rose Garden," (excerpted below), was written about 1258. The fifth chapter of the *Gulestan* is devoted to the love of young people, mostly male. In Sadi's poetry, as in a great deal of Persian poetry, the love of a beautiful young man—or *shahid,* "witness of beauty"—is the means by which the poet focuses on and praises the Divine Beloved. "God is Beauty" says the Qur'an; for many great Persian mystics that beauty was most exquisitely and profoundly seen, tasted, and adored in the beauty of a beardless young man. The love of young men, in this vision, did not separate the seeker from God; on the contrary, as in the vision of Plato, it could be an initiation into divine splendor and bliss.

ONE NIGHT

I remember that, one night, a dear friend of mine entered the door; I jumped up from my place so elated that the lamp was put out by my sleeve.

POETRY

An apparition of one who lighted up the darkness with his
*   countenance came at night,*
An imaginary form, traveling with me at night as a guide:
He whom I love came to me in brightness,
And I said to him, "Welcome! welcome! welcome! friend."

I was astonished at my luck,
Saying to myself : Whence this good fortune!

Thereupon he sat down, and commenced scolding me, saying, "Why didst thou put out the lamp the moment thou sawest me?" I replied, "I thought the sun rose; and, moreover, (of) what the witty say:

STANZA

'If an obnoxious person come before the light,
Jump up and put it out in the midst of the party;

And if he be one with a sweet smile, and sweet lips,
Take hold of his sleeve, and extinguish the light.'"

I remember that, in the days of my youth, I had to pass through a
certain street, and I set eyes on a face most sweet, at the height of such
a hot season, that the heat thereof was parching my mouth, and the
hot wind thereof setting the marrow of my bones a-boiling. Through
the feebleness of human nature, I had not the strength to bear the sun,
and took shelter in the shade of a wall, watching for someone to allay
the heat of my system with a draught of iced water. All of a sudden a
light shone forth from the darkness of the antechamber of a house—
that is to say, a lovely boy appeared, such that the tongue of eloquence
would fail to describe his beauty—just as morn breaks upon a dark
night, or as the water of life issues from the dark regions, holding a
goblet of iced water in his hand, with sugar dissolved in it, and rose-
water mixed. I know not whether he had perfumed it with rose-water,
or distilled some drops from the roses of his own face into it. I took
the sherbet from his beautiful hand, and drank it, and received new
life, and said:

POETRY

*"There is a thirst in my heart which the sucking in of cool, sweet,
      water,
Would not go nigh to allay, even though I drank seas-full* (of it).

STANZA

Happy (is it) for the fortune-favored mortal whose eyes
Fall on such a face every morning!
He who is intoxicated with the wine may wake at midnight;
He who is intoxicated with the (beauty of the) cup-bearer will
      not wake till the morn of the day of resurrection."

LOVE'S REALITY

There was an honorable and pure-lived young man,
Whose heart was pledged to a lovely youth.
I have so read, that in the ocean,

They fell together into a vortex.
When a sailor came to seize his hand,
Lest he should perish in that situation,
He was crying out from the midst of the waves of anguish,
"Leave me, and seize the hand of my beloved."
While he was in the act of uttering this, a world of confusion closed
    upon him.
They heard him saying, as he was dying,
"Listen not to love's tale from that false one
Who forgets love in the midst of distress."
Thus do lovers live;
Pay heed to him who has had to do with the matter, in order that
    thou mayst know;
For Sadi the ways and modes of love-making
Knows as well as they know Arabic in Baghdad
The beloved that thou hast, fix thy heart on him alone,
And thenceforth close thine eyes to all the world beside.
Were Majnun and Laila living,
They would copy the story of (their) love from this Book.

STORY OF A RAINDROP

A raindrop fell from a spring cloud, and, seeing the wide expanse of
the sea, was shamed. "Where the sea is, " it reflected, "where am I?
Compared with that, forsooth, I am extinct."

While thus regarding itself with an eye of contempt, an oyster
took it to its bosom, and Fate so shaped its course that eventually the
raindrop became a famous royal pearl.

It was exalted, for it was humble. Knocking at the door of extinc-
tion, it became existent.

STORY ILLUSTRATIVE OF PIOUS MEN REGARDING THEMSELVES WITH CONTEMPT

A sagacious youth of noble family landed at a seaport of Turkey, and,
as he displayed piety and wisdom, his baggage was deposited in a
mosque.

One day the priest said to him: "Sweep away the dust and rubbish from the mosque."

Immediately, the young man went away and no one saw him there again. Thus, did the elder and his followers suppose he did not care to serve.

The next day, a servant of the mosque met him on the road and said: "Thou didst act wrongly in thy perverse judgment. Knowest thou not, O conceited youth, that men are dignified by service?"

Sorrowfully, the youth began to weep. "O soul-cherishing and heart-illuminating friend!" he answered; "I saw no dirt or rubbish in that holy place but mine own corrupt self. Therefore, I retraced my steps, for a mosque is better cleansed from such."

Humility is the only ritual for a devotee. If thou desire greatness, be humble; no other ladder is there by which to climb.

HAFIZ

Muhammad Shams ud-Din Hafiz (1307–88) was born, like Sadi, in Shiraz, where he died after a long, rich, and creative life. With Rumi, he is perhaps the most famous of the Persian mystical poets in the West, largely due to Goethe's discovery of him (in German translation) in the early nineteenth century and his imitation of some of Hafiz's forms and exotic imagery in his own *West-östlicher Divan.* Hafiz, like Attar and Sadi, was at once an impassioned and serious Sufi mystic of the deepest and highest inner experience and an ecstatic lover of young men. Like Sadi, he celebrated the young men he adored as *shahids*, witnesses, to that beauty that is creating all the worlds and so whether consciously or not, initiators into the *Kibriya,* or Glory of the Divine.

Although upon his moonlike cheek delight and beauty glow,
Nor constancy nor love is there: O Lord! These gifts bestow.

A child makes war against my heart; and he in sport one day
Will put me to a cruel death, and law shall not gainsay.

What seems for my own good is this: my heart from him to guard;
For one who knows not good from ill its guardianship were hard.

Agile and sweet, of fourteen years that idol whom I praise:
His earrings in her soul retains the moon of fourteen days.

A breath as the sweet smell of milk comes from those sugary lips;
But from those black and roguish eyes behold what blood there drips!

My heart to find that newborn rose has gone upon its way;
But where can it be found, O Lord? I've lost it many a day.

If the young friend who owns my heart my center thus can break,
The Pasha will command him soon the lifeguard's rank to take.

> I'd sacrifice my life in thanks,
> If once that pearl of sheen
> Would make the shell of HAFIZ' eye
> Its place of rest serene.

PAEAN OF A DREG-DRINKER

The splendor of youth, again
Has come to the garden.
The fragrance of the rose carries
A sweet message to the nightingale.

Soft breeze,
If you reach the meadow where
The cypress, rose, and sweet basil lie—
Give them my greetings.

If the young wine selling mage
Should thus choose to come,
I will make my eyelash a broom
And sweep the walkway clean.

Oh moon, do not eclipse your white beauty
With your dark flowing hair.
For then my tortured mind
Shall be a frenzy of perplexity.

Though the sophisticated scoff
At those who drink the dregs
They will lose their faith
When they arrive at the tavern door.

Stand near the blessed few.
In Noah's ark a little dust
Inherited everything.
While a drop of water was repaid
With total devastation.

Go forth from the world and seek not bread
For within the dark cup is a deadly potion.
To all whose future is to be dust
What use is it to build a tower to the sky?

My Moon of Canaan,
the Throne of Egypt,
Is yours. The hour is near.
It is time to bid the prison farewell.

So drink in joy, Hafiz!
And balance on the brink.
But do not twist as others have
The sacred word of God
Into a hypocritical snare of lies.

IN LOVE'S GREAT OCEAN

In love's great ocean, whose calm shelter's shore
Must he for ever leave, whose soul is bound
On farthest quest, life's wonders to explore—

That mightiest flood, all-whelming, torment-toss'd,
Wherein must ev'ry lover's self be lost
Ere the Beloved's lovelier self be found—

Think not, O searcher, in that sea to find
Food for thine earthborn strength and lustful show,
Nor glorious pearl to deck thy worldly mind,

Nor isle of ease; all such doth he forego
Who, recking nought of hurt to pride or limb,
Heark'neth to love's unchallengeable call:

Yea, who would venture, no help is for him
Save whole surrender; health, strength, life and all.

WHEN THE STRONG CLIMBER

When the strong climber his last mountain crest
Attaineth, and the point for which he strove
Is reached, and his desire made manifest,

and seating him the topmost heights above
He gazeth on each aspect leisurely,
Considering the path by which he clomb

and which so many attempted, and how he
The first of all his race had strength to come
Unto that eminence, and how this throne

Shall men hereafter to his name recall;
Then more than ever is he strangely lone,
Seeing earth's dwellings spread out far and small;

and more unfathom'd seemeth and more high,
Eternal heaven's unchanged immensity.

IRAQI

Fahkruddin Iraqi was born in the village of Kamajan, near the city of Hamadan, about 1213, and died in Damascus, an honored sheikh and mystic, on November 23, 1289. By the time Iraqi was eight, he was famous throughout Hamadan for his singing voice and learning; by seventeen he had learned all the sciences both "transmitted" and "intellectual" and had started to teach himself. The decisive event of his life happened when he was about twenty; he ran off—first to Persia and then to India—with a group of wandering Sufi dervishes known as Kalendars, who cultivated the Way of Drunkenness and Abandon. What he learned from them changed him forever into an impassioned mystic who also loved young men, and loved them in an open ecstatic way that drew criticism from the more staid and orthodox. His habits and eccentricities did not, however, cause him to forfeit his place of honor among his contemporaries; in middle age he became the sheikh of an order and his masterpiece, the *Lama'at* ("Divine Flashes"), is thought of by many to be, with Shabestari's *The Rosegarden of Mystery* and Rumi's odes, among the greatest and most sublime works of Sufi mysticism.

Although you may not know it,
If you love anyone, it is Him you love;
If you turn your head in any direction,
it is toward Him you turn.

Let go of everything,
Completely lose yourself on this path,
Then your every doubt will be dispelled.
With absolute conviction you'll cry out—
I am God!
I am the one I have found!

In the light I praised you
And never knew it.
In the dark I slept with you
And never knew it.
I always thought that I was me,
But no, I was you
and never knew it.

I LOOK INTO THE MIRROR

I look into the mirror and see my own beauty;
I see the Truth of the universe revealing itself as me.

I rise in the sky as the morning Sun, do not be surprised,
Every particle of creation is me alone.

What are the holy spirits? My essence revealed.
And the human Body? The vessel of my own form.

What is the ocean that encircles the world?
A drop of my abundant Grace;
And the purest light that fills every soul?
A spark of my own illumination.

I am Light itself, reflected in the heart of everyone;
I am the treasure of the Divine Name,
the shining Essence of all things.

I am every light that shines,
Every ray that illumines the world.

From the highest heavens to the bedrock of the earth
All is but a shadow of my splendor.

If I dropped the veil covering my true essence
The world would be gone—lost in a brilliant light.

What is the water that gives eternal life?
A drop of my divine nectar.
And the breath that brings the dead back to life?
A puff of my breath, the breath of all life. . . .

FLASH II

King Love desired to pitch His tent in the desert, open the door of His
warehouse, and scatter treasures to the world;

> then raised His parasol,
>   hoisted His banners
> to mingle Being
>   and nothingness.
> Ah, the restlessness
>   of enrapturing Love
> has thrown the world
>   in tumult!

But if He had not done so, the world would have slumbered on, at rest with existence and nonexistence, at ease in the Retreat of Vision where "God was, and nothing was with Him."

> In those days
>   before a trace
> of the two worlds,
>   no "other" yet imprinted
> on the Tablet of Existence,
>   I, the Beloved, and Love
> lived together
>   in the corner
> of an uninhabited
>   cell.

But suddenly Love the Unsettled flung back the curtain from the whole show, to display Its perfection as the "Beloved" before the entity of the world;

> and when Its ray of loveliness appeared
> at once the world came into being
> at once the world borrowed sight
> from Love's Beauty, saw the loveliness of Its Face
> and at once went raving mad;
> borrowed sugar from Love's lips
> and tasting it at once began to speak.

> One needs Thy Light
> To see Thee. . . .

The Morning of Manifestation sighed, the breeze of Grace breathed gently, ripples stirred upon the sea of Generosity. The clouds of Effusion poured down the rain of "He sprinkled creation with His Light" upon the soil of preparedness; so much rain that *the earth shone with the Light of its Lord.* The lover, then, satiated with the water of life, awoke from the slumber of nonexistence, put on the cloak of being and tied round his brow the turban of contemplation; he cinched the belt of desire about his waist and set forth with the foot of sincerity upon the path of the Search.

> He came from theory to actuality,
> from hearsay to the Embrace! (Sana'i)

As soon as he opened his eyes his gaze fell upon the Beloved, and he said, "I have never beheld anything without seeing God before it" ('Ali); he looked at himself, found that all of him was HE, and exclaimed,

> "So only Reality peers out of my eyes!
> A peculiar business, indeed!
> If I have become the Beloved,
> who is the lover?"

Here indeed the lover is the very Beloved, for he has no existence of his own to call "the lover." He still sleeps in his original nonexistence, just as the Beloved remains forever in His Eternity: "He is now as He was."

> Beloved, Love and lover—three-in-one.
> There is no place for Union here
> so what's this talk of "separation"?

From Divine Flashes

FLASH XVII

Each moment from each of the myriad windows of the Attributes the Beloved shows the lover a different face, and from these rays of light the lover's inner eye gains illumination with each flash, fresh vision with each passing instant. The more beauty is displayed, the more overpowering the love; the more overpowering the love, the more beauty is displayed . . . and all the while the gap grows wider between Beloved and lover. Finally the lover flees the Loved-one's cruelty, flies to the Refuge of Love Itself, and clings to Oneness that he may escape duality.

The Manifestation of Lights, so it has been said, extends as far as the preparedness, and the Effusion of Gnosis as far as the receptivity.

> No fault of the sun if the owl
> gains nothing from its light.

The more you purify the face of your heart
   the better prepared for theophany. (Sana'i)

True enough . . . but "O Thou who makest blessings to appear before they are deserved!" That is, when the Beloved would display
Himself in the lover's mystic eye, He lends that organ a glimmer of
His own Beauty-ray. With this light the lover can see and take pleasure in that Divine loveliness.

After the lover has enjoyed through that light his share of contemplation, again the radiance of the Beloved's Face bestows upon his eye a
brighter light—with which yet greater lights can be perceived. And so
and so it goes, like a thirsty man gulping saltwater: The more he drinks,
the more rages his thirst. The more you acquire, the more you aspire.

> The more I gaze
>   at Your face, the more
> my eyes incline
>   toward Your vision
> like one who dies of thirst
>   by the ocean shore,
> lips to the wave,
>   thirstier and thirstier.
>
> Seek not, find not—
>   except in this one case:
> Until you find the Friend
>   you'll never seek Him.

One who thirsts for *this* water can never be satisfied.

From Divine Flashes

JAMI

Muwlana Nur ud-Din Jami (1414–90) was born in Jam, a small town of
Khorassan, from which he took his *takhalus,* or poetic name, Jami. Educated first at Herat and then in Samarcand, Jami returned to Herat in his
early twenties at the prompting of a dream to study under a famous Sufi

master there, Sheikh Mehmed Kaschgari. Soon after his religious apprenticeship began, Jami began to write the rich mystical poetry for which he quickly became famous all over the Islamic world. By the time of his death in Herat in 1490, Jami was the most famous mystical poet of his day. He never made any secret of his passion for young men and wrote of it in the *shahid* tradition of Sadi and Hafiz; he was also married, with five children.

All through eternity
Beauty unveils His exquisite form
in the solitude of nothingness;
He holds a mirror to His Face
and beholds His own beauty.
He is the knower and the known,
the seer and the seen;
No eye but His own
has ever looked upon this Universe.

His every quality finds an expression:
Eternity becomes the verdant field of Time and Space;
Love, the life-giving garden of this world.
Every branch and leaf and fruit
Reveals an aspect of His perfection—
The cypress give hint of His majesty,
The rose gives tidings of His beauty.

Wherever Beauty looks,
Love is also there;
Wherever Beauty shows a rosy cheek
Love lights Her fire from that flame.
When Beauty dwells in the dark folds of night
Love comes and finds a heart
entangled in her tresses.
Beauty and Love are as body and soul.
Beauty is the mine, Love is the diamond.

They have been together
since the beginning of time—
Side by side, step by step.

CHAPTER SIX

FIERY LOVE

THE RENAISSANCE AND AFTER

MICHELANGELO

Michelangelo (1475–1564) was born in Caprese, a village near Florence. During the course of his long and complex life, he established himself as the greatest artist of the Renaissance. The colossal statue of David, the frescoes of the Sistine Chapel, and the Dome of St. Peter's Cathedral are among his many masterpieces recognized as landmarks in the history of art.

When he was fifty-seven, in 1532, Michelangelo met and fell in love with the "infinitely beautiful" Tommaso Cavalieri, a Roman aristocrat. At twenty-three, Cavalieri, in his strong and tender beauty, symbolized to the aging artist that ideal of masculine physical and spiritual perfection that he had been searching for all his life. Cavalieri respected and was moved by Michelangelo's devotion, but it is unlikely that they were physical lovers. Cavalieri later married; Michelangelo was tormented by religious scruples. Yet his passion for the young Roman gave birth to some great mystical love poetry. In his sonnets, Michelangelo explores poignantly and with great honesty the mystery of the relationship between human and divine beauty and the rich, sometimes harrowing, tensions he endured in the sacred task he set for himself of transmuting human desire into divine love.

This glorious light I see with your own eyes
Since mine are blind and will not let me see.
Your feet lend me their own security
To carry burdens far beyond my size.

Supported by your wings I now am sped,
And by your spirit to heaven I am borne.
According to your will, I'm pale or red—
Hot in the harshest winter, cold in sun.

All my own longings wait upon your will,
Within your heart my thoughts find formulation,
Upon your breath alone my words find speech.

Just as the moon owes its illumination
To the sun's light, so I am blind until
To every part of heaven your rays will reach.

The first day I beheld so much unique
Beauty, I trusted that I might be one
Who, like the eagle soaring to the sun,
Finds such a radiance makes its own eyes weak.

The fault was mine; I knew that I had failed,
Since he who follows angels and lacks wings
Is sowing seeds on stone, his words are whirled
Away by wind; God takes his questionings.

My heart will not support me when I know
So great a beauty's near; my eyes grow blind
Though, from a distance, it persuades me still.

What will become of me? What guide will show
Some value in myself I still may find?
When near, you burn me, when far off, you kill.

Only through fire can the smith pull and stretch
Metal into the shape of his design.

Only through fire can the artist reach
Pure gold which only furnaces refine.

Nor can the phoenix rare itself remake
Unless it first be burnt. For my part, I
Hope to ascend triumphantly on high
Where death fulfills, where time itself must break.

The fire of which I speak has brought salvation,
I find in it new powers and restoration
Although I seemed already with the dead.

Since fire by nature reaches up to heaven
I may, through it, be reconciled, forgiven,
For it must surely bear me overhead.

To others merciful and only to
Itself unkind, this lowly creature who
Sloughs off its skin in pain that it may give
Pleasure to others, dies that they may live.

So do I long for such a destiny—
That from my death, my Lord, you might alone
Take life; then by my death I too might be
Changed like the worm which casts its skin on stone.

For if that skin were mine I could at least
Be woven in a gown to clasp that breast,
And so embrace the beauty which I crave.

Then would I gladly die. Or could I save
My Lord's feet from the rain by being shoes
Upon his feet—this also would I choose.

The living portion of my love is not
My heart; the love with which I love has no
Heart, for in human hearts things mean and low
Always exist, in impulse or in thought.

Love which came, like the soul, from God's own hands
Made me without eyes, made you full of light;
That light cannot be seen in what death ends—
The mortal part which hurts me with delight.

Just as from fire the heat cannot be parted,
Neither can I be separated from
That Beauty in whose likeness she is made.

Ardent, I run to joys which cannot fade,
That paradise where your own beauty started,
Eternal loveliness from which you come.

I see in your fair face, my dearest Lord,
That which in life I cannot fitly tell.
Your soul already, though flesh holds it still,
Has many times ascended to its God.

And if the vulgar and malignant crowd
Misunderstand the love with which we're blest,
Its worth is not affected in the least:
Our faith and honest love can still feel proud.

Earth is the meager source of all that we
Can know while still fleshbound. To those who see
In the right way, it gives most copiously.

All that we have of wisdom and of faith
Derives from earth, and if I love you with
Fervor, I shall reach God and find sweet death.

When you came back into this earthly prison,
It was as if an angel had sprung forth;
You were so full of that divine compassion
Which heals the mind and dignifies the earth.

This only draws me and with this alone
I fall in love, not with the outward grace

Of gentle features. Love will not grow less
When such a lasting good it fixes on.

In this way value always is detected
In proud and natural things. Heaven will not fail
To give what's needful when their birth takes place.

God in no other way has shown His grace
Than in a lovely and a mortal veil
In which I find He is Himself reflected.

Then let me see you everywhere I go.
If merely mortal beauty make me burn,
How much more strongly shall I shine and glow
When to your fiery love at last I turn.

Dear God, I call and plead with you alone,
For only you can help my blinding pain;
You only have the power to sustain
My courage. I am helpless on my own.

This everlasting spirit, which you gave
To me on earth, is locked within a frail
Body and doomed to an unhappy fate.

What can I do? Myself I cannot save;
Without your strength I certainly shall fail.
Only divine power can improve my state.

SHAKESPEARE

William Shakespeare (1564–1616) is universally recognized as the greatest
dramatist and one of the greatest poets of humankind. His sonnets record
the inner history of a three-way love affair, with a beautiful young man
and a wild Dark Lady who both betray him with each other. The poems

to the young man burn with a passion at once sensual and revelatory, sexual and religious. As the poet Thomas Beddoes wrote to his friend Thomas Kelsall in 1827, "The sonnets are deep and ardent expressions in which Shakespeare turns his heart out and reveals the root of a love as firm and sacred as the foundations of the world."

Very few modern scholars now dispute Shakespeare's bisexuality, although for centuries any mention of "homosexuality" in the sonnets was considered blasphemy. What is more controversial now is the extent of Shakespeare's religious belief. In recent years, many excellent studies have revealed the depth and complexity of the Rosicrucian and alchemical references in the later plays (notably in *The Winter's Tale, Pericles,* and *The Tempest*). These suggest that, in the last decades of his life, Shakespeare turned to different, but linked, kinds of mystical philosophy to deepen his understanding of the working of providence and redemption in our lives —the great theme of all his last great works.

FIVE SONNETS

Shall I compare thee to a summer's day?
Thou art more lovely and more temperate:
Rough winds do shake the darling buds of May,
And summer's lease hath all too short a date:
Sometime too hot the eye of heaven shines,
And often is his gold complexion dimmed:
And every fair from fair sometime declines,

By chance, or nature's changing course untrimm'd;
But thy eternal summer shall not fade,
Nor lose possession of that fair thou ow'st,
Nor shall death brag thou wander'st in his shade,
When in eternal lines to time thou grow'st
So long as men can breathe, or eyes can see,
So long lives this, and this gives life to thee.

When in disgrace with fortune and men's eyes
I all alone beweep my outcast state,

And trouble deaf heaven with my bootless cries,
And look upon myself, and curse my fate,
Wishing me like to one more rich in hope,
Featur'd like him, like him with friends possess'd
Desiring this man's art, and that man's scope,
With what I most enjoy contented least;
Yet in these thoughts myself almost despising,
Haply I think on thee—and then my state,
Like to the lark at break of day arising
From sullen earth, sings hymns at heaven's gate;
For thy sweet love remember'd such wealth brings
That then I scorn to change my state with kings.

Why didst thou promise such a beauteous day,
And make me travel forth without my cloak,
To let base clouds o'ertake me in my way,
Hiding thy bravery in their rotten smoke?
'Tis not enough that through the cloud thou break,
To dry the rain on my storm-beaten face,
For no man well of such a salve can speak
That heals the wound and cures not the disgrace:
Nor can thy shame give physic to my grief;
Though thou repent, yet I have still the loss:
The offender's sorrow lends but weak relief
To him that bears the strong offense's cross.
Ah! But those tears are pearl which thy love sheds,
And they are rich and ransom all ill deeds.

Let me not to the marriage of true minds
Admit impediments. Love is not love
Which alters when it alteration finds,
Or bends with the remover to remove:
O, no! it is an ever-fixed mark,
That looks on tempests and is never shaken;
It is the star to every wandering bark,

Whose worth's unknown, although his height be taken.
Love's not Time's fool, though rosy lips and cheeks
Within his bending sickle's compass come;
Love alters not with his brief hours and weeks
But bears it out even to the edge of doom.
If this be error, and upon me prov'd
I never writ, nor no man ever lov'd.

Poor soul, the center of my sinful earth,
Fool'd by these rebel powers that thee array,
Why dost thou pine within and suffer dearth,
Painting thy outward walls so costly gay?
Why so large cost, having so short a lease,
Dost thou upon thy fading mansion spend?
Shall worms, inheritors of this excess,
Eat up thy charge? Is this thy body's end?
Then, soul, live thou upon thy servant's loss,
And let that pine to aggravate thy store;
Buy terms divine in selling hours of dross;
Within be fed, without be rich no more:
So shalt thou feed on Death, that feeds on men,
And Death once dead, there's no more dying then.

THE PHOENIX AND THE TURTLE

Let the bird of loudest lay,
On the sole Arabian tree,
Herald sad and trumpet be,
To whose sound chaste wings obey.

But thou shrieking harbinger,
Foul precursor of the fiend,
Augur of the fever's end,
To this troop come thou not near.

From this session interdict
Every fowl of tyrant wing,

Save the eagle, feather'd king:
Keep the obsequy so strict.

Let the priest in surplice white
That defunctive music can,
Be the death-divining swan,
Lest the requiem lack his right.

And thou treble-dated crow,
That thy sable gender mak'st
With the breath thou giv'st and tak'st
'Mongst our mourners shalt thou go.

Here the anthem doth commence:
Love and constancy is dead;
Phoenix and the turtle fled
In a mutual flame from hence.

So they lov'd, as love in twain
Had the essence but in one;
Two distincts, division none:
Number there in love was slain.

Hearts remote, yet not asunder;
Distance, and no space was seen
'Twixt the turtle and his queen:
But in them it were a wonder.

So between them love did shine,
That the turtle saw his right
Flaming in the phoenix's sight;
Either was the other's mine.

Property was thus appall'd,
That the self was not the same;
Single nature's double name
Neither two nor one was call'd

Reason, in itself confounded,
Saw division grow together;

To themselves yet either neither,
Simple were so well compounded,

That it cried, "How true a twain
Seemeth this concordant one!
Love hath reason, reason none,
If what parts can so remain."

Whereupon it made this threne
To the phoenix and the dove,
Co-supremes and stars of love,
As chorus to their tragic scene.

THRENOS

Beauty, truth, and rarity
Grace in all simplicity,
Here enclos'd in cinders lie.

Death is now the phoenix' nest;
And the turtle's loyal breast
To eternity doth rest,

Leaving no posterity:
'Twas not their infirmity,
It was married chastity.

Truth may seem, but cannot be;
Beauty brag, but 'tis not she;
Truth and beauty buried be.

To this urn let those repair
That are either true or fair;
For these dead birds sigh a prayer.

CORDELIA: We are not the first
Who, with best meaning, have incurr'd the worst.
For thee, oppressed king, am I cast down;

Myself could else out-frown false Fortune's frown.
Shall we not see these daughters and these sisters?

LEAR: No, no, no, no! Come, let's away to prison;
We two alone will sing like birds i' the cage:
When thou dost ask me blessing, I'll kneel down,
And ask of thee forgiveness: so we'll live,
And pray, and sing, and tell old tales, and laugh
At gilded butterflies, and hear poor rogues
Talk of court news; and we'll talk with them too,
Who loses and who wins; who's in, who's out;
And take upon's the mystery of things,
As if we were God's spies: and we'll wear out,
In a wall'd prison, packs and sects of great ones
That ebb and flow by the moon.

　　From King Lear, *Act 5, Scene 3*

CROMWELL: O my lord!
Must I then, leave you? Must I needs forego
So good, so noble, and so true a master?
Bear witness all that have not hearts of iron,
With what a sorrow Cromwell leaves his lord.
The king shall have my service; but my prayers
For ever and for ever, shall be yours.

WOLSEY: Cromwell, I did not think to shed a tear
In all my miseries; but thou hast forc'd me,
Out of thy honest truth, to play the woman.
Let's dry our eyes: and thus far hear me, Cromwell;
And, when I am forgotten, as I shall be,
And sleep in dull cold marble, where no mention
Of me more must be heard of, say, I taught thee,
Say, Wolsey, that once trod the ways of glory,
And sounded all the depths and shoals of honor,
Found thee a way, out of his wrack, to rise in;
A sure and safe one, though thy master miss'd it.
Mark but my fall, and that that ruin'd me.

Cromwell, I charge thee, fling away ambition:
By that sin fell the angels; how can man then,
The image of his Maker, hope to win by't?
Love thyself last: cherish those hearts that hate thee;
Corruption wins not more than honesty.
Still in thy right hand carry gentle peace,
To silence envious tongues: be just, and fear not.
Let all the ends thou aim'st at be thy country's,
Thy God's, and truth's; then if thou fall'st, O Cromwell!
Thou fall'st a blessed martyr. Serve the king;
And—prithee, lead me in:
There take an inventory of all I have,
To the last penny; 'tis the king's: my robe,
And my integrity to heaven is all
I dare now call mine own. O Cromwell, Cromwell!
Had I but serv'd my God with half the zeal
I serv'd my king, he would not in mine age
Have left me naked to mine enemies.

CROMWELL: Good sir, have Patience.

WOLSEY: So I have. Farewell
The hopes of court! My hopes in heaven do dwell.

   From Henry VIII, *Act 3, Scene 2*

THE MIRACULOUS REUNION OF PERICLES
AND HIS LONG-LOST DAUGHTER, MARINA

PERICLES: Where were you bred?
And how achiev'd you these endowments, which
You make more rich to owe?

MARINA: Should I tell my history, it would seem
Like lies, disdain'd in the reporting.

PERICLES: Prithee, speak;
Falseness cannot come from thee, for thou look'st
Modest as justice, and thou seem'st a palace
For the crown'd truth to dwell in. I believe thee,

And make my senses credit thy relation
To points that seem impossible; for thou lookest
Like one I lov'd indeed. What were thy friends?
Didst thou not say when I did push thee back—
Which was when I perceiv'd thee—that thou cam'st
From good descending?

MARINA: So indeed I did.

PERICLES: Report thy parentage. I think thou said'st
Thou hadst been toss'd from wrong to injury,
And that thou thought'st thy griefs might equal mine,
If both were open'd.

MARINA: Some such thing
I said, and said no more but what my thoughts
Did warrant me was likely.

PERICLES: Tell thy story;
If thine consider'd prove the thousandth part
Of my endurance thou art a man, and I
Have suffer'd like a girl; yet thou dost look
Like Patience gazing on kings' graves, and smiling
Extremity out of act. What were thy friends?
How lost thou them? Thy name, my most kind virgin?
Recount, I do beseech thee. Come, sit by me.

MARINA: My name is Marina.

PERICLES: O! I am mock'd,
And thou by some incensed god sent hither
To make the world to laugh at me.

MARINA: Patience, good sir,
Or here I'll cease.

PERICLES: Nay, I'll be patient.
Thou little know'st how thou dost startle me,
To call thyself Marina.

MARINA: The name
Was given me by one that had some power;
My father, and a king.

PERICLES: How! A king's daughter?
And call'd Marina?

MARINA: You said you would believe me;
But, not to be a troubler of your peace,
I will end here.

PERICLES: But are you flesh and blood?
Have you a working pulse? And are no fairy?
Motion! Well; speak on. Where were you born?
And wherefore call'd Marina?

MARINA: Call'd Marina
For I was born at sea.

PERICLES: At sea! what mother?

MARINA: My mother was the daughter of a king;
Who died the minute I was born,
As my good nurse Lychorida hath oft
Deliver'd weeping.

PERICLES: O! stop there a little.
This is the rarest dream that e'er dull sleep
Did mock sad fools withal; this cannot be.
My daughter's buried. Well; where were you bred?
I'll hear you more to the bottom of your story,
And never interrupt you.

MARINA: You'll scorn to believe me; 'twere best I did give o'er.

PERICLES: I will believe you by the syllable
Of what you shall deliver. Yet, give me leave:
How came you in these parts? where were you bred?

MARINA: The king my father did in Tarsus leave me,
Till cruel Cleon, with his wicked wife,
Did seek to murder me; and having woo'd
A villain to attempt it, who having drawn to do't,
A crew of pirates came and rescu'd me;
Brought me to Mitylene. But, good sir,
Whither will you have me? Why do you weep? It may be
You think me an impostor; no, good faith;

I am the daughter to King Pericles,
If good King Pericles be.

PERICLES: Ho, Helicanus!

HELICANUS: Calls my lord?

PERICLES: Thou art a grave and noble counsellor,
Most wise in general; tell me, if thou canst,
What this maid is, or what is like to be,
That thus hath made me weep?

HELICANUS: I know not; but
Here is the regent, sir, of Mitylene,
Speaks nobly of her.

LYSIMACHUS: She never would tell
Her parentage; being demanded that,
She would sit still and weep.

PERICLES: O Helicanus! strike me, honor'd sir;
Give me a gash, put me to present pain,
Lest this great sea of joys rushing upon me
O'erbear the shores of my mortality,
And drown me with their sweetness. O! come hither,
Thou that begett'st him that did thee beget;
Thou that wast born at sea, buried at Tarsus,
And found at sea again. O Helicanus!
Down on thy knees, thank the holy gods as loud
As thunder threatens us; this is Marina.
What was thy mother's name? tell me but that,
For truth can never be confirm'd enough,
Though doubts did ever sleep.

MARINA: First, sir, I pray,
What is your title?

PERICLES: I am Pericles of Tyre: but tell me now
My drown'd queen's name, as in the rest you said
Thou hast been god-like perfect;

Thou'rt heir of kingdoms, and another life
To Pericles thy father.

MARINA: Is it no more to be your daughter than
To say my mother's name was Thaisa?
Thaisa was my mother, who did end
The minute I began.

PERICLES: Now, blessing on thee! rise; thou art my child,
Give me fresh garments. Mine own, Helicanus;
She is not dead at Tarsus, as she should have been,
By savage Cleon; she shall tell thee all;
When thou shalt kneel, and justify in knowledge
She is thy very princess. Who is this?

HELICANUS: Sir, 'tis the governor of Mitylene,
Who, hearing of your melancholy state,
Did come to see you.

PERICLES: I embrace you.
Give me my robes. I am wild in my beholding.
O heavens! bless my girl. But, hark! what music?
Tell Helicanus, my Marina, tell him
O'er point by point, for yet he seems to doubt,
How sure you are my daughter. But, what music?

HELICANUS: My lord, I hear none.

PERICLES: None!
The music of the spheres! List, my Marina.

LYSIMACHUS: It is not good to cross him; give him way.

PERICLES: Rarest sounds! Do ye not hear?

LYSIMACHUS: My lord, I hear.

PERICLES: Most heavenly music:
It nips me unto list'ning, and thick slumber
Hangs upon mine eyes; let me rest.

From Pericles, *Act 5, Scene 1*

Sor Juana Inés de la Cruz is one of the greatest mystical writers in Spanish literature. She was born Juana Ramirez de Asbaje in San Miguel Nepantla in New Spain (Mexico) in 1648 or 1651. At fifteen Juana joined the court of the viceroy and vicereine of New Spain in Mexico City as lady-in-waiting and astonished the court by her learning. At twenty, to escape marriage, she later said, Juana became a nun at the convent of San Jerónimo. From her cell, she poured out a river of brilliant work of every kind and kept up a series of passionate relationships with aristocratic women, including several succeeding vicereines. In 1693, after years of being attacked for her "unfeminine" love of learning and her "advanced" views on the education of women, Sor Juana was forced to sign by the church a new profession of faith, was stripped of all her possessions (including her four-thousand-book library), and seems to have given writing up altogether for a life of silence and penance. She died two years later in an epidemic that decimated the convent.

It is impossible to doubt that Sor Juana was lesbian from her letters and poems to the close women friends in her life; they have a far more than conventional intimacy and passion. Her spiritual poetry—especially in her "songs" to the Virgin and in her play *The Divine Narcissus*—combine erudition, clarity of expression, and ecstatic illumination with force and brilliance.

My love, this evening when I spoke with you,
and in your face and actions I could read
that arguments of words you would not heed,
my heart I longed to open to your view.
In this intention, Love my wishes knew
and, though they seemed impossible, achieved:
pouring in tears that sorrow had conceived,
with every beat my heart dissolved anew.
Enough of suffering, my love, enough:
let jealousy's vile tyranny be banned,
let no suspicious thought your calm corrupt

with foolish gloom by futile doubt enhanced,
for now, this afternoon, you saw and touched
my heart, dissolved and liquid in your hands.

Since Love is shivering
in the ice and cold,
since hoarfrost and snow
have ringed him round,
who will come to his aid?
Water!
Earth!
Air!
No, Fire will!
Since the Child is assailed
by pains and ills
and has no breath left
to face his woes,
who will come to his aid?
Fire!
Earth!
Water!
No, but Air will!
Since the loving Child
is burning hot,
that he breathes a volcanic
deluge of flame,
who will come to his aid?
Air!
Fire!
Earth!
No, Water will!
Since today the Child
leaves heaven for earth
and finds nowhere to rest
his head in this world,

who will come to his aid?
Water!
Fire!
Air!
No, but Earth will!

> *From the First* Villancico,
> *Written for the Nativity of our Lord, Pueblo, 1689*

Because my Lord was born to suffer,
let Him stay awake.

Because for me He is awake,
let Him fall asleep.

Let Him stay awake—
there is no pain for one who loves
as painlessness would be.

Let Him sleep—
for one who sleeps, in dreaming,
prepares himself to die.

Silence, now He sleeps!
Careful, He's awake!
Do not disturb Him, no!
Yes, He must be waked!
Let Him wake and wake!
Let Him have his sleep!

> *From the Fifth* Villancico, *in alternating voices,*
> *Written for the Feast of the Nativity in Pueblo, 1689*

[*Refrain:*]
Seraphim, come,
come here and ponder
a Rose that, when cut,
lives all the longer.

So far from wilting
it will be revived
when cruelly tortured,
be fructified
by its own sweet moisture:
    And thus to cut it
renews the wonder.
Gardeners, come,
come here and ponder
a Rose that, when cut,
lives all the longer.

[*Verses:*]
Against one frail Rose
a thousand storm winds plot.
Sheer envy is its lot,
though one brief span is all the life it knows.
    Men envy the Rose its beauty,
its wiseness they resent.
Far too long the world has known
that virtue attracts sin as complement.
    Thus they guarantee
that the slash of whirling knives
from one breath will draw a thousand,
give one heart thorns to pierce a thousand lives.
    Rancor, ever a coward,
is afraid of a simple death:
to snuff out a single life,
it finds a thousand ways to stifle breath.
    But wily, witless evil
is blind and cannot see
that the wicked torturer's wheel
is destined for the chariot of victory.
    Thus, the whirling instrument,
considerate in its blades,
makes its every revolution
one more song in glorious Catherine's praise.

The Rose can hardly find it new
to feel the piercing barbs,
since every rose since time began
has made the prickly thorns its regal guards.

From the Fifth Villancico,
Saint's Day of Catherine of Alexandria, Oaxaca, 1691

NARCISSUS:
Here at last—but what greets my eyes?
What surpassing beauty is this
beside whose purest light
the whole celestial sphere turns pale?
The glistening band of the sun
in all his shining course
from Occident to Orient
will never shed in signs and stars
a light like this, will never flash
as bright as this one Fount.
Heaven and earth joined hands
to form this burst of brilliance,
heaven supplying the beacon,
the meadow giving the bloom.
The sky came down entire
in eagerness to adorn it.
But no, for beauty so peerless
could never have been devised
by all the loving care
of heaven and earth combined. . . .

With but one of those lovely eyes
my heart has been set afire.
With a single twist of the hair
my breast has been transfixed. . . .

Break the crystalline seal
on the clear, cold glass of this fountain

and allow my love to enter.
See how my golden curls
are overspread with hoarfrost,
are wet with dewy pearls.
Come, my Spouse, to your Love,
rend that clear curtain,
make your countenance seen,
let me hear your voice in my ear!
Come with me from Lebanon;
ah, if only you come,
I will place a crown on the Ophir
of your precious locks—
even the sweet-smelling crown
of Amana, Sanir, and Hermon!

    From The Divine Narcissus, *Tableau 4, Scene 9*

CHAPTER SEVEN

THE GODS IN THE BODY

THE NINETEENTH CENTURY

HENRY DAVID THOREAU

Henry David Thoreau was born in Concord, Massachusetts, on July 12, 1817. He attended the newly established Concord Academy and went on to graduate from Harvard with the class of 1837. His most famous work is *Walden* (1854), which chronicles the inner history of his revelatory stay at Walden Pond. He also wrote *A Week on the Concord and Merrimack Rivers* —about a canoe trip he took with his brother John—in addition to journals and essays about nature and science, many of which were published posthumously. He died on May 6, 1862, of tuberculosis.

Thoreau's journals, poems, and essays, especially his essay "Chastity and Sensuality" and the long discourse on "friendship" in *A Week on the Concord and Merrimack Rivers,* all contain naked and vibrant expressions of the beauty, power, and suffering of love between men. In one of his journals Thoreau writes, "I love man with the same distinction that I love woman—as if my friend were of some third sex—some other or some stranger and still my friend" (2:245).

Thoreau is among the most life-affirming and celebratory of mystic writers in any language; the exalted but precise sensuality of his vision of the divine presence in nature and in the ordinary activities of life continues to inspire seekers everywhere.

ON FRIENDSHIP

What is commonly honored with the name of Friendship is no very profound or powerful instinct. Men do not, after all, love their Friends greatly. I do not often see the farmers made seers and wise to the verge of insanity by their Friendship for one another. They are not often transfigured and translated by love in each other's presence. I do not observe them purified, refined, and elevated by the love of a man.

But sometimes we are said to love one another, that is, to stand in a true relation to him, so that we give the best to, and receive the best from, him. Between whom there is hearty truth there is love; and in proportion to our truthfulness and confidence in one another, our lives are divine and miraculous, and answer to our ideal. There are passages of affection in our intercourse with mortal men and women, such as no prophecy has taught us to expect, which transcend our earthly life, and anticipate heaven for us. What is this Love that may come right into the middle of a prosaic Goffstown day, equal to any of the gods? that discovers a new world, fair and fresh and eternal, occupying the place of this old one, when to the common eye a dust has settled on the universe? which world cannot else be reached, and does not exist. What other words, we may also ask, are memorable and worthy to be repeated than those which love has inspired?

From A Week on the Concord and Merrimack Rivers

LATELY, ALAS, I KNEW A GENTLE BOY

Lately, alas, I knew a gentle boy,
    Whose features were all cast in Virtue's mold,
As one she had designed for Beauty's toy,
    But after manned him for her own stronghold.

On every side he open was as day,
    That you might see no lack of strength within,

For walls and ports do only serve alway
　　For pretense to feebleness and sin.

Say not that Caesar was victorious,
　　With toil and strife who stormed the House of Fame,
In other sense this youth was glorious,
　　Himself a kingdom wheresoe'er he came.

No strength went out to get him victory,
　　When all was income of its own accord;
For where he went none other was to see,
　　But all were parcel of their noble lord.

He forayed like the subtile haze of summer,
　　That stilly shows fresh landscapes to our eyes,
And revolutions works without a murmur,
　　Or rustling of a leaf beneath the skies.

So was I taken unawares by this,
　　I quite forgot my homage to confess;
Yet now am forced to know, though hard it is,
　　I might have loved him had I loved him less.

Each moment as we nearer drew to each,
　　A stern respect withheld us farther yet,
So that we seemed beyond each other's reach,
　　And less acquainted than when first we met.

We two were one while we did sympathize,
　　So could we not the simplest bargain drive;
And what avails it now that we are wise,
　　If absence doth this doubleness contrive?

Eternity may not the chance repeat,
　　But I must tread my single way alone,
In sad remembrance that we once did meet,
　　and know that bliss irrevocably gone.

The spheres henceforth my elegy shall sing,
　　For elegy has other subject none;

Each strain of music in my ears shall ring
   Knell of departure from the other one.

Make haste and celebrate my tragedy;
   With fitting strain resound ye woods and fields;
Sorrow is dearer in such case to me
   Than all the joys other occasion yields.

     . . .

Is't then too late the damage to repair?
   Distance, forsooth, from my weak grasp hath reft
The empty husk, and clutched the useless tare,
   But in my hands the wheat and kernel left.

If I but love that virtue which he is,
   Though it be scented in the morning air,
Still shall we be truest acquaintances,
   Nor mortals know a sympathy more rare.

NOW AND HERE

Men esteem truth remote, in the outskirts of a system, behind the farthest star, before Adam and after the last man. In eternity there is indeed something true and sublime. But all these times and places and occasions are now and here. God himself culminates in the present moment, and will never be more divine in the lapse of all the ages. And we are enabled to apprehend at all what is sublime and noble only by the perpetual instilling and drenching of the reality that surrounds us. . . .

Let us spend one day as deliberately as Nature, and not be thrown off the track by every nutshell and mosquito's wing that falls on the rails. Let us rise early and fast, gently and without perturbation; let company come and let company go, let the bells ring and the children cry—determined to make a day of it. Why should we knock under and go with the stream? . . .

Let us settle ourselves, and work and wedge our feet downward through the mud and the slush of opinion, and prejudice, and tradition, and delusion, and appearance, that alluvion which covers the globe, through Paris and London, through New York and Boston and Concord, through Church and State, through poetry and philosophy and religion, till we come to a hard bottom and rocks in place, which we can call reality, and say, This is, and no mistake; and then begin, having a *point d'appui,* below freshet and frost and fire, a place where you might found a wall or a state, or set a lamppost safely, or perhaps a gauge, not a Nilometer, but a Realometer, that future ages might know how deep a freshet of shams and appearances had gathered from time to time. If you stand right fronting and face to face to a fact, you will see the sun glimmer on both its surfaces, as if it were a cimeter, and feel its sweet edge dividing you through the heart and marrow, and so you will happily conclude your mortal career. Be it life or death, we crave only reality. If we are really dying let us hear the rattle in our throats and feel cold in the extremities; if we are alive, let us go about our business.

Time is but the stream I go a-fishing in. I drink at it; but while I drink I see the sandy bottom and detect how shallow it is. Its thin current slides away, but eternity remains.

From Walden

THE POND IN WINTER

After a still winter night I awoke with the impression that some question had been put to me, which I had been endeavoring in vain to answer in my sleep, as what—how—when—where? But there was dawning Nature, in whom all creatures live, looking in at my broad windows with serene and satisfied face, and no question on her lips. I awoke to an answered question, to Nature and daylight. The snow lying deep on the earth dotted with young pines, and the very slope of the hill on which my house is placed, seemed to say, "Forward!" Nature puts no question and answers none which we mortals ask. She has long ago taken her resolution. "O Prince, our eyes contemplate with admiration and transmit to the soul the wonderful and varied spectacle of this universe. The night veils without doubt a part of this glorious creation; but day comes to reveal to us this great work, which extends from earth even into the plains of the ether."

Then to my morning work. First I take an axe and pail and go in search of water, if that be not a dream. After a cold and snowy night it needed a diving rod to find it. Every winter the liquid and trembling surface of the pond, which was so sensitive to every breath, and reflected every light and shadow, becomes solid to the depth of a foot or a foot and a half, so that it will support the heaviest teams, and perchance the snow covers it to an equal depth, and it is not to be distinguished from any level field. Like the marmots in the surrounding hills, it closes its eyelid and becomes dormant for three months or more. Standing on the snow-covered plain, as if in the pastures amid the hills, I cut my way first through a foot of snow, and then a foot of ice, and open a window under my feet, where, kneeling to drink, I look down into the quiet parlor of the fishes, pervaded by a soften light as through a window of grounded glass, with its bright sanded floor the same as summer; there a perennial waveless serenity reigns as in the amber twilight sky, corresponding to the cool and even temperament of the inhabitants. Heaven is under our feet as well as over our heads. . . .

From Walden

HERMAN MELVILLE

Herman Melville (1819–91) was born into a prosperous and distinguished family in New York City. In 1830 his father went bankrupt and Melville began a long period of wandering that led him first to England and then, as a sailor in a whaling ship, all over the South Seas. Out of his experiences of these years he wrote his first novels, *Redburn, Typee,* and *Omoo.* Melville married in 1847 and lived in New York until 1850, then moved to Pittsfield, Massachusetts, where he wrote *Moby Dick* (1851), which is generally considered to be the greatest American novel.

Melville's marriage has obscured, until recently, any discussion of the homosexual themes that run throughout his work, from his wonder at the beauty of Polynesian men and the richness of their relationships in *Typee* and *Omoo,* through his lengthy exploration of the ecstatic friendship of

Ishmael and Queequeg in *Moby Dick*, to his last story, *Billy Budd*. Modern gay critics recognize in Melville's work a sustained, poignant, and dark meditation on the ways patriarchy encourages homophobia and so thwarts the natural love between men. Like Walt Whitman, Melville sees in passionate male bonding a revolutionary social potential that is linked to the democratic mission of America. This vision finds its erotic apotheosis in the chapter entitled "A Squeeze of the Hand" in *Moby Dick*.

The mystical depth of Melville's work is apparent to anyone who reads it seriously. Few writers have meditated so profoundly on the mystery of good and evil and their invisible war within the human soul.

FROM FATHER MAPPLE'S SERMON IN *MOBY DICK*

"I have read ye by what murky light may be mine the lesson that Jonah teaches to all sinners; and therefore to ye, and still more to me, for I am a greater sinner than ye. And now how gladly would I come down from this masthead and sit on the hatches there where you sit, and listen as you listen, while some one of you reads me that other and more awful lesson which Jonah teaches to me, as a pilot of the living God. How being an anointed pilot-prophet, or speaker of true things, and bidden by the Lord to sound those unwelcome truths in the ears of a wicked Nineveh, Jonah, appalled at the hostility he should raise, fled from his mission, and sought to escape his duty and his God by taking ship at Joppa. But God is everywhere; Tarshish he never reached. As we have seen, God came upon him in the whale, and swallowed him down to the living gulfs of doom, and with swift slantings tore him along "into the midst of the seas," where the eddying depths sucked him ten thousand fathoms down, and "the weeds were wrapped about his head," and all the watery world of woe bowled over him. Yet even then beyond the reach of any plummet—"out of the belly of hell"—when the whale grounded upon the ocean's utmost bones, even then, God heard the engulphed, repenting prophet when he cried. Then God spake unto the fish; and from the shuddering cold and blackness of the sea, the whale came breeching up toward the warm and pleasant sun, and all the delights of air and earth; and "vomited out Jonah upon the dry land"; when the word of the Lord came a second time; and Jonah, bruised and beaten—his ears, like two sea shells, still multitudinously murmuring of the ocean—Jonah did the Almighty's bidding. To preach the Truth to the face of the Falsehood! That was it!

"This, shipmates, this is that other lesson; and woe to that pilot of the living God who slights it. Woe to him whom this world charms from Gospel duty! Woe to him who seeks to pour oil upon the waters when God has brewed them into a gale! Woe to him who seeks to please rather than appall! Woe to him whose good name is more to him than goodness! Woe to him who, in this world, courts not dishonor! Woe to him who would not be true, even though to be false were salvation! Yea, woe to him who, as the great Pilot Paul has it, while preaching to others is himself a castaway!"

He drooped and fell away from himself for a moment; then lifting his face to them again, showed a deep joy in his eyes, as he cried out in a heavenly enthusiasm—"But oh! shipmates! on the starboard hand of every woe, there is a sure delight; and higher the top of that delight, than the bottom of the woe is deep. Is not the main truck higher than the kelson is low? Delight is to him—a far, far upward, and inward delight—who against the proud gods and commodores of this earth, ever stands forth his own inexorable self. Delight is to him whose strong arms yet support him, when the ship of this base treacherous world has gone down beneath him. Delight is to him, who gives no quarter in the truth, and kills, burns, and destroys all sin though he pluck it out from under the robes of Senators and Judges. Delight—top-gallant delight is to him, who acknowledges no law or lord, but the Lord his God, and is only a patriot to heaven. Delight is to him, who all the waves of the billows of the seas of the boisterous mob can never shake from this sure Keel of the Ages. And eternal delight and deliciousness will be his, who coming to lay him down, can say with his final breath—O Father!—chiefly known to me by thy rod—mortal or immortal, here I die. I have striven to be Thine, more than to be this world's, or mine own. Yet this is nothing; I leave eternity to Thee; for what is man that he should live out the lifetime of his God?"

He said no more, but slowly waving a benediction, covered his face with his hands, and so remained kneeling, till all the people had departed, and he was left alone in the place.

From Moby Dick

Though among the holy pomps of the Romish faith, white is specially employed in the celebration in the Passion of our Lord; though in the Vision of St. John, white robes are given to the redeemed, and the four and twenty elders stand clothed in white before the white throne, and the Holy One that sitteth there white like wool; yet for all of these accumulated associations, with whatever is sweet and honorable, and sublime, there yet lurks an elusive something in the innermost idea of this hue, which strikes more of panic to the soul than that redness which affrights in blood.

This elusive quality it is, which causes the thought of whiteness, when divorced from more kindly associations, and coupled with any object terrible in itself, to heighten that terror to the furthest bounds. Witness the white bear of the poles, and the white shark of the tropics; what but their smooth, flaky whiteness makes them the transcendent horrors they are?. . .

But not yet have we solved the incantation of this whiteness, and learned why it appeals with such power to the soul; and more strange and far more portentous—why, as we have seen, it is at once the most meaning symbol of spiritual things, nay, the very veil of the Christian Deity; and yet should be as it is, the intensifying agent in things the most appalling to mankind.

It is that by its indefiniteness it shadows forth the heartless voids and immensities of the universe, and thus stabs us from behind with the thought of annihilation, when beholding the white depths of the milky way? Or is it, that in essence whiteness is not so much a color but the visible absence of color, and at the same time the concrete of all colors; it is for these reasons that there is such a dumb blankness, full of meaning, in a wide landscape of snows—a colorless, all-color of atheism from which we shrink? And when we consider that other theory of the natural philosophers, that all other earthly hues—every stately or lovely emblazoning—the sweet tinges of sunset skies and woods; yea, and the gilded velvets of butterflies, and the butterfly cheeks of young girls; all these are but subtile deceits, not actually inherent in substances, but only laid on from without; so that all deified Nature absolutely paints like the harlot, whose allurements cover nothing but the charnel-house within; and when we proceed further, and consider that the mystical cosmetic which produces every one of her hues, the great principle of light, for ever remains white or colorless in itself, and if operating without medium upon matter, would touch all objects, even tulips and roses, with its own blank tinge— pondering all this, the palsied universe lies before us a leper; and like willful travelers in Lapland, who refuse to wear colored and coloring glasses upon their eyes, so the wretched infidel gazes upon himself blind at the monumental white shroud that wraps all the prospect around him. And all of these things the Albino Whale the symbol. Wonder ye then at the fiery hunt?

From Moby Dick

A SQUEEZE OF THE HAND

That whale of Stubb's, so dearly purchased, was duly brought to the *Pequod*'s side, where all those cutting and hoisting operations previously detailed, were regularly gone through, even to the baling of the Heidelburgh Tun, or Case.

While some were occupied with this latter duty, others were employed in dragging away the larger tubs, so soon as filled with the sperm; and when the proper timed arrived, this same sperm was carefully manipulated ere going to the try-works, of which anon.

It had cooled and crystallized to such a degree, that when, with several others, I sat down before a large Constantine's bath of it, I found it strangely concreted into lumps, here and there rolling about in the liquid part. It was our business to squeeze these lumps back into fluid. A sweet and unctuous duty! No wonder that in old times this sperm was such a favorite cosmetic. Such a clearer! such a sweetener! such a softener! such a delicious mollifier! After having my hands in it for only a few minutes, my fingers felt like eels, and began, as it were, to serpentine and spiralize.

As I sat there at my ease, cross-legged on the deck; after the bitter exertion at the windlass; under a blue tranquil sky; the ship under indolent sail, and gliding so serenely along; as I bathed my hands among those soft, gentle globules of infiltrated tissues, woven almost within the hour; as they richly broke to my fingers, and discharged all their opulence, like fully ripe grapes their wine; as I snuffed up that uncontaminated aroma—literally and truly, like the smell of spring violets; I declare to you, that for the time I lived in musky meadow . . . in that inexpressible sperm, I washed my hands and my heart of it; I almost began to credit the old Paracelsan superstition that sperm is of rare virtue in allaying the heat of anger: while bathing in that bath, I felt divinely free of all ill will, or petulance, or malice, of any sort whatsoever.

Squeeze! squeeze! squeeze! all the morning long; I squeezed that sperm till I myself almost melted into it; I squeezed that sperm till a strange sort of insanity came over me; and I found myself unwittingly squeezing my co-laborers' hands in it, mistaking their hands for the gentle globules. Such an abounding, affectionate, friendly, loving feeling did this avocation beget; that at last I was continually squeezing their hands, and looking up into their eyes sentimentally; as much as to say— Oh! my dear fellow beings, why should we longer cherish any social acerbities, or know the slightest ill humor or envy! Come; let us squeeze hands all round; nay, let us all squeeze ourselves into each other; let us squeeze universally into the very milk and sperm of kindness.

Would that I could keep squeezing that sperm for ever! For now, since by many prolonged, repeated experiences, I have perceived that in all cases man must eventually lower, or at least shift, his conceit of attainable felicity; not placing it anywhere in the intellect or the fancy; but in the wife, the heart, the bed, the table, the saddle, the fireside, the country; now that I have perceived all this, I am ready to squeeze case eternally. In thoughts of the visions of the night, I saw long rows of angels in paradise, each with his hands in a jar of spermaceti.

From Moby Dick

EMILY DICKINSON

Emily Dickinson was born on December 10, 1830, in Amherst, Massachusetts. After the age of thirty—except for a few trips to Cambridge— Dickinson remained at her home in Amherst, seeing only her immediate family and a select group of children. She became in fact a recluse; local gossips referred to her as "The Myth" and were fascinated by her habit of wearing white. Only a handful of her poems were published in her lifetime; the rest, found after her death in 1886 in parcels in her room, were published to an astonished reception.

It is only recently that scholars and critics have faced the passionate lesbian content of her work and life. Dickinson wrote many more of her 1,776 poems to women than to men, particularly to her sister-in-law, Susan (Sue) Gilbert Dickinson. Emily was clearly in love with Sue; in one of her letters to her she writes, "Susan knows that she is a siren—and that at a word from her, Emily would forfeit righteousness." Modern scholarship is revealing Sue more and more as one of Dickinson's two crucial muses—the other being the man to whom she wrote what are known as the "Master" poems (probably Samuel Bowles, editor of a prominent local newspaper).

Dickinson is a great mystic poet of supreme passion and force; her original address and diction still astound by their modernity.

I showed her Heights she never saw—
"Would'st climb?" I said.
She said—"Not so"—
"With me—" I said—"With me?"
I showed her Secrets—Morning's Nest—
The Rope the Nights were put across—
And now—"Would'st have me for a Guest?"
She could not find her Yes—
And then, I brake my life—And Lo,
A Light, for her, did solemn glow,
The larger, as her face withdrew—
And could she, further, "No"?

Not "Revelation" —'tis—that waits,
But our unfurnished eyes—

The Soul's Superior instants
Occur to Her—alone—

When friend—and Earth's occasion
Have infinite withdrawn—

Or She—Herself—ascended
To too remote a Height
For lower Recognition
Than Her Omnipotent—

This Mortal Abolition
Is seldom—but as fair
As Apparition—subject
To Autocratic Air—

Eternity's disclosure
To favorites—a few—
Of the Colossal substance
Of Immortality

Wild Nights—Wild Nights!
Were I with thee
Wild Nights should be
Our luxury!

Futile—the Winds—
To a Heart in port—
Done with the Compass—
Done with the Chart!

Rowing in Eden—
Ah, the Sea!
Might I but moor—Tonight—
In Thee!

I had been hungry, all the Years—
My Noon had Come—to dine—
I trembling drew the Table near—
And touched the Curious Wine—

'Twas this on Tables I had seen—
When turning, hungry, Home
I looked in Windows, for the Wealth
I could not hope—for Mine—

I did not know the ample Bread—
'Twas so unlike the Crumb
The Birds and I, had often shared
In Nature's—Dining Room—

The Plenty hurt me—'twas so new—
Myself felt ill—and odd—
As Berry—of a Mountain Bush—
Transplanted—to the Road—

Nor was I hungry—so I found
That Hunger—was a way
Of Persons outside Windows—
The Entering—takes away—

I dwell in Possibility—
A fairer House than Prose—
More numerous of Windows—
Superior—for Doors—

Of Chambers as the Cedars—
Impregnable of Eye—
And for an Everlasting Roof
The Gambrels of the Sky—

Of Visitors—the fairest—
For Occupation—This—
The spreading wide my narrow Hands
To gather Paradise—

The Brain—is wider than the Sky—
For—put them side by side—

The one the other will contain
With ease—and You—beside—

The Brain is deeper than the sea—
For—hold them—Blue to Blue—
The one the other will absorb—
As Sponges—Buckets—do—

The Brain is just the weight of God—
For—Heft them—Pound for Pound—
And they will differ—if they do—
As Syllable from Sound

Nature—the Gentlest Mother is,
Impatient of no Child—
The feeblest—or the waywardest—
Her Admonition mild—

In Forest—and the Hill—
By Traveler—be heard—
Restraining Rampant Squirrel—
Or too impetuous Bird—

How fair Her Conversation—
A Summer Afternoon—
Her Household—Her Assembly—
And when the Sun go down—

Her Voice among the Aisles
Incites the timid prayer
Of the minutest Cricket—
The most unworthy Flower—

When all the Children sleep—
She turns as long away
As will suffice to light Her lamps—
Then bending from the Sky—

With infinite Affection—
And infiniter Care—

Her Golden finger on Her lip—
Wills Silence—Everywhere—

The Soul selects her own Society—
Then—shuts the Door—
To her divine Majority—
Present no more—

Unmoved—she notes the Chariots—pausing—
At her low Gate—
Unmoved an Emperor be kneeling
Upon her Mat—

I've known her—from an ample nation—
Choose One—
Then—close the Valves of her attention—
Like Stone—

No Rack can torture me—
My Soul—at Liberty—
Behind this mortal Bone
There knits a bolder One—

You cannot prick with saw—
Nor pierce with Scimitar—
Two Bodies—therefore be—
Bind one—The Other fly—

The Eagle of his Nest
No easier divest—
And gain the Sky
Than mayest Thou—

Except Thyself may be
Thine Enemy—
Captivity is Consciousness—
So's Liberty.

Walt Whitman is the pivotal visionary in the history of gay mysticism and a key figure for an understanding of the sacred significance of homosexual liberation in particular and sexual liberation in general.

Born in West Hills, Long Island, in 1819, Whitman was the first author of working-class origins to reach prominence in the United States. Whitman was a product of the unsettled and mobile life of the poor, and he was largely self-taught. In his early years he worked as a carpenter, printer, and country schoolteacher. In 1841 Whitman went to New York, where he worked first as a printer and then as a writer for the *Aurora,* the *Brooklyn Daily Eagle,* and other papers.

Whitman's decisive mystical and personal breakthrough came in 1848, when he went on an extended trip to New Orleans. In this period, he seems to have had a simultaneously mystic and erotic awakening. From this explosion of new awareness and from the edenic rapturous visions it gave him, Whitman started to write his vast visionary epic poem, *Leaves of Grass,* which became his life's work. The first edition of *Leaves of Grass* was published in 1855; in 1860 Whitman added the great homosexual masterpieces of the "Calamus" section.

When Whitman died in 1892 he had, despite years of neglect and poverty, come to be recognized internationally—and by other such sympathetic homosexual visionaries as Edward Carpenter and John Addington Symonds—as having done the pioneering mystical and sexual healing work of the modern age and as having opened up to the whole of humanity what Symonds calls "extraordinary freedoms."

Nothing can be grasped of the larger mystical meanings of Whitman's work and philosophy unless it is realized that Whitman became, through his inner experiences and through a fearless opening to sexual passion, a tantric master—a profoundly awake, wise, ecstatic, *direct seer* of the highest realities, a figure comparable to Rumi in immensity of awakening and capacity for literary expression.

In many ways, Whitman can now be seen as prefiguring the great return to the Divine Feminine that the last part of the twentieth century is witnessing. Again and again, and with thrilling precision and abandon, Whitman sings the great liberating truths of the Mother, truths that patriarchal culture has kept imprisoned too long: that the divine is in the core of every individual and not in some great "external" spirit; that the body and soul are not separate but one, two equally sacred parts of a divine human whole; that the aim of human life is not some impossible "perfection" that denies life, but a wholeness that integrates with—and in—divine love all of life's powers; that the world, the universe, and life are one vast interlinked symphony of divine consciousness; and that the next stage of human evolution (a stage that Whitman believed it was America's destined mission to engender) would have to see a wild and joyful going beyond of all inherited shames, fears, dogmas, and hierarchies into the sisterhood and brotherhood of authentic, sacred democracy.

IN PATHS UNTRODDEN

In paths untrodden,
In the growth by margins of pond-waters,
Escaped from the life that exhibits itself,
From all the standards hitherto unpublish'd, from the pleasures,
     profits, conformities,
Which too long I was offering to feed my soul,
Clear to me now standards not yet publish'd, clear to me that my
     soul,
That the soul of the man that I speak for rejoices in comrades,
Here by myself away from the clank of the world,
Tallying and talk'd to here by tongues aromatic,
No longer abash'd, (for in this secluded spot I can respond as I would
     not dare elsewhere,)
Strong upon me the life that does not exhibit itself, yet contains all
     the rest,
Resolv'd to sing no songs to-day but those of manly attachment,
Projecting them along that substantial life,
Bequeathing hence types of athletic love,
Afternoon this delicious Ninth-month in my forty-first year,
I proceed for all who are or have been young men,
To tell the secrets of my nights and days,
To celebrate the need of comrades.

Of the terrible doubt of appearances,
Of the uncertainty after all, that we may be deluded,
That maybe reliance and hope are but speculations after all,
That maybe identity beyond the grave is a beautiful fable only,
Maybe the things I perceive, the animals, plants, men, hills, shining
    and flowering waters,
The skies of days and night, colors, densities, forms, maybe these are
    (as doubtless they are) only apparitions, and the real something has
    yet to be known,
(How often they dart out of themselves as if to confound me and
    mock me!
How often I think neither I know, nor any man knows, aught of
    them,)
Maybe seeming to me what they are (as doubtless they indeed but
    seem) as from my present point of view, and might prove (as of
    course they would) nought of what they appear, or nought anyhow,
    from entirely changed points of view;
To these and the like of these are curiously answer'd by my lovers, my
    dear friends,
When he whom I love travels with me or sits a long while holding me
    by the hand,
When the subtle air, the impalpable, the sense that words and reason
    hold not, surrounds us and pervades us,
Then I am charged with untold and untellable wisdom, I am silent, I
    require nothing further,
I cannot answer the question of appearances or that of identity
    beyond the grave,
But I walk or sit indifferent, I am satisfied,
He ahold of my hand has completely satisfied me.

WHEN I HEARD AT THE CLOSE OF THE DAY

When I heard at the close of the day how my name had been receiv'd
    with plaudits in the capitol, still it was not a happy night for me
    that follow'd,

And else when I carous'd, or when my plans were accomplish'd, still I
  was not happy,
But the day when I rose at dawn from the bed of perfect health,
  refreshed, singing, inhaling the ripe breath of autumn,
When I saw the full moon in the west grow pale and disappear in the
  morning light,
When I wander'd alone over the beach, and undressing bathed,
  laughing with the cool waters, and saw the sun rise,
And when I thought how my dear friend my lover was on his way
  coming, O then I was happy,
O then each breath tasted sweeter, and all that day my food nourish'd
  me more, and the beautiful day pass'd well,
And the next day came with equal joy, and with the next at evening
  came my friend,
And that night while all was still I heard the waters roll slowly
  continually up the shores,
I heard the hissing rustle of the liquid and sands as directed to me to
  congratulate me,
For the one I love most lay sleeping by me under the same cover in the
  cool night,
In the stillness in the autumn moonbeams his face was inclined
  toward me,
And his arm lay lightly around my breast—and that night I was happy.

I SAW IN LOUISIANA A LIVE-OAK GROWING

I saw in Louisiana a live-oak growing,
All alone stood it and the moss hung down from the branches,
Without any companion it grew there uttering joyous leaves of dark
  green,
And its look, rude, unbending, lusty, made me think of myself,
But I wonder'd how it could utter joyous leaves standing alone there
  without its friend near, for I knew could not,
And I broke off a twig with a certain number of leaves upon it, and
  twined around it a little moss,
And brought it away, and I have placed it in sight in my room,

It is not needed to remind me as of my own dear friends,
(For I believe lately I think of little else than of them,)
Yet it remains to me a curious token, and it makes me think of manly
love;
For all that, and though the live-oak glistens there in Louisiana
solitary in a wide flat space,
Uttering joyous leaves all its life without a friend a lover near,
I know very well I could not.

O TAN-FACED PRAIRIE-BOY

O tan-faced prairie-boy,
Before you came to camp came many a welcome gift,
Praises and presents came and nourishing food, till at last among the
recruits,
You came, taciturn, with nothing to give—we but look'd on each other,
When lo! more than all the gifts of the world you gave me.

All beauty comes from beautiful blood and beautiful brain. If the
greatnesses are in conjunction in a man or woman it is enough . . . the
fact will prevail through the universe . . . but the gaggery and gilt of a
million years will not prevail. Who troubles himself about his orna-
ments or fluency is lost. This is what you shall do: Love the earth and
the sun and animals, despise riches, give alms to every one that asks,
stand up for the stupid and the crazy, devote your income and labor to
others, hate tyrants, argue not concerning God, have patience and in-
dulgence toward the people, take off your hat to nothing known or
unknown or to any man or number of men, go freely with powerful
uneducated persons and with the young and with the mothers of fam-
ilies, read these leaves in the open air every season of every year of your
life, re-examine all you have been told at school or church or in any
book, dismiss whatever insults your own soul, and your very flesh
shall be a great poem and have the richest fluency not only in its
words but in the silent lines of its lips and face and between the lashes
of your eyes and in every motion and joint of your body . . .

From the Preface to Leaves of Grass *(1855)*

O my body! I dare not desert the likes of you in other men and
women, nor the likes of the parts of you,
I believe the likes of you are to stand or fall with the likes of the soul,
(and that they are the soul,)
I believe the likes of you shall stand or fall with my poems, and that
they are my poems,
Man's, woman's, child's, youth's, wife's, husband's, mother's, father's,
young man's, young woman's poems,
Head, neck, hair, ears, drop and tympan of the ears,
Eyes, eye-fringes, iris of the eye, eyebrows, and the waking or sleeping
of the lids,
Mouth, tongue, lips, teeth, roof of the mouth, jaws, and the jaw-
hinges,
Nose, nostril of the nose, and the partition,
Cheeks, temple, forehead, chin, throat, back of the neck, neck-
slue,
Strong shoulders, manly beard, scapula, hind-shoulders, and the
ample side-round of the chest . . .
Hips, hip-sockets, hip strength, inward and outward round, man-
balls, man-root,
Strong set of thighs, well carrying the trunk above,
Leg-fibers, knee, knee-pan, upper-leg, under-leg,
Ankles, instep, foot-ball, toes, toe-joints, the heel;
All attitudes, all the shapeliness, all the belongings of my or your body
or of any one's body, male or female . . .
The curious sympathy one feels when feeling with the hand the naked
meat of the body,
The circling rivers the breath, and breathing it in and out,
The beauty and the waist, and thence of the hips, and thence
downward toward the knees,
The thin red jellies within you or within me, the bones and the
marrow in the bones,
The exquisite realization of health;
O I say these are not the parts and poems of the body only, but of the
soul,
O I say now these are the soul!

From "I Sing the Body Electric"

5

I believe in you my soul . . . the other I am must not abase itself to
   you,
And you must not be abased to the other.

Loafe with me on the grass . . . loose the stop from your throat,
Not words or music or rhyme I want . . . not custom or lecture, not
   even the best,
Only the lull I like, the hum of your valved voice.

I mind how we lay in June, such a transparent summer morning;
You settled your head athwart my lips and gently turned over upon
   me,
And parted the shirt from my bosom-bone, and plunged your tongue
   to my barestript heart,
And reached till you felt my beard, and reached till you held my feet.

Swiftly arose and spread around me the peace and knowledge that
   pass all the arguments of the earth;
And I know that the hand of God is the elderhand of my own,
And I know that the spirit of God is the eldest brother of my own,
And that all the men ever born are also my brothers . . . and the
   women my sisters and lovers,
And that a kelson of the creation is love;
And limitless are leaves stiff or drooping in the fields,
And brown ants in the little wells beneath them,
And mossy scabs of the wormfence, and heaped stones, and elder and
   mullen and pokeweed.

48

I have said that the soul is not more than the body,
And I have said that the body is not more than the soul,
And nothing, not God, is greater to one than one's-self is,
And whoever walks a furlong without sympathy walks to his own
   funeral, dressed in his shroud,
And I or you pocketless of a dime may purchase the pick of the
   earth,

And to glance with an eye or show a bean in its pod confounds the
learning of all times,
And there is no trade or employment but the young man following it
may become a hero,
And there is no object so soft but it makes a hub for the wheeled
universe,
And any man or woman shall stand cool and supercilious before a
million universes.

And I call to mankind, Be not curious about God,
For I who am curious about each am not curious about God,
No array of terms can say how much I am at peace about God and
about death.

I hear and behold God in every object, yet I understand God not in
the least,
Nor do I understand who there can be more wonderful than myself.

Why should I wish to see God better than this day?
I see something of God in each hour of the twenty-four, and each
moment then,
In the faces of men and women I see God, and in my own face in the
glass;
I find letters from God dropped in the street, and every one is signed
by God's name,
And I leave them where they are, for I know that others will
punctually come forever and ever.

49

And as to you death, and you bitter hug of mortality . . . it is idle to
try to alarm me.

To his work without flinching the accoucheur comes,
I see the elderhand pressing receiving support,
I recline by the sills of the exquisite flexible doors . . . and mark the
outlet, and mark the relief and escape.

And as to you corpse, I think you are good manure, but that does not
offend me,

I smell the white roses sweet-scented and growing,
I reach to the leafy lips . . . I reached to the polished breasts of melons.

And as to you life, I reckon you are the leavings of many deaths,
No doubt I have died myself ten thousand times before.

I hear you whispering there O stars of heaven,
O suns . . . O grass of graves . . . O perpetual transfers and
    promotions . . . if you do not say anything how can I say anything?

Of the turbid pool that lies in the autumn forest,
Of the moon that descends the steeps of the soughing twilight,
Toss, sparkles of day and dusk . . . toss on the black stems that decay
    in the muck,
Toss to the moaning gibberish of the dry limbs.

I ascend from the moon . . . I ascend from the night,
And perceive of the ghastly glimmer the sunbeams reflected,
And debouch to the steady and central from the offspring great or
    small.

50

There is that in me . . . I do not know what it is . . . but I know it is in
    me.

Wrenched and sweaty . . . calm and cool then my body becomes;
I sleep . . . I sleep long.

I do not know it . . . it is without name . . . it is a word unsaid,
It is not in any dictionary or utterance or symbol.

Something it swings on more than the earth I swing on,
To it the creation is the friend whose embracing awakes me.

Perhaps I might tell more . . . Outlines! I plead for my brothers and
    sisters.

Do you see O my brothers and sisters?
It is not chaos or death . . . It is form and union and plan . . . it is
    eternal life . . . it is happiness.

Edward FitzGerald, English poet and translator, was born in Bedfield, Suffolk, on March 31, 1809, and died in Norfolk on June 14, 1883. He possessed a private income and lived most of his life in retirement; his letters and diaries reveal his discreet, but fervent, homosexuality. Among his many famous friends were William Makepeace Thackeray, Alfred, Lord Tennyson, and Thomas Carlyle. His first translation of the *Rubaiyat* of Omar Khayyam (a Sufi mystic of the twelfth century) appeared in 1859 anonymously; it was ignored by the public and remaindered. A year later, a copy was discovered by the well-known contemporary poet Dante Gabriel Rossetti and its extraordinary fame began. Five subsequent editions of his *Rubaiyat* appeared, but the best is generally considered to be the first (the version quoted here). FitzGerald's *Rubaiyat* is far more than the moving, elegiac, "exotic" work the Victorians so admired: careful readers acquainted with the themes of Sufi mysticism will see in it a great and precise mystic masterpiece, at once full of profound grief at life's illusions and transience and illumined from within by a subtle rapture at divine identity.

> Dreaming when Dawn's left hand was in the Sky,
> I heard a Voice within the Tavern cry,
> "Awake, my Little ones, and fill the Cup
> Before Life's Liquor in its Cup be dry."

> Now the New Year reviving old Desires,
> The thoughtful Soul to Solitude retires,
> Where the WHITE HAND OF MOSES on the Bough
> Puts out, and Jesus from the Ground suspires.

> Iram indeed is gone with all its Rose,
> And Jamshyd's Sev'n-ring'd Cup where no one knows;
> But still the Vine her ancient Ruby yields,
> And still a Garden by the Water blows.

Here with a Loaf of Bread beneath the Bough,
A Flask of Wine, a Book of Verse—and Thou
Beside me singing in the Wilderness—
And Wilderness is Paradise enow.

One Moment in Annihilation's Waste,
One Moment, of the Well of Life to taste—
The Stars are setting and the Caravan
Starts for the Dawn of Nothing—Oh, make haste!

The Moving Finger writes; and, having writ,
Moves on: nor all thy Piety nor Wit
Shall lure it back to cancel half a Line,
Nor all thy Tears wash out a Word of it.

And this I know: whether the one True Light
Kindle to Love, or Wrath-consume me quite,
One Glimpse of It within the Tavern caught
Better than in the Temple lost outright.

That ev'n my buried Ashes such a Snare
Of Perfume shall fling up into the Air,
As not a True Believer passing by
But shall be overtaken unaware.

From The Rubaiyat of Omar Khayyam

GERARD MANLEY HOPKINS

Gerard Manley Hopkins (1844–89) was born in Essex, the eldest son of a middle-class family. He was educated at Highgate school and Balliol College, Oxford, where he read classics and began his lifelong friendship with the poet Robert Bridges, who was later to be his editor and champion. In 1866 Hopkins joined the Roman Catholic church; two years later he became a member of the Society of Jesus. In 1877 Hopkins was ordained; he served in a number of parishes including one in a slum district in Liverpool. From 1882 Hopkins taught at Stonyhurst College; in 1884 he became Classics Professor at University College, Dublin. In his lifetime Hopkins, like Emily Dickinson, was hardly known as a poet, except to a few friends; it wasn't until 1918 that his marvelous, completely original visionary poems were published, in a volume edited by Robert Bridges. Like Dickinson, too, when Hopkins's poems were finally released, they were immediately recognized as being among the most important of the nineteenth century.

In his life, it seems, Hopkins never completely accepted his homosexuality; his poetry, however, is permeated with sensual and passionate evocations of male beauty. Throughout it, in fact, male beauty is celebrated as one of the most splendid witnesses to the divine power that creates all things. For Hopkins, "the world is charged with the grandeur of God"; and his entire oeuvre is dedicated to a fearless and ecstatic celebration of that whole beauty which, as he writes in "Pied Beauty," is "past change."

GOD'S GRANDEUR

The world is charged with the grandeur of God.
  It will flame out, like shining from shook foil;
  It gathers to a greatness, like the ooze of oil
Crushed. Why do men then now not reck his rod?
Generations have trod, have trod, have trod;
  And all is seared with trade; bleared, smeared with toil;
  And wears man's smudge and shares man's smell: the soil
Is bare now, nor can foot feel, being shod.

And for all this, nature is never spent;
  There lives the dearest freshness deep down things;
And though the lasts lights off the black West went
  Oh, morning, at the brown brink eastward, springs—
Because the Holy Ghost over the bent
  World broods with warm breast and with ah! bright wings.

SPRING

Nothing is so beautiful as Spring—
    When weeds, in wheels, shoot long and lovely and lush;
    Thrush's eggs look little low heavens, and thrush
Through the echoing timber does so rinse and wring
The ear, it strikes like lightnings to hear him sing;
    The glassy peartree leaves and blooms, they brush
    The descending blue; that blue is all in a rush
With richness; the racing lambs too have fair their fling.

What is all this juice and all this joy?
    A strain of the earth's sweet being in the beginning
In Eden garden.—Have, get, before it cloy,
    Before it cloud, Christ, lord, and sour with sinning,
Innocent mind and Mayday in girl and boy,
    Most, O maid's child, thy choice and worthy thy winning.

THE WINDHOVER
TO CHRIST OUR LORD

I caught this morning morning's minion, kingdom of daylight's
    dauphin, dapple-dawn-drawn Falcon, in his riding
        Of the rolling level underneath him steady air, and striding
High there, how he rung upon the rein of a wimpling wing
In his ecstasy! then off, off forth on swing,
    As a skate's heel sweeps smooth on a bow-bend: the hurl and
        gliding
    Rebuffed the big wind. My heart in hiding
Stirred for a bird,—the achieve of, the mastery of the thing!

Brute beauty and valor and act, oh, air, pride, plume, here
    Buckle! AND the fire that breaks from thee then, a billion
Times told lovelier, more dangerous. O my chevalier!

    No wonder of it: sheer plod makes plough down sillion
Shine, and blue-bleak embers, ah my dear,
    Fall, gall themselves, and gash gold-vermilion.

PIED BEAUTY

Glory be to God for dappled things—
    For skies of couple-color as a brinded cow;
       For rose-moles in all stipple upon trout that swim;
Fresh-firecoal chestnut-falls; finches' wings;
    Landscape plotted and pieced—fold, fallow, and plough;
      And all trades, their gear and tackle and trim.
All things counter, original, spare, strange;
    Whatever is fickle, freckled (who knows how?)
      With swift, slow; sweet, sour; adazzle, dim;
He fathers-forth whose beauty is past change:
        Praise him.

AS KINGFISHERS CATCH FIRE . . .

As kingfishers catch fire, dragonflies draw flame;
As tumbled over rim in roundy wells
Stones ring; like each tucked string tells, each hung bell's
Bow swung finds tongue to fling out broad its name;
Each mortal thing does one thing and the same:
Deals out that being indoors each one dwells;
Selves—goes itself; myself it speaks and spells,
Crying What I do is me: for that I came.

I say more: the just man justices;
Keeps grace: that keeps all his goings graces;
Acts in God's eye what in God's eye he is—
Christ—for Christ plays in ten thousand places,
Lovely in limbs, and lovely in eyes not his
To the Father through the features of men's faces.

HARRY PLOUGHMAN

Hard as hurdle arms, with a broth of goldish flue
Breathed round; the rack of ribs; the scooped flank; lank
Rope-over thigh; knee-nave; and barreled shank—
      Head and foot, shoulder and shank—

The Gods in the Body: The Nineteenth Century   155

By a grey eye's heed steered well, one crew, fall to;
Stand at stress. Each limb's barrowy brawn, his thew
That onewhere curded, onewhere sucked or sank—
        Soared or sank—,
Though as a beechbole firm, finds his, as at a roll-call, rank
And features, in flesh, what deed he each must do—
        His sinew-service where do.

He leans to it, Harry bends, look. Back, elbow, and liquid waist
In him, all quail to the wallowing o' the plough's cheek crimsons; curls
Wag or crossbridle, in a wind lifted, windlaced—
        See his wind-lilylocks-laced;
Churlsgrace, too, child of Amansstrength, how it hangs or hurls
Them—broad in bluff hide his frowning feet lashed! raced
With, along them, cragiron under the cold furls—
        With-a-fountain's shining-shot furls.

THAT NATURE IS A HERACLITEAN FIRE AND OF THE COMFORT OF THE RESURRECTION

Cloud-puffball, torn tufts, tossed pillows flaunt forth, then chevy on the air-
built thoroughfare: heaven-roysterers, in gay-gangs they throng; they glitter in marches.
Down roughcast, down dazzling whitewash, wherever an elm arches,
Shivelights and shadowtackle in long lashes lace, lance, and pair.
Delightfully in the bright wind boisterous ropes, wrestles, beats earth bare
Of yestertempest's creases; in pool and rut peel parches
Squandering ooze to squeezed dough, crust, dust; stanches, starches
Squadroned masks and manmarks treadmire toil there
Footfretted in it. Million-fueled, nature's bonfire burns on.
But quench her bonniest, dearest to her, her clearest-selved spark
Man, how fast his firedint, his mark on mind, is gone!
Both are in an unfathomable, all is in an enormous dark
Drowned. O pity and indignation! Manshape, that shone
Sheer off, disseveral, a star, death blots black out; nor mark
        Is any of him at all so stark

But vastness blurs and time beats level. Enough! the Resurrection,
A heart's-clarion! Away grief's gasping, joyless days, dejection.
　　　　　Across my foundering deck shone
A beacon, an eternal beam. Flesh fade, and mortal trash
Fall to the residuary worm; world's wildfire, leave but ash:
　　　　　In a flash, at a trumpet crash,
I am all at once what Christ is, since he was what I am, and am
This Jack, joke, poor potsherd, patch, matchwood, immortal
　　diamond,
　　　　　Is immortal diamond.

Sept. 24. First saw the Northern Lights. My eye was caught by beams
of light and dark very like the crown of horny rays the sun makes behind a cloud. At first I thought of silvery cloud until I saw that these
were more luminous and did not dim the clearness of the stars in the
Bear. They rose slightly radiating thrown out from the earthline. Then
I saw soft pulses of light one after another rise and pass upwards arched
in shape but waveringly and with the arch broken. They seemed to
float, not following the warp of the sphere as falling stars look to do but
free though concentrical with it. This busy working of nature wholly
independent of the earth and seeming to go in a strain of time not
reckoned by our reckoning of days and years but simpler and as if cor-
recting the preoccupation of the world by being preoccupied with the
appealing to and dated to the day of judgment was like a new witness
to God and filled me with delightful fear.

　From his journal (1870)

There met in Jesus Christ all things that can make man lovely and
loveable. In his body he was most beautiful. This is known first by the
tradition in the Church that it was so and by holy writers agreeing to
suit those words to him/ Thou art beautiful in mold above the sons
of men: we have even accounts of him written in early times. They tell
us that he was moderately tall, well built and slender in frame, his features straight and beautiful, his hair inclining to auburn, parted in the
midst, curling and clustering about the ears and neck as the leaves of a

filbert, so they speak, upon the nut. He wore also a forked beard and this as well as the locks upon his head were never touched by razor or shears; neither, his health being perfect, could a hair ever fall to the ground. . . . Another proof of his beauty may be drawn from the words *proficiebat sapientia et aetate et gratia apud Deum et homines* (Luc. ii 52) / he went forward in wisdom and bodily frame and favor with God and men; this is / he pleased both God and men daily more and more by his growth of mind and body. But he could not have pleased by growth of body unless the body was strong, healthy, and beautiful that grew. But the best proof of all is this, that his body was the special work of the Holy Ghost. He was not born in nature's course, no man was his father; had he been born as others are he must have inherited some defect of figure or of constitution, from which no man born as fallen men are born is wholly free unless God interfere to keep him so. But his body was framed directly from heaven by the power of the Holy Ghost, of whom it would be unworthy to leave any the least botch or failing in his work. So the first Adam was molded by God himself and Eve built up by God too out of Adam's rib and they could not but be pieces, both, of faultless workmanship: the same then and much more must Christ have been. . . . I leave it to you, brethren, then to picture him, in whom the fullness of the godhead dwelt bodily, in his bearing how majestic, how strong and yet how lovely and lissome in his limbs, in his look how earnest, grave but kind. In his Passion all this strength was spent, this lissomness crippled, this beauty wrecked, this majesty beaten down. But now it is more than all restored, and for myself I make no secret I look forward with eager desire to seeing the matchless beauty of Christ's body in the heavenly light.

THE ROOT OF CHRIST: HOLINESS

Christ's life and character are such as appeal to all the world's admiration, but there is one insight St. Paul gives us of it which is very secret and seems to me more touching and constraining than everything else is: This mind, he says, was in Christ Jesus—he means as man: being in the form of God—that is, finding, as in the first instant of his incarnation he did, his human nature informed by the godhead—he thought it nevertheless no snatching-matter for him to be equal with God, but annihilated himself, taking the form of servant; that is, he could not but see what he was, God, but he would see it as if he did not see it, and be it as if he were not and instead of snatching at once at what all the time was his, or was himself, he emptied or exhausted himself so far as that was possible, of godhead and behaved only as God's slave, as his creature, as man, which also he was, and then being in the guise of man humbled himself to death, the death of the cross. It is this holding of himself back, and not snatching at the truest and highest good, the good that was his right, nay his possession from a past eternity in his other nature, his own being and self, which seems to me the root of all his holiness and the imitation of this the root of all moral good in other men.

EDWARD CARPENTER

Edward Carpenter was born in Brighton, England, in 1844, the son of upper-middle-class parents, and died in Guildford, Surrey, in 1929. He was educated at Oxford and Cambridge. At Cambridge, he was elected a clerical fellow and later ordained a deacon. Soon, however, his liberalism brought him into the conflict with the tenets of Anglicanism; in 1871 he resigned his church roles to concentrate on his work as a lecturer. During this period, Carpenter fell passionately, but unhappily, in love with a contemporary, Andrew Beck, who rejected him to pursue a conventional life and career (Beck married and later rose to become Master of Trinity Hall).

The devastation that followed his breakup with Beck led Carpenter to a reconsideration of his whole life—and to his most important discovery, that of the work of Walt Whitman. Whitman's thrilling mystical celebration of the holiness of all life and of the body, the splendor of his homosexual love poems in the "Calamus" section of *Leaves of Grass*, and his vision of a sacred democracy inspired and sustained by the free love between men and women profoundly moved Carpenter and confirmed his own deepest feelings and aspirations. After a brief teaching stint at Sheffield, Carpenter retired to a small cottage at Millthorpe in the Sheffield countryside. In

1891 he met a workman, George Merrill, and lived the rest of his life with him. This union inspired E. M. Forster to create *Maurice.*

In his great works *Towards Democracy, The Intermediate Sex,* and *Love's Coming of Age,* Carpenter fuses a socialist vision of justice and social equality with a mystical celebration of the "healed" and "resurrected" body, the body freed from agelong religious and material oppression to enshrine the full glory of the spirit. This extremely powerful vision is now largely unknown, but it in its day deeply influenced Forster, D. H. Lawrence, and Aurobindo; Aurobindo's later explorations of the links between spirit and matter owe a great deal to Carpenter. In *Towards Democracy,* Carpenter writes of his great dream of happiness for the human race: "I conceive of a millennium on earth—a millennium not of riches, nor of mechanical facilities, nor of intellectual facilities, nor absolutely of immunity from pain; but a time when men and women all over the earth shall ascend and enter into relation with their bodies—shall attain freedom and joy."

ON SEX

Our public opinion, our literature, our customs, our laws, are saturated with the notion of the uncleanness of Sex, and are so making the conditions of its cleanness more and more difficult. . . .

Till this dirty and dismal sentiment with regard to the human body is removed there can be little hope of anything like a free and gracious public life. With the regeneration of our social ideas the whole conception of Sex as a thing covert and to be ashamed of, marketable and unclean, will have to be regenerated. That inestimable freedom and pride which is the basis of all true manhood and womanhood will have to enter into this most intimate relation to preserve it frank and pure—pure from the damnable commercialism which buys and sells all human things, and from the religious hypocrisy which covers and conceals; and a healthy delight in and cultivation of the body and all its natural functions, and a determination to keep them pure and beautiful, open and sane and free, will have to become a recognized part of national life. . . .

LOVE'S COMING OF AGE

Sex is the allegory of Love in the physical world. It is from this fact that it derives its immense power. The aim of Love is non-differentiation—

absolute union of being; but absolute union can only be found at the center of existence. Therefore whoever has truly found another has found not only that other, and with that other himself, but has found a third—who dwells at the center and holds the plastic material of the universe in the palm of his hand, and is a creator of sensible forms. . . .

THE INTERMEDIATE SEX

While the Uranian temperament has, in cases, specially fitted its possessors to become distinguished in art or education or war or administration, and enabled them to do valuable work in these fields; it remains perhaps true that above all it has fitted them, and fits them, for distinction and service in affairs of the heart.

It is hard to imagine human beings more skilled in these matters than are the Intermediates. For indeed no one else can possibly respond to and understand, as they do, all the fluctuations and interactions of the masculine and feminine in human life. . . .

It is strange to see how even an unlettered person of this type will often read Love's manuscript easily in cases where the normal man or woman is groping over it like a child in the dark. . . .

I say that I think perhaps of all the services the Uranian may render to society it will be found some day that in this direction of solving the problems of affection and of the heart he will do the greatest service. If the day is coming as we have suggested—when Love is at last to take its rightful place as the binding and directing force of society (instead of the Cash-nexus), and society is to be transmuted in consequence to a higher form, then undoubtedly the superior types of Uranians—prepared for this service by long experience and devotion, as well as by much suffering—will have an important part to play in the transformation. For that the Urnings in their own lives put Love before everything else—postponing to it the other motives like money-making, business success, fame, which occupy so much space in most people's careers—is a fact which is patent to everyone who knows them. This may be saying little or nothing in favor of those of this class whose conception of love is only of a poor and frivolous sort; but in the case of those others who see the god in his true light, the fact that they serve him in singleness of heart and so unremittingly raises them at once into the position of the natural leaders of mankind.

THE GODS IN THE BODY

The gods, in fact, may be said not only to be aspects of the life of the race, but to dwell in some sense in the organic nuclei and plexuses of the body, and to be the centers of command and service there. . . .

The body is not vile. It is not only a Temple of God, but it is a collection of temples; and just as the images of the gods dwell in the temples of a land, and are the objects of service and the centers of command there, so, we may say, the gods themselves dwell in the centers and sacred places of the body. The one thing is an allegory or symbol of the other. . . . Every organ and center of the body is the seat of some great emotion, which in its proper activity and due proportion is truly divine. It is through this bodily and physiological center that the emotion, the *enthusiasm*, that portion of the divine Being, expresses itself; and in the pure and perfect body that expression, that activity, is itself a revelation. The total physiology of Man is, or should be, the nearest expression of divinity compete, and the replica or image of physiology of the Cosmos itself. . . .

We are arriving at one of the most fruitful and important turning-points in the history of the race. The Self is entering into relation with the Body. For, that the individual should conceive and know himself, not as a toy and chance-product of his own bodily heredity, but as identified and continuous with the Eternal Self of which his body is a manifestation, is indeed to begin a new life and to enter a hitherto undreamed world of possibilities. . . .

When the individual self, reaching union with the universal, becomes consciously and willingly the creator and inspirer of the body —that is indeed a Transfiguration. The individual is no longer under the domination of the body and its heredity, but rising out of this tomb becomes lord and master of the body's powers, and identified with the immortal Self of the world.

This transformation, whilst the greatest and most wonderful, is also of course the most difficult in Man's evolution, for him to effect. It may roughly be said that the whole of the civilization-period in Man's history is the preparation for it.

LVI

Slowly on You, too, the meanings: the light-sparkles on water, tufts of
    weed in winter—the least things—dandelion and groundsel.
Have you seen the wild bees' nest in the field, the cells, the grubs, the
    transparent white baby-bees, turning brown, hairy, the young bees
    beginning to fly, raking the moss down over the disturbed cells? the
    parasites?
Have you seen the face of your brother or sister? have you seen the
    little robin hopping and peering under the bushes? have you seen
    the sun rise, or set? I do not know—I do not think that I have.
When your unquiet brain has ceased to spin its cobwebs over the calm
    and miraculous beauty of the world;
When the Air and the Sunlight shall have penetrated your body
    through and through; and the Earth and Sea have become part
    of it;
When at last, like a sheath long concealing the swelling green shoot,
    the love of learning and the regard for elaborate art, wit manners,
    dress, or anything rare or costly whatever, shall drop clean off from
    you;
When your Body—for to this it must inevitably return—is become
    shining and transparent before you in every part (however
    deformed);
Then (O blessed One!) these things also transparent possibly shall
    surrender themselves—the least thing shall speak to you words of
    deliverance.

The stones are anywhere and everywhere: the temple roof is the sky.
The materials are the kettle boiling on the fire, the bread in the oven,
    the washing dolly, the axe, the gavelock—the product is God;
And the little kitchen where you live, the shelves, the pewter, the
    nightly lamp, the fingers and faces of your children—a finished
    and beautiful Transparency of your own Body.

LIX

Out of Night and Nothingness a Body appears.
The threads of a thousand past ages run together in it; out of its loins
    and the look of its eyes a thousand ages part their way into the future.

The Gods in the Body: The Nineteenth Century   163

Eyes out of which I see, Ears through which I hear—formed in my
   mother's womb in silence;
Mother of mine, walking the earth no more (to me closer than ever),
   out of all tears, suffusing light over the world, equal with God—for
   whose sake Night and Day evermore are sacred;
Body, by which I ascend and know Myself—Mysteries of life and
   death slowly parting and transforming around me
O glad, not for one year or two but for how many thousands, I out of
   deep and infinite Peace salute you.
The doctor does not give Health, but the winds of heaven;
Happiness does not proceed by chance, nor is got by supplication, but
   is inevitable wherever the Master is.
Doubt parts aside. I hear grown and bearded men shouting in the
   woods for joy, shouting singing with the birds; I hear the immense
   chorus over all the world, of the Return of Joy.

THE SOUL TO THE BODY

Now at last after thousands of years, dear Body, from thy prison
   emerging,
[Where, with what swathing-bands, like Lazarus, what mummy-cloths,
   what cerements of fashion custom ignorance, thou wast bound,]
Strange chrysalis, thy dead sheath bursting!
Strange glorious Lover!
To feel again thy arms enfolding, to breathe the fragrance of thy sun-
   kist skin, how sweet!

What long estrangement, dear, what nightmare has it been, divided us?
From far away what long slow exodus?
Why to the tomb in ages past didst thou descend—of Death and
   dread Corruption?—
While I, poor ghost, went wandering belated, and homeless and
   forlorn about the world?
For, as the delicate vein-winged gnat from its watery case, as Eve from
   Adam's side, as Psyche from the dark embrace of Eros,
So from thee gliding, far-back, long ago—dimly I mind me now—
Slow-differenced, this wondering wandering Self was I.

[Dimly I mind the agelong alienation:
    Thou body, of thy mate bereft, and falling unclean, diseased, by
    devils possest, in mire and filth—
Blind Maenad by thy own senses led astray!
While I, poor soul, half formed and maimed of half,
Abstract, absurd, amazed, and crucified,
To arid and unending toils was doomed, and loneliness.]

After it all to thee, dear, to return,
To feel again thy close-enfolding arms—how sweet!
To know Thee now at last—(long veiled and hidden)—
Through Nature moving, as the Sun and Moon
Move through the crystal heaven, self-sent, divine,
Transparent, timeless, more than spirit or matter;
Dear body, brushing with thy feet the grasses, or resting outlined by
    the rocks and sea—
To rest with thee, content, in perfect union,
O in such deep and fathomless joy to rest beside thee,
Thy mate and friend, stricken with doubts no more . . .

LOVE'S VISION

At night in each other's arms,
Content, overjoyed, resting deep deep down in the darkness,
Lo! the heavens opened and He appeared—
Whom no mortal eye may see,
Whom no eye clouded with Care,
Whom none who seeks after this or that, whom none who has not
    escaped from self.

There—in the region of Equality, in the world of Freedom no longer
    limited,
Standing as a lofty peak in heaven above the clouds,
From below hidden, yet to all who pass into that region most clearly
    visible—
He the Eternal appeared.

ARTHUR RIMBAUD

Arthur Rimbaud was born on October 20, 1854, in Charleville in northern France of rural parents. Rimbaud studied at Charleville's Institution Rossat and then, in spring 1865, began to attend the Collège de Charleville, where he obtained his degree. He began writing very early, first in Latin, then in French; by the age of sixteen he had already published several poems in the journal *Le Parnasse Contemporain.* In February 1871 he visited Paris for the first time and there met the poet Paul Verlaine and his circle. Invited back in the following year, in September 1871, Rimbaud began with Verlaine (who was married and ten years older) a turbulent homosexual affair that was to last a year and a half and be lived out dramatically in Paris, London, and Brussels. This ended in July 1873 when Verlaine shot Rimbaud in the wrist during a violent quarrel. Soon after, increasingly disgusted by the literary world and the limitations of language, Rimbaud began to abandon his career as a poet. In 1876 he enlisted in the Dutch army, only to leave it soon afterward and travel to Sweden, Denmark, Greece, and Egypt; he was employed as a coffee buyer in 1880 and in 1887 sold guns in the Middle East. Rimbaud died at thirty-seven on November 10, 1891, in a hospital in Marseille.

Paul Claudel called Rimbaud "the supreme mystical visionary of France"; his wildly original poetry is inspired throughout by a vision of the alchemical power of words to transform reality by evoking and creating the divine truths latent within it. Rimbaud consciously thought of himself as a prophet and seer and "inaugurator of a new freedom." Toward the end of his creative life, however, this sometimes vain vision gives way to a more authentically mystical understanding of the necessity for humility and charity. Rimbaud's quest for a transformatory "magic" became a discovery of the transforming power of love and of the surrender to the mystery of God.

> I say that one must be a *seer*, make oneself a *seer*. The poet makes himself a *seer* by a long, prodigious, and rational *disordering of all the senses*. Every form of love, of suffering, of madness; he searches himself, he consumes all the poisons in him, and keeps only their quintessence. This is an unspeakable torture during which he needs all his faith and superhuman strength, and during which he becomes the

great patient, the great criminal, the great accursed—and the great learned one!—among men. —For he arrives at the *unknown*! Because he has cultivated his own soul—which was rich to begin with—more than any other man! He reaches the unknown; and even if, crazed, he ends up by losing the understanding of his visions, at least he has seen them! Let him die charging through those unutterable, unnamable things: other horrible workers will come; they will begin from the horizons where he has succumbed!

From Letters

DAWN

I embraced the summer dawn.

Nothing was stirring yet on the facades of the palaces. The water was dead. The camps of shadows in the woodland road had not been struck. I walked, awakening vivid warm breaths, and the precious stones looked up, and wings rose without a sound.

The first adventure was, in the path already filled with a cool, pale gleams, a flower which told me its name.

I laughed at the blond waterfall, disheveled between the fir trees: in the silvery peak I recognized the goddess.

Then I lifted the veils, one by one. In the avenue, waving my arms. On the plain, where I declared her to the cock. In the city, she fled among the belfries and domes, and I, running like a beggar across the marble quays, chased after her.

At the top of the road, near a laurel wood, I surrounded her with her heaped-up veils, and I felt, a little, her immense body. Dawn and the child fell down at the bottom of the wood.

When I woke up it was noon.

from Les Illuminations

GENIE

He is affection and the present because he has made the house which is open to the frothy winter and to the murmur of summer, he who has purified drink and food, he who is the charm of fugitive places and the superhuman delight of halts. He is affection and the future, the strength and the love which we, standing in rage and boredom, see passing in the stormy sky among banners of ecstasy.

He is love, the measure perfect and reinvented, marvelous and unexpected reason, and eternity: beloved machine of the fatal powers. We have all known the terror of his yielding and of our own: O delight in our health, impetus of our faculties, selfish affection and passion for him, him who loves us for his eternal life . . .

And we call him back to us and travels on . . . And if Adoration goes away, ring, his promise rings: "Away with these superstitions, these old bodies, these couples and these ages. It is this epoch that has sunk!"

He will not go away, he will not descend from any heaven again, he will not achieve the redemption of woman's anger and men's gaieties and all that sin: because it is done, because he exists and is loved.

O his breaths, his heads, his runnings: the terrible swiftness of the perfection of forms and of action.

O fruitfulness of the mind and immensity of the universe!

His body! The dreamed-of redemption, the shattering of grace meeting with new violence!

The sight of him, the sight of him! all the old kneelings and pains *lifted* at his passing.

His light! the abolition of all audible and moving suffering in more intense music.

His step! migrations more enormous than the old invasions.

O He and we! pride more benign than wasted charities.

O world! and the clear song of new misfortunes!

He has known us all and has loved us all. May we know, this winter night, from promontory, from the tumultuous pole to the country house, from the multitude to the beach, from looks to looks, strength and feelings wearied, how to hail him and see him, and to send him away, and, beneath the tides and at the top of the deserts of snow, to follow his vision, his breath, his body, his light.

From Les Illuminations

CHARITY IS THE KEY

Once, if I remember correctly, my life was a feast at which all hearts opened and all wines flowed.

One evening I sat Beauty on my knees—And I found her bitter—And I reviled her.

I armed myself against justice.

I fled. O witches, O misery, O hatred, it was to you that my treasure was entrusted!

I managed to erase in my mind all human hope. Upon every joy, in order to strangle it, I made the muffled bound of the wild beast.

I called up executioners in order to bite their gun-butts as I died. I called up plagues, in order to suffocate myself with sand and blood. Bad luck was my god. I stretched myself out in the mud. I dried myself in the air of crime. And I played some fine tricks on madness.

And spring brought me the hideous laugh of the idiot.

But just lately, finding myself on the point of uttering the last croak, I thought of looking for the key to the old feast, where perhaps I might find my appetite again.

Charity is this key—This inspiration proves that I have been dreaming!

"You'll go on being a hyena, etc. . . ." cries indignantly with the demon who crowned me with such pleasing poppies. "Reach death with all your appetites, your selfishness, and all the deadly sins."

Ah! I have brought too many—But my dear Satan, I beg you, an eye a little less inflamed! And while we are waiting for the few little overdue dirty deeds, you, who like in a writer the absence of descriptive or instructive talent, for you I tear off these few hideous pages from my notebook of a damned soul . . .

ONLY DIVINE LOVE

Only divine love bestows the key of knowledge. I see that nature is only a display of kindness. Farewell, chimeras, ideals, errors.

The reasoned song of the angels rises from the rescue ship: it is divine love—Two loves! I can die of earthly love or die of devotion. I have left souls whose pain will grow for my departure! You have chosen me from among the shipwrecked; are those who are left behind not my friends?

Save them!

Reason is born in me. The world is good. I will bless life. I will love my brothers. These are no longer childhood vows. Nor are they the hope of escaping old age and death. God is my strength, and I praise God.

From Les Illuminations

ETERNITY

The fox howled under the leaves, spitting out the bright feathers of his feast of fowl: like him, I consume myself.

Salads and fruits are only waiting to be picked; but the hedge spider eats nothing but violets.

Let me sleep! let me simmer on Solomon's altars. The scum runs down over the rust, and mingles with the Kedron.

from Fêtes de la Patience

At last, O happiness, O reason, I removed from the sky the azure, which is a blackness, and I lived, a spark of gold of the *natural* light. Out of joy, I took on the most clownish and exaggerated mode of expression possible:

It has been found again! What? eternity. It is the sea mingled with the sun.

My immortal soul, keep your vow despite the lonely night and the day on fire.

Thus you detach yourself from human approval, from common impulses! You fly off as you may . . .

—No hope, never; and no *orietur*. Knowledge and fortitude, torture is certain.

No more tomorrow, satiny embers, your own heat is the [only] duty.

It has been found again—What? Eternity. It is the sea mingled with the sun.

from Les Illuminations

CHRISTINA ROSSETTI

Christina Rossetti was born on December 5, 1830, to Gabriele and Frances Polidori Rossetti. With an Italian father and a half-Italian and half-English mother, Christina grew up fluent in both languages. One of four extremely talented and precocious children (one of her brothers was the Pre-Raphaelite painter and poet Dante Gabriel Rossetti), Christina published her first book of poems at seventeen. Mysterious illnesses kept her confined to her home, however, for many years. From 1850 onwards, she lived with her parents, nursing her sick father until his death in 1854.

In the 1850s and 1860s Christina came out of her relative seclusion to do social work for the Mary Magdalen Home for fallen women in Highgate. Always religious, Christina became increasingly devoted to God and to the poetry and prose her devotion inspired. Recent biographers claim that she loved both men and women, both in a repressed and unfulfilled way; her poem "Goblin Market" has become a favorite among lesbian feminist writers because of its astonishing female eroticism. Christina Rossetti died of cancer in 1894, leaving behind a body of exquisitely crafted and spiritually profound religious lyrics in which she takes us with great integrity and courage into the heart of an inner life lived for, and in, God.

TWO PURSUITS

A voice said, "Follow, follow": and I rose
　　And followed far into the dreamy night,
　　　Turning my back upon the pleasant light.
It led me where the bluest water flows,
And would not let me drink: where the corn grows
　　I dared not pause, but went uncheered by sight
　　　Or touch: until at length in evil plight
It left me, wearied out with many woes.
Some time I sat as one bereft of sense:
　　But soon another voice from very far
　　　Called, "Follow, follow": and I rose again.
Now on my night has dawned a blessed star:

Kind steady hands my sinking steps sustain,
And will not leave me till I shall go hence.

AFTER COMMUNION

Why should I call Thee Lord, Who art my God?
  Why should I call Thee Friend, Who art my Love?
  Or King, Who art my very Spouse above?
Or call Thy Scepter on my heart Thy rod?
  Lo now Thy banner over me is love,
All heaven flies open to me at Thy nod:
For Thou hast lit Thy flame in me a clod,
  Made me a nest for dwelling of Thy Dove.
  What wilt Thou call me in our home above,
Who now has called me friend? how will it be
  When Thou for good wine settest forth the best?
Now Thou dost bid me come and sup with Thee,
  Now Thou dost make me lean upon Thy breast:
How will it be with me in time of love?

AMEN

It is over. What is over?
  Nay, how much is over truly:
Harvest days we toiled to sow for;
  Now the sheaves are gathered newly,
  Now the wheat is garnered duly.

It is finished. What is finished?
  Much is finished known or unknown:
Lives are finished; time diminished;
  Was the fallow field left unsown?
  Will these buds be always unblown?

It suffices. What suffices?
  All suffices reckoned rightly:
Spring shall bloom where now the ice is,
  Rose make the bramble sightly,

And the quickening sun shine brightly,
And the latter wind blow lightly,
And my garden teem with spices.

IN PROGRESS

Ten years ago it seemed impossible
    That she should ever grow as calm as this,
    With self-remembrance in her warmest kiss
And dim dried eyes like an exhausted well.
Slow-speaking when she has some fact to tell,
    Silent with long-unbroken silences,
    Centered in self yet not unpleased to please,
Gravely monotonous like a passing bell.
Mindful of drudging daily common things,
    Patient at pastime, patient at her work,
        Wearied perhaps but strenuous certainty.
        Sometimes I fancy we may one day see
Her head shoot forth seven stars from where they lurk
And her eyes lightnings and her shoulders wings.

LATER LIFE: A DOUBLE SONNET OF SONNETS

Tread softly! all the earth is holy ground.
    It may be, could we look with seeing eyes,
    This spot we stand on is a Paradise
Where dead have come to life and lost been found,
Where Faith has triumphed, Martyrdom been crowned,
    Where fools have foiled the wisdom of the wise;
    From this same spot the dust of saints may rise,
And the King's prisoners come to light unbound.
O earth, earth, earth, hear thou thy Maker's Word:
    "Thy dead thou shalt give up, nor hide thy slain"—
    Some who went weeping forth shall come again
        Rejoicing from the east or from the west,
As doves fly to their windows, love's own bird
    Contented and desirous to the nest.

John Addington Symonds (1840–93) was the most daring innovator in the history of nineteenth-century British homosexual writing. While at Harrow in his teens, he read Plato's *Phaedrus* and *Symposium,* which gave him the "true freedom to love at last . . . the sanction of the love which had been ruling me from childhood." Six years later, in 1871, he discovered Walt Whitman's poetry and started to correspond with Whitman about the homosexual meanings of "Calamus," thrilled to have found a poet who voiced so completely his own visions and dreams. In 1864, inner tension about his homosexuality and fear of social rejection led him to marry (he went on to father four children). Persistent health crises followed, leading to a diagnosis of tuberculosis in 1865, a move to the Swiss Alps in 1877, and in 1868 a mental breakdown and contemplation of suicide.

Such inner torment and physical and mental distress did not prevent him from writing many pioneering works, some of which he had to keep private during his lifetime—several books of poems and essays in defense of homosexuality, *A Problem in Greek Ethics* (1873), and *A Problem in Modern Ethics* (1891), as well as a surprisingly frank biography. After his death his memoirs were found. Because of their sometimes scandalous honesty, they were not published until 1984.

Symonds understood from his deep reading of Whitman and from his love of the Renaissance and classical Greece that sexual freedom was part of a larger and wider liberation of the spiritual and creative power of the human race, a next stage in humanity's progression toward full divine-human identity. Symonds had always believed in God, but age made him increasingly mystical and anxious that humanity should retain through its age of "scientific" progress that "humble reverence" that would keep it open to the powers of grace.

A MYSTERY

The love wherewith my heart is big for thee,
    Hath found no home with cowards or with slaves;
It blooms a deathless flower among the free,
    And on untrodden heights unbroken waves.

No little heart can hold it, for it springs
    Twinned with eternity and scorn of death,
Feeding on hopes and high imaginings
    That fail not with our fitful human breath.

With those sweet strivings of the blood that stir
    Our souls in youth, and make our manhood great,
By interchange of love and life with her
    Who clings to us in bonds of equal fate,

This passion hath no part—nor on the roots
    Of sense and yearning stationed, nor upborne
By tenderness; nor are its sterner fruits
    Shown in dear kisses given at night or morn.

Be it enough that thou and I are one,
    That years and days seem nothing in the shine
Of that perpetual and unsinking sun
    Which nerves our souls with energy divine . . .

THE DESERT

A young man in a barren land
Wandered, where shrubs on burning sand
    Clustered eight dead-sea apples dry:
The ground beneath his feet was dust,
Shining with salt and scurf and crust:
    But, where the desert met the sky,

Rose domes that glimmered, fret and frieze
Sculptured on endless terraces,
    With pearly pyramid and palm;
All quivering in a silver haze,
Growing and fading 'neath the blaze
    Of light inexorably calm.

Then came a Spirit; one who trod
That land alone with Love and God;
    Crying: "If thou wert strong, O youth,

Those trees would bear thee fruit and flowers,
Those phantom palaces and bowers
    Would prove an everlasting truth!"

The Spirit promised—but in vain.
The youth, possessed of aching pain,
    Plucked apples dry as dust, that charred
His loathing lips, and saw the bright
Mirage dissolve in mist and light,
    Leaving the skyline sharp and hard.

So that he said: "Poor Spirit, born
To be the butt of simple scorn!
    Dwell in the wilderness, and taste
Apples with ashes at their core,
Deceived, deceiving evermore!
    I turn and leave thee to the waste."

Then too the Spirit went and trod
That land without or Love or God;
    And all around him into cloud
Faded the unsubstantial show
Of palm and palace; till with woe
    His head upon his breast was bowed.

Yet forasmuch as he was wrung
With pain surpassing mortal tongue,
    Believing still beyond belief,
Nor resting, nor resigning life,
But struggling with continual strife,
    God placed a limit to his grief:

For after many years there came
A day when earth dissolved in flame;
    When neither dust nor sand nor sheen
Phantasmal seared his aching eyes,
But shining through the limpid skies
    The City of the Lord was seen.

The greatest poet of the lyric age, the lyricist *par excellence* Pindar, adds much to our conception of Greek love at this period. Not only is the poem to Theoxenos, whom he loved, and in whose arms he is said to have died in the theater at Argos, one of the most splendid achievements of his art; but its choice of phrase . . . helps us to comprehend the serious intensity of this passion. "The flashing rays of his forehead" and "is storm-tossed with desire," and "the young-limbed bloom of boys," are phrases which it is impossible adequately to translate. So, too, are the images by which the heart of him who does not feel the beauty of Theoxenos is said to have been forged with cold fire out of adamant, while the poet himself is compared to wax wasting under the sun's rays. In Pindar, passing from Ibycus and Anacreon, we ascend at once into a purer and more healthful atmosphere, fraught, indeed, with passion and pregnant with storm, but no longer simply sensual. Taken as a whole, the Odes of Pindar, composed for the most part in the honor of young men and boys, both beautiful and strong, are the work of a great moralist as well as a great artist. He never fails to teach by precept and example; he does not, as Ibycus is reported to have done, adorn his verse with legends of Ganymede and Tithonus, for the sake of insinuating compliments. Yet no one shared in fuller measure the Greek admiration for health and grace and vigor of limb. This is obvious in the many radiant pictures of masculine perfection he has drawn, as well as in the images by which he loves to bring the beauty-bloom of youth to mind. The true Hellenic spirit may be better studied in Pindar than in any other poet of his age; and after we have weighed his high morality, sound counsel, and reverence for all things good, together with the passion he avows, we shall have done something toward comprehending the inner nature of Greek love.

THE LIMITS OF KNOWLEDGE

It may be demanded of me, then, why, holding these views, professing the Agnostic creed, I speak of God as Law, brought back to us by modern science?

The answer is simple. It rests upon the root-conception that man, in all his qualities, but most essentially in the highest part of him, his mind, forms a real portion of the world. Being a portion, he cannot apprehend the whole: to do that was the pretension of theologians and ontologists. Yet this part, this man, raised to self-consciousness, increasing always in his grasp on partial knowledge, is brought continually more and more into the presence of a Force, a Life, a Being, call it what you will, which he is bound to recognize and worship as the essence which fashioned him and which keeps him in existence.

Man has the right to use time-honored language, and to designate his apprehension of the unity in Nature by that venerable title, God. He is only doing now what all the men from whom he is descended did before him. Mumbo Jumbo, Indra, Shiva, Jahve, Zeus, Odin, Balder, Christ, Allah—what are these but names for the Inscrutable, adapted to the modes of thought which gave them currency? God is the same, and His years do not change. It is only our way of presenting the unknown to human imagination which varies.

TOWARD A NEW SYNTHESIS

The revolution in all our conceptions of the world which has been performed during the last three centuries is so tremendous, that no dogmatic theology of any sort can gain a hold upon our minds. At this stage, it is surely enough if, having displaced the old conception of an extra-mundane Creator, who governed a universe which had man for its center, we have not thereby abandoned the belief in God. Let us, in reverence and humility, retain our religious attitude. Let us, so far as we are able, refer our aspirations to God, as the only Life, the only Love, the only Law, the ground of all Reality, the source of all Being. So long as we do this, we keep alive the sacred flame in Vesta's temple of the human heart, and march in the procession of saints, martyrs, and confessors. What must of necessity remain at present blank and abstract in our idea of God may possibly again be filled up and rendered concrete when the human mind is prepared for a new synthesis of faith and science. That, in its turn, will have to be decomposed like older, simpler syntheses; and so forth perpetually, until the inevitable day of *Götter-Dämmerung* [twilight of the gods], the day of dying for our planet, comes. Meanwhile for man, through all these transformations of the religious idea, abides one motto fixed: "While living do thy duty."

OSCAR WILDE

Oscar Wilde was born to accomplished but eccentric parents in Dublin, Ireland, in 1854. Wilde was educated at Trinity College, Dublin, and Magdalen College, Oxford, where he was almost equally influenced by the practically incompatible doctrines of the moralistic John Ruskin and the epicurean Walter Pater. Leaving Oxford in 1878, he proclaimed prophetically, "Somehow or other I'll be famous, and if not famous, I'll be notorious." Before the end of his life, Wilde was to be both. First, he set about being famous. A stream of brilliantly observant and hilarious plays—most notably *Lady Windermere's Fan* (1892) and *The Importance of Being Earnest* (1895)—made him the toast of London. His prose works and poems— among them *The Picture of Dorian Gray* (1890) and *The Soul of Man Under Socialism* (1891)—unveiled a more probing and politically passionate side of his genius, which won him the admiration of the serious artists of his time.

The seeds of notoriety, however, were growing under his fame. In 1884, anxious for social acceptance, Wilde married a young conventional socialite named Constance Lloyd and quickly fathered two sons. He could not long deny his sexual nature, however; in 1891 he met the man who was to be both his great love and his ruin—Lord Alfred Douglas, the twenty-one-year-old son of the ninth Marquess of Queensberry. On February 18, 1895—only four days after the triumphant opening of *The Importance of Being Earnest*—the marquess left a card for Wilde at his club, "To Oscar Wilde, posing as somdomite (*sic*)." Whipped on by Douglas, who detested his father, Wilde sued Queensberry for criminal libel—a suit that was won by the bitter, half-crazy marquess and that culminated in Wilde's own prosecutions for "gross indecency between males," his appalling public humiliation, his years of imprisonment in Reading Gaol, and his subsequent exile and early death (1900).

While in Reading Gaol, Wilde produced what for many people are his two greatest works, *The Ballad of Reading Gaol*, a poem on his experience in prison, and *De Profundis,* a long, agonized, marvelously eloquent "letter" to Lord Alfred Douglas. In both these works, Wilde reveals those depths of soul-knowledge that humiliation, horror, and grief had taught him; they give us what is undoubtedly the finest mystical meditation on suffering and its role in inner transformation that the nineteenth century produced as well as an inspired, radical portrait of Christ and Christ consciousness. What destroyed Wilde as a "figure" made him as a soul; from the ashes of the world-famous dandy emerged a mystic visionary of great power.

E TENEBRIS (OUT OF DARKNESS)

Come down, O Christ, and help me! reach thy hand,
    For I am drowning in a stormier sea
    Than Simon on thy lake of Galilee:
The wine of life is spilt upon the sand,
My heart is as some famine-murdered land
    Whence all good things have perished utterly,
    And well I know my soul in Hell must lie
If I this night before God's throne should stand.
"He sleeps perchance, or rideth to the chase,
    Like Baal, when his prophets howled that name
    From morn to noon on Carmel's smitten height."
Nay, peace, I shall behold, before the night,
    The feet of brass, the robe more white than flame,
    The wounded hands, the weary human face.

EACH IN HIS SEPARATE CELL

But though lean Hunger and green Thirst
    Like asp with adder fight,
We have little care of prison fare,
    For what chills and kills outright
Is that every stone one lifts by day
    Becomes one's heart by night.

With midnight always in one's heart,
    And twilight in one's cell,

We turn the crank, or tear the rope,
    Each in his separate Hell,
And the silence is more awful far
    Than the sound of a brazen bell.

And never a human voice comes near
    to speak a gentle word:
And the eye that watches through the door
    Is pitiless and hard:
And by all forgot, we rot and rot,
    With soul and body marred.

And thus we rust Life's iron chain
    Degraded and alone:
And some men curse, and some men weep,
    And some men make no moan:
But God's eternal Laws are kind
    And break the heart of stone.

And every human heart that breaks,
    In prison-cell or yard,
Is as that broken box that gave
    Its treasure to the Lord,
And filled the unclean leper's house
    With the scent of costliest nard.

Ah! happy they whose hearts can break
    And peace of pardon win!
How else may man make straight his plan
    And cleanse his soul from Sin?
How else but through a broken heart
    May Lord Christ enter in?

    From The Ballad of Reading Gaol

THE TREASURE IN THE FIELD

I have lain in prison for nearly two years. Out of my nature has come
wild despair; an abandonment to grief that was piteous even to look

at: terrible and impotent rage: bitterness and scorn: anguish that wept aloud: misery that could find no voice: sorrow that was dumb. I have passed through every possible mood of suffering. Better than Wordsworth himself I know what Wordsworth meant when he said:

> Suffering is permanent, obscure, and dark
> And has the nature of Infinity.

But while there were times when I rejoiced in the idea that my sufferings were to be endless, I could not bear them to be without meaning. Now what I find hidden away in my nature, like a treasure in a field, is Humility.

It is the last thing left in me, and the best: the ultimate discovery at which I have arrived: the starting-point for a fresh development. It has come to me right out of myself, so I know that it has come at the proper time. It could not have come before, nor later. Had anyone told me of it, I would have rejected it. Had it been brought to me, I would have refused it. As I found it, I want to keep it. I must do so. It is the one thing that has in it the elements of life, of a new life, a *Vita Nuova* for me. Of all things it is the strangest. One cannot give it away, and another may not give it to one. One cannot acquire it, expect by surrendering everything that one has. It is only when one has lost all things, that one knows that one possesses it.

From De Profundis

THE REVELATION OF SUFFERING

Sorrow, and all that it teaches one, is my new world. I used to live entirely for pleasure. I shunned sorrow and suffering of every kind. I hated both. I resolved to ignore them as far as possible, to treat them, that is to say, as modes of imperfection. They were not part of my scheme of life. They had no place in my philosophy. My mother, who knew life as a whole, used often to quote to me Goethe's lines—written by Carlyle in a book he had given her years ago—and translated, I fancy, by him also:

> Who never ate his bread in sorrow,
> Who never spent the midnight hours

Weeping and waiting for the morrow,
He knows you not, ye Heavenly Powers.

They were lines my mother often quoted in the troubles of her later life: I absolutely declined to accept or admit the enormous truth hidden in them. I could not understand it. I remember quite well how I used to tell her that I did not want to eat my bread in sorrow, or to pass any night weeping and watching for a more bitter dawn. I had no idea that it was one of the special things that the Fates had in store for me; that for a whole year of my life, indeed, I was to do little else. But so has my portion been meted out to me; and during the last few months I have, after terrible struggles and difficulties, been able to comprehend some of the lessons hidden in the heart of pain. Clergymen, and people who use phrases without wisdom, sometimes talk of suffering as a mystery. It is really a revelation. One discerns things that one never discerned before. One approaches the whole of history from a different standpoint. What one had felt dimly through instinct, about Art, is intellectually and emotionally realized with perfect clearness of vision and absolute intensity of apprehension. . . . There are times when Sorrow seems to me to be the only truth. Other things may be illusions of the eye or the appetite, made to blind the one and cloy the other, but out of Sorrow have the worlds been built, and at the birth of a child or a star there is pain. . . .

I remember talking once on this subject to one of the most beautiful personalities I have ever known: a woman, whose sympathy and noble kindness to me both before and since the tragedy of my imprisonment have been beyond power and description. . . . On the occasion of which I am thinking I recall distinctly how I said to her that there was enough suffering in one narrow London lane to show God did not love man, and that wherever there was any sorrow, though but that of a child in some little garden weeping over a fault that it had or had not committed, the whole face of creation was completely marred. I was entirely wrong. She told me so, but I could not believe her. I was not in the sphere in which such belief was to be attained to. Now it seems to me that Love of some kind is the only possible explanation of the extraordinary amount of suffering that there is in the world. I cannot conceive any other explanation. I am convinced that there is no other, and that if the worlds have indeed, as I have said, been built out of Sorrow, it has been by the hands of Love, because in no other way could the Soul of man for whom the worlds are made reach the full stature of its perfection.

THE FULL PERSONALITY

It is a question whether we have ever seen the full expression of a personality, except on the imaginative plane of art. . . . It will be a marvelous thing—the true personality of man—when we see it. It will grow naturally and simply, flowerlike, or as a tree grows. It will not be discord. It will never argue or dispute. It will not prove things. It will know everything. And yet it will not busy itself about knowledge. It will have wisdom. Its value will not be measured by material things. It will have nothing. And yet it will have everything, and whatever one takes from it, it will still have, so rich will it be. It will not be always meddling with others, or asking them to be like itself. It will love them because they will be different. And yet while it will not meddle with others, it will help all, as a beautiful thing helps us, by being what it is. The personality of man will be very wonderful. It will be as wonderful as the personality of a child.

In its development it will be assisted by Christianity, if men desire that; but if men do not desire that, it will develop none the less surely. For it will not worry itself about the past, nor care whether things happened or did not happen. Nor will it admit any laws but its own laws; nor any authority but its own authority. Yet it will love those who sought to intensify it, and speak often of them. And of these Christ was one.

"Know thyself!" was written over the portal of the antique world. Over the portal of the new world, "Be thyself" shall be written. And the message of Christ to man was simply "Be thyself." That is the secret of Christ. . . .

CHAPTER EIGHT

RAGE, MY BLIZZARD-FIRE

EARLY TWENTIETH CENTURY

ANDRÉ GIDE

André Gide (1869–1951) was born in Paris and discovered writing as a means to heal confused childhood feelings due to his father's early death and the rigors of his consequent Protestant upbringing. Gide's literary career began with *The Notebooks of André Walter,* which was published anonymously in 1891. This work was followed, among others, by *The Immoralist,* a psychological novel published in 1902, and *Corydon,* published in 1924, one of the first—and finest—modern defenses of homosexuality. Gide's last major work, *Theseus* (1946), earned him the Nobel Prize for literature in 1947. Gide's work is marked by fierce and probing brilliance of mind and psychological understanding. While he despised "formal" religion, his early work *Fruits of the Earth* shows his innate spirituality and sense of divine presence in reality.

Know that God is that which lies ahead of you. Do not seek Him elsewhere than everywhere.

Understand that at every single moment of the day you can possess God in totality. Do not wait for God. To wait for God means not to understand that you already have Him.

Look upon evening as if the day were meant to die and upon morning as if everything were being born again.

Let your vision be new at every single moment. The wise man is he who stands in wonderment before all things.

Never on this earth have I seen anything beautiful without immediately wishing to touch it with all my love.

I wanted to embrace all the smiles on the lips; drink all the tears in the eyes; bite the pulp of all the fruits bending toward me. Before each tavern I felt new hunger; in front of each spring new thirst. . . .

In the Gospels I have always admired, and continue to admire, the superhuman effort toward joy. The first word attributed to Christ is "Happy . . ." His first miracle, the transformation of water into wine.

The true Christian is he who gets drunk on water. It is inside him that the Cana miracle is being repeated. Only due to the outrageously incorrect interpretation of men, the consecration of sadness and woe was imposed upon the Gospels.

Know that joy is rarer, more difficult and more beautiful than sadness. Once you make this all-important discovery, you must embrace joy as a moral obligation.

From Fruits of the Earth

JEAN COCTEAU

Jean Cocteau (1889–1963) was born and brought up in pre–World War I Paris. He published *The White Paper,* an ecstatic and shameless celebration of homosexuality, in 1928. Cocteau, equally expert in poetry, novels, and filmmaking, collaborated with Nijinsky, Pablo Picasso, and Igor Stravinsky. At thirty, he and his fifteen-year-old lover, Raymond Radiguet, wrote four of the most celebrated novels of post–World War I French literature: Cocteau's *The Great Split* (1923) and *The Imposter* (1923) and Radiguet's *The Devil in the Flesh* (1923) and *Count d'Orgel* (1924). After Radiguet's death from typhoid in 1923, Cocteau branched out into film and scriptwriting, which led to the creation of the extraordinary films *Orpheus* (1950) and *Testament to Orpheus* (1960). Cocteau's famous novel *The Holy Terrors* (1929) became a film in 1950. All of Cocteau's work is infused by an electric sense of the mystery of the universe and of the power of mythic and mystical archetypes.

THE TWO-WAY MIRROR

You went into a dark cabin and opened a shutter. This shutter revealed a metallic canvas through which the eye could see a small bathroom. On the other side of the canvas was a mirror that reflected so well from such a smooth surface that it was impossible to guess that it was full of eyes.

Due to financial reasons I happened to spend a Sunday there. Out of the twelve mirrors in the twelve bathrooms it was the only one of this sort. The owner had acquired it for a very high price and had had it brought from Germany. His staff were unaware of the observatory. The young working-class men supplied the show.

They all followed the same routine. They undressed and hung up their new suits carefully. Once they were out of their Sunday best their delightful professional deformities made it possible to guess their jobs. Standing up on the bath, they would look at themselves (and me) and begin by a Parisian grimace that bares the gums. Then they would rub one shoulder, pick up the soap and make it lather. The soaping turned into a caress. Suddenly their eyes left the world, their head would fall back and their body spit like a furious animal.

Some of them sank down exhausted into the steaming water, while others began the same procedure all over again; the youngest ones were distinguishable because they climbed out of the bath and wiped from the tiles the sap that their blind stems had hurled distantly, madly, toward love. Once, a Narcissus who was pleasuring himself, brought his mouth up to the mirror, glued it to the glass and completed the adventure with himself. Invisible as a Greek god, I pressed my lips against his and imitated his gestures. He never knew that the mirror, instead of reflecting, was participating, that it was alive and loved him.

From The White Album

The bizarre nature of the fact alone compels one to say it: Greece is an idea one develops, and develops endlessly beneath a sky that lends itself to this kind of illusion, to the point where one wonders whether Greece even exists, whether we exist when traveling there, and whether all its islands and its Athens where the peppermills fill the air with their pepper, are not simply some fable, a presence as strong and as dead as that of Pallas Athena, for instance, or of Neptune. One wonders, climbing like a goat over the bones of kings, embalmed by those immortals in whom the storm unleashes a web of odors as alive and as extinct as that oracle who walks, his feet motionless, through the centuries, his gaze like the white cane of the blind. An idea built up and destroyed, immortal and mortal, like those immortals who desiccate beneath the sun around the cave where the sibyl prophesied and before her door where the Sunday crowd lined up. An idea, yes, an obsession, so obsessive that it remains standing on its oracle's feet, watching us with an eye that sees us not. And this eye of an idea sends out its gaze over everything, over Delphi, crowned with its dead theater, over Crete, where we were nearly lost in the open labyrinth of Knossos that conceals ideas of red bulls and bees, to which the hillside hives, and the waists of princes and princesses, mercilessly crushed against the walls and bloody columns, bear witness. Over Santorini, which escapes its volcano only by a white flight to the summit of its lava peaks. Over that idea, the idea which the sea chews like cud, over and over, to the point where it mumbles, over and over, to the point where one would sacrifice one's daughter to silence it, to calm its mumbling upheaval of one's boat, which is an idea of a boat . . .

ON THE BIRTH OF A POEM

Whence came visibility in the notion of angels, the human shape taken by these inhumans? Surely, from man's need to explain certain forces, to overcome an abstract presence, to embody it somewhat in our own image, that it might be less frightening.

The phenomena of nature—lightning, eclipses, floods—would seem less inscrutable at the hands of some perceptible host, acting on God's orders.

In bearing human features, the lineaments of this host would lose that vagueness against which the mind revolts, that nameless quality that terrifies children and makes them leap breathlessly for the nearest lamp. . . .

Graceful monsters, cruel, dreadfully masculine and androgynous— such was the notion I held of angels, of *flying angels,* before I discovered that their invisibility could be captured in a poem and made visible, *without running the risk of being seen.*

I had originally intended my play *Orphée* to be a story about the Virgin and Joseph, about the backbiting at their expense that was instigated by the angel (a carpenter's assistant), the malevolence of Nazareth confronted by an unaccountable pregnancy, and the necessity of the couple's flight occasioned by the village's spite.

The plot lent itself to so many misapprehensions that I was forced to abandon it. In its place I used the Orphic theme, in which the unaccountable birth of poems would replace that of the Holy Infant.

The angel was to have a part in it, in the guise of a glazier. But I was not to write the act until much later, at the Hotel Welcome in Villefranche. . . .

If I run ahead of myself, it is only in order to make it quite clear that the character of the angel lived platonically within me and gave me no cause for uneasiness before the poem, and that once I had finished the poem I considered him to be harmless. I kept only his name in the play and in the film. Having become a poem, he was but little concerned over whether or not I gave him any thought.

Here is the passage from *Opium* that shed light on my impotence to write this chapter. It dates from 1928. I had placed it in 1930.

> One day, on my way to visit Picasso in rue La Boétie, I felt that something terrible and eternal was growing within and next to me in the elevator. A voice called out to me: "My name is on the plate," a jolt brought me to my senses, and I read on the brass plate affixed to the hand lever: HEURTEBISE ELEVATORS.
>
> I recall that, later, Picasso and I spoke about miracles. Picasso said that everything is a miracle, that it's a miracle that we don't dissolve in our baths.

In retrospect, I see how deeply that sentence influenced me. It sums up the style of a play in which miracles must appear not to be miraculous, must reflect both comedy and tragedy, must fascinate in the way that the adult world fascinates children.

I thought no more about the incident in the elevator. Then, suddenly, everything changed. The outline of my projected play became blurred. At night, I would fall asleep then awaken abruptly, unable to go back to sleep. During the day, I floundered and stumbled in a quagmire of daydreams. This agitation became atrocious. The angel had taken up residence within me without my knowing it, and it had taken this name Heurtebise, with which I became ever more obsessed, to make me aware of it. . . .

In giving it a name, I hoped that it would leave me alone. I was sadly mistaken. The mythical creature became unbearable. It grew burdensome, spread its wings, thrashed about, kicked like a baby in its mother's womb. I could confide in no one. I was compelled to bear the torture. . . .

The angel couldn't have cared less about my rebellion. I was only its vehicle, and it treated me like one. It made ready for its departure. My crises came more and more frequently, becoming one single crisis akin to labor pains. But it was a monstrous birth, one which would benefit neither from the maternal instinct nor from the closeness it engenders. Imagine a parthenogenesis, a couple formed of one body that gives birth. At last, after a night in which I had contemplated suicide, the delivery took place, on the Rue d'Anjou. It lasted seven days, during which the character's gall exceeded all bounds, compelling me to write against my will.

From Diary of an Unknown

WILFRED OWEN

Wilfred Owen was born in 1893 and brought up in Shropshire, England. After failing to get into the university, he worked for a vicar and then as an English teacher in France before enlisting at the beginning of World War I at the age of twenty-one. His earliest poetry is in the homoerotic tradition of Housman's *A Shropshire Lad* and Tennyson's *In Memoriam,* poems that at once mourn and exalt the beauty of a dead young man.

The terrible experience of trench warfare stripped his style of all preciousness and transformed him into the fiercest and most eloquent of all the war poets. War's horrors revealed to him the limitations of all organized religion, but engendered in his soul the Christlike agony of pity that inspires his greatest work.

Wilfred Owen was killed in battle on November 4, 1918; the news reached his parents as the bells rang to celebrate the armistice.

INSENSIBILITY

Happy are men who yet before they are killed
Can let their veins run cold.
Whom no compassion fleers
Or makes their feet
Sore on the alleys cobbled with their brothers.
The front line withers,
But they are troops who fade, not flowers
For poets' tearful fooling:
Men, gaps for filling:
Losses, who might have fought
Longer; but no one bothers.

And some cease feeling
Even themselves or for themselves.
Dullness best solves
The tease and doubt of shelling,
And Chance's strange arithmetic
Comes simpler than the reckoning of their shilling.
They keep no check on armies' decimation.

Happy are those who lose imagination:
They have enough to carry with ammunition.
Their spirit drags no pack,
Their old wounds, save with cold, can not more ache.
Having seen all things red,
Their eyes are rid
Of the hurt of the color of blood for ever.
And terror's first constriction over,
Their hearts remain small-drawn.

Their senses in some scorching cautery of battle
Now long since ironed,
Can laugh among the dying, unconcerned.

Happy the soldier home, with not a notion
How somewhere, every dawn, some men attack,
And many sighs are drained.
Happy the lad whose mind was never trained:
His days are worth forgetting more than not.
He sings along the march
Which we march taciturn, because of dusk,
The long, forlorn, relentless trend
From larger day to huger night.

We wise, who with a thought besmirch
Blood over all our soul,
How should we see our task
But through his blunt and lashless eyes?
Alive, he is not vital overmuch;
Dying, not mortal overmuch;
Nor sad, nor proud,
Nor curious at all.
He cannot tell
Old men's placidity from his.

But cursed are dullards whom no cannon stuns,
That they should be as stones;
Wretched are they, and mean
With paucity that never was simplicity.
By choice they made themselves immune
To pity and whatever moans in man
Before the last sea and the hapless stars;
Whatever mourns when many leave these shores;
Whatever shares
The eternal reciprocity of tears.

STRANGE MEETING

It seemed that out of battle I escaped
Down some profound dull tunnel, long since scooped

Through granites which titanic wars had groined.
Yet also there encumbered sleepers groaned,
Too fast in thought or death to be bestirred.
Then, as I probed them, one sprang up, and stared
With piteous recognition in fixed eyes,
Lifting distressful hands as if to bless.
And by his smile, I knew that sullen hall
By his dead smile I knew we stood in Hell.
With a thousand pains that vision's face was grained;
Yet no blood reached there from the upper ground,
And no guns thumped, or down the flues made moan.
"Strange friend," I said, "here is no cause to mourn."
"None," said that other, "save the undone years,
The hopelessness. Whatever hope is yours,
Was my life also; I went hunting wild
After the wildest beauty in the world,
Which lies not calm in eyes, or braided hair,
But mocks the steady running of the hour,
And if it grieves, grieves richlier than here.
For by my glee might many men have laughed,
And of my weeping something had been left,
Which must die now. I mean the truth untold,
The pity of war, the pity war distilled.
Now men will go content with what we spoiled,
Or, discontent, boil bloody, and be spilled.
They will be swift with swiftness of the tigress,
None will break ranks, though nations trek from progress.
Courage was mine, and I had mystery,
Wisdom was mine, and I had mastery;
To miss the march of this retreating world
Into vain citadels that are not walled.
Then, when much blood had clogged their chariot-wheels
I would go up and wash them from sweet wells,
Even with truths that lie too deep for taint.
I would have poured my spirit without stint
But not through wounds; not on the cess of war.
Foreheads of men have bled where no wounds were.
I am the enemy you killed, my friend.

I knew you in this dark; for so you frowned
Yesterday through me as you jabbed and killed.
I parried; but my hands were loath and cold.
Let us sleep now. . . ."

SERGEI ESENIN

Sergei Esenin (1895–1925) is best known in the West due to his brief marriage to the dancer Isadora Duncan. Although he was married to three
women, his only meaningful love poetry was addressed to other men.
Esenin's two-year relationship with the poet Nikolai Kliuev was inspiration for Esenin as well as Kliuev, and their love was expressed in the work
of both poets during this time. His last poem, which was also his suicide
note, was addressed to a young Jewish poet whom he had spent the night
with a few days earlier. Esenin's precise and transparent lyricism is permeated by echoes of the mystical imagery and liturgy of the Russian Orthodox tradition. At their best, Esenin's poems have, as Pasternak wrote, the
"dazzling and somber radiance of a medieval icon."

AUTUMN

Along the bluff the juniper grove is still.
Autumn like a red mare combs her mane.

Along the banks that guard the river
You hear the blue clink of her hoofs.

The monkish wind with cautious tread
Disturbs the leaves along the highway wall

And kisses on the rowan tree
The scarlet ulcers of the unseen Christ.

Beyond the hills, beyond the yellow valleys,
The village footpath stretches, unmetaled;

I see the forest in the evening's blaze,
The fences twined with nettles.

There from morning the sands of the sky
Turned blue above the church's towers.
Damp breezes off the lakes fly,
Ringing through the roadside flowers.

Not for the spring song over the plains
Are the green spaces dear to me still.
I love with the love of the yearning cranes
The monastery on the hill.

At evening when the sky turns misty,
And sunset hangs the bridge above,
At this hour, you go my wretched country
And bow to the Cross and to love.

Gentle souls of that cloistered place,
Avidly hearing the Angelus toll,
Before the Savior's gentle face,
Pray for my shipwrecked soul.

NOT FOR NOTHING

Not for nothing have the winds
and thunder roared and raved.
Some secret being slaked
my eyes with peaceful light.

With something of a springtime
tenderness, I ceased to grieve
into the azure haze
of earth's unearthly beautiful
enigma.

The silent galaxies do not oppress me now,
nor the starry terror appall me:
for I have learned to love
the world and eternity as I have loved
the hearth of home.

Everything in them is blessed
and holy, all horrors are sublime.
The scarlet poppy of sunset slowly
stains the glass lake. Despite

my will, resistlessly, the image
in the sea of corn is torn
from the tongue: the calving sky
licks the red calf just born.

MIKHAIL KUZMIN

Mikhail Alekseyevich Kuzmin (1872–1936), the Russian writer and multi-
lingual translator, was first published in 1905 with *The History of the Knight
d'Alessio.* Kuzmin gained recognition with the publication of *Alexandrian
Songs,* a collection of twelve poems, and his novel *Wings* (1906), which
deals with the love of young men. Among Kuzmin's major works are the
plays *Dangerous Precaution* (1907), a bold affirmation of homosexual love,
and *The Venetian Madcaps* (1915), which depicts a woman meddling in
gay male relations. In 1910, Kuzmin fell in love and published *The Caril-
lon of Love,* a collection of poems set to music. The openly homosexual
Lakes in Autumn (1912) and the collections of verse entitled *Echo* (1921)
and *Parabolas* (1922) preceded two chapters of *Roman Wonders* (1922),
which Kuzmin felt to be his finest prose. Kuzmin's final great work, *The
Trout Breaks the Ice* (1929), was completed seven years before he died of
pneumonia in 1936.

Kuzmin's work is at once profoundly sophisticated and ironic in its use
of masks, myths, and historical "personae" and saturated with sensual,
mystical love of bodies and nature.

Love joins. The source of love is God, and creation is the work of His
love. The primal law—love. The revelation of this law—truth. Truth
and love—Divine Wisdom.
That which has an immortal soul is guided by inner forces.
That which has no soul is guided by external forces, but forces
which have their beginning in love. Love for oneself is the primal in-

stinct, the capacity for perfection; the goal is love toward everything in its entirety, deviation from the goals is disorder.

Virtue—the readiness to regulate one's actions according to the relationships of universal love.

God is fullness, Creation, oneness. As soon as there is a creation, there are two: the Creator and the created. Division. But at once there is love as union and active fullness. That is why there is no Nirvana, no inertia.

Christ's passion is the exertion of the Divine love. Is it not sexual? The channel of love is the cross. The Phallus. Only in the life of the flesh is there the union of creation and oneness.

ALEXANDRIAN SONGS

7

Were I a general of olden times,
I would subdue the Ethiops and the Persians,
I would dethrone Pharaoh,
I would build myself a pyramid
higher than Cheops',
and I would become
more glorious than any man in Egypt.

Were I a nimble thief,
I would rob the tomb of Menkaure,
I would sell the gems to the Jews of Alexandria,
I would buy up land and mills,
and I would become
richer than any man in Egypt.

Were I a second Antinous,
he who drowned in the sacred Nile—
I would drive all men mad with my beauty,
temples would be raised to me while I yet lived,
and I would become
more powerful than any man in Egypt.

Were I a sage steeped in wisdom,
I would squander all my wealth,

I would shun office and occupation,
I would guard other men's orchards,
and I would become
freer than any man in Egypt.

Were I your lowliest slave,
I would sit in a dungeon
and once a year or once in two years
I would glimpse the golden tracery of your sandals
when you chanced to walk by the prison house,
and I would become
happier than any man in Egypt.

THE DEATH OF ANTINOUS

5

Three times I saw him face to face.
The first time was in the gardens—
I had been sent to fetch food for my comrades,
and to make the journey shorter
I took the path by the palace wing;
suddenly I caught the tremor of strings,
and, being tall of stature,
I peered through the broad window
And saw him:
he was sitting alone and sad,
his slender fingers idly plucking the strings of a lyre;
a white dot
lay silent at his feet,
and only the fountain's plashing
mingled with the music.
Sensing my gaze,
he put down his lyre
and lifted his lowered face.
Magic to me his beauty
and his silence in the empty room,
in the noontide stillness.
Crossing myself, I ran away in fear,

away from the window . . .
Later, on guard duty at Lochias,
I was standing in the passage
leading to the quarters of the imperial astrologer.
The moon cast a bright square on the floor,
and the copper buckles of my sandals
glinted
as I trod the patch of brightness.
Hearing footsteps,
I halted.
From the inner chamber,
a slave bearing a torch before them,
three men came forth,
he being one.
He was pale,
but it seemed to me
that the room was lit
not by the torch, but by his countenance.
As he passed, he glanced at me
and said, "I've seen you before, my friend,"
and withdrew to the astrologer's quarters.
Long after his white robes were lost to view
and the torch had been swallowed in darkness,
I stood there, not moving, not breathing,
and afterwards in the barracks,
feeling Martius, who slept next to me,
touch my hand in his usual way,
I pretended to be asleep.
And then one evening
we met again.
We were bathing
near the tents of Caesar's camp,
when suddenly a cry went up.
We ran, but it was too late.
Dragged from the water, the body
lay on the sand,
and that same unearthly face,
the face of a magician,

stared with wide-open eyes.
Still far off, the Emperor was hurrying toward us,
shaken by the grievous tidings;
but I stood seeing nothing,
not feeling tears unknown to me since childhood
running down my cheeks.
All night I whispered prayers,
raving of my native Asia, of Nicomedia,
and angel voices sang:
"Hosanna!
A new god
is given unto men!"

MARINA TSVETAEVA

Marina Tsvetaeva (1892–1941) is considered to be one of the greatest Russian poets of the twentieth century. Tsvetaeva began writing poetry at age six and published her first volume of poetry, *Evening Album,* in 1910 at age eighteen. Her self-acknowledged bisexuality and lesbianism served as overt inspiration in her writings, including the most artistically mature work of her early period, *Girlfriend* (1914–15). Tsvetaeva's most famous collection of poetry, *Mileposts I* (1922), was followed by her "*Lettre a l'Amazone*" (1932, rev. 1934), which is based upon her relationships with poet Sophia Parnok and writer Natalie Clifford Barney.

Tsvetaeva's exalted vision of the poet as seer and of poetry as prophetic utterance combined with her wild, intensely poignant understanding of suffering of all kinds, private and political, make her one of the few authentically religious poets of the century.

She left Russia with her husband in 1922 and lived first in Prague, then Paris. In 1939, she followed her husband back to the Soviet Union, where he was arrested and executed. In 1941, penniless and ostracized, Tsvetaeva hanged herself.

GOD (3)

No, you never will bind him
To your signs and your burdens!

The least chink—he's inside it,
Like the supplest of gymnasts.

By the drawbridges
And flocks in migration,
By the telegraph poles,
God's escaping us.

No, you never will train him
To abide and to share!
He, in feelings' resident slush,
Is a gray floe of ice.

No, you never will catch him!
On a thrifty dish, God
Never thrives in the window
Like domestic begonias!

All, beneath the roof's vault,
Were awaiting the builder,
The call. Poets and pilots
—All gave up in despair.

He's the sprint—and he's moving.
The whole volume of stars
Is, from Alpha to Omega,
Just a trace of his cloak.

Translation by Paul Graves

Strange and beautiful brother—take this
city no hands built—out of my hands!

Church by church—all the forty times forty, and
the small pigeons also that rise over them.

Take the Spassky gate, with its flowers, where
the orthodox remove their caps, and

the chapel of stars, that refuge from evil,
where the floor is—polished by kisses.

Take from me the incomparable circle
of five cathedrals, ancient, holy friend!

I shall lead you as a guest from another
country to the Chapel of the Inadvertent Joy

where pure gold domes will begin to shine
for you, and sleepless bells will start thundering.

There the Mother of God will drop her
cloak upon you from the crimson clouds

and you will rise up filled with wonderful powers.
Then, you will not repent that you have loved me!

From Verses About Moscow

THE POET

I

A poet's speech begins a great way off.
A poet is carried far away by speech

by way of planets, signs, and the ruts
of roundabout parables, between *yes* and *no,*
in his hands even sweeping gestures from a bell-tower
become hook-like. For the way of comets

is the poet's way. And the blown-apart
links of causality are his links. Look up
after him without hope. The eclipses of
poets are not foretold in the calendar.

He is the one that mixes up the cards
and confuses arithmetic and weight,
demands answers from the school bench,
the one who altogether refutes Kant,

the one in the stone graves of the Bastille
who remains like a tree in its loveliness.
And yet the one whose traces have always vanished,

the train everyone always arrives
too late to catch

                for the path of comets
is the path of poets: they burn without warning,
pick without cultivating. They are: an explosion, a breaking in—
and the mane of their path makes the curve of a
graph cannot be foretold by the calendar.

3

Now what shall I do here, blind and fatherless?
Everyone else can see and has a father.
Passion in this world has to leap anathema
as it might be over the walls of a trench
and weeping is called a cold in the head.

What shall I do, by nature and trade
a singing creature (like a wire—sunburn! Siberia!)
as I go over the bridge of my enchanted
visions, that cannot be weighed, in a
world that deals only in weights and measures?

What shall I do, singer and firstborn, in a
world where the deepest black is grey,
and inspiration is kept in a thermos?
with all this immensity
in a measured world?

A SOUL'S BEEN REALIZED

The gold that was my hair has turned
silently to gray. Don't pity me!
Everything's been realized,
in my breast all's blended and attuned.

—Attuned, as all of distance blends
In the smokestack moaning on the outskirts.
And Lord! A soul's been realized:
The most deeply secret of your ends.

    Translated by Paul Graves

Sophia Parnok (1885–1933), Russia's only openly lesbian poet of her time, published a book of verse entitled *Poems* in 1916. This book was delayed for many years due to her poor relations with her father, who disapproved of her lesbianism, and to a short-lived marriage that stifled her creativity. Parnok's *Poems* was published near the end of her relationship with poet Marina Tsvetaeva, which was followed by a new love affair that inspired the creation of the dramatic poem "Almast" (1917). Parnok's mature lesbian voice appears in the collections *Roses of Pieria* (1922), *The Vine* (1923), *Music* (1926), and *Half-Voiced* (1928). Her greatest lesbian poems come from *Ursa Major* and *Useless Goods* (both written in the late 1920s). These two lyrical cycles were inspired by her love affair with physicist Nina Vedeneyeva, which ended only at Parnok's death in 1933.

Like that of her lover Marina Tsvetaeva, Sophia Parnok's poetry has as its core an exalted and exacting vision of the poet as spirit guide, as the champion of the soul's ordeals and revelations.

TO MARINA TSVETAEVA

Blindly staring eyes of the
Holy Mother and Savior Child.
Smell of incense, wax, and oil.
Sounds of soft weeping filling the church.
Melting tapers held by young, meek women
in fists stiff with cold and rough-skinned.
Oh, steal me away from my death,
you, whose arms are tanned and fresh,
you, who passed by, exciting me!
Isn't there in your desperate name a
wind from all storm-tossed coasts,
Marina, named after the sea!

For long I lived in love with liberty,
with no more thought of God than has a bird,
directing my flight merely for the sake of flight.

And the Lord remembered me—and so,
like heat lightning, the soul in me was sparked,
everything lit up. And I found you,
to die in you and to be born again
for other days and for other heights.

The Lord has made note of me too,
I dream of mysterious sounds:
for names I do not search in books,
I carry my calendars in me.
I baptize in a sacred font,
—the one I had hurt with a nickname,
I haven't endeavored to try
gold locks with a burglar's lockpick.
My world may be sparsely settled,
but I have my godchildren with me,
and in the eternity of names
the name I have given blossoms.

RONDEAU

I'll remember everything. In one boundless moment,
the obedient herds of all my days will crowd before me.
On the paths I've trodden I shall not overlook
one track, like the lines in my reference book,
and to the evil of all my days I shall softly say "yes."
Are we not summoned here by the whim of love—
love, I have not endeavored to break your chains!
And without fear, without shame, without despair
I'll remember everything.
Even if my toil has yielded me a pitiful harvest,
and my barns are full of wormword rather than corn,
and even if my god has lied, my faith is firm,
I won't be like some contemptible defrocked monk
in that endless moment, the last moment, when
I'll remember everything.

Rage, my blizzard-fire
My heart will burn to ashes,
my spirit rise from them.
I pray to all the martyrs
that the flame won't dim.
Rage, my blizzard-fire,
in your thicket black,
until my spirit finds a
baptismal font inside the
blaze of seething fire.

CONSTANTINE CAVAFY

Constantine Cavafy (1863–1933) was born in Alexandria, Egypt, into a family of rich Greek merchants and, after brief periods of living in England and Constantinople at an early age, made his home in his native city the rest of his life. He is considered to be, with George Seferis, one of the two great modern Greek poets of the century; both W. H. Auden and Marguerite Yourcenar wrote memorable essays about him and some of David Hockney's finest etchings were inspired by his terse, explicit homosexual love poems.

The canon of Cavafy's poems contains only 154 works, most of them short. Their detached, austere, and nakedly unsentimental tone has assured them an unique place in world literature. What makes Cavafy sometimes a mystical poet is the depth of his often painful rapture at beauty and sensual passion; both have for him, as his poetry clearly shows, the shocking force of religious revelation.

GROWING IN SPIRIT

He who hopes to grow in spirit
will have to transcend obedience and respect.
He will hold to some laws
but he will mostly violate
both law and custom, and go beyond

the established, inadequate norm.
Sensual pleasures will have much to teach him.
He will not be afraid of the destructive act:
half the house will have to come down.
This way he will grow virtuously into wisdom.

CHANDELIER

In a room—empty, small, four walls only,
covered with green cloth—
a beautiful chandelier burns, all fire;
and in each of its flames a sensual fever,
a lascivious urge, glows with heat.

In the small room, radiantly lit
by the chandelier's hot fire,
no ordinary light breaks out.
Not for timid bodies
the rapture of this heat.

THE BANDAGED SHOULDER

He said he'd hurt himself against a wall or had fallen down.
But there was probably some other reason
for the wounded, the bandaged shoulder.

Because of a rather abrupt gesture,
as he reached for a shelf to bring down
some photographs he wanted to look at,
the bandage came undone and a little blood ran.

I did it up again, taking my time
over the binding; he wasn't in pain
and I liked looking at the blood.
It was a thing of my love, that blood.

When he left, I found, in front of his chair,
a bloody rag, part of the dressing,
a rag to be thrown straight into the garbage;

and I put it to my lips
and kept it there a long while—
the blood of love against my lips.

ONE NIGHT

The room was cheap and sordid,
hidden above the suspect taverna.
From the window you could see the alley,
dirty and narrow. From below
came the voices of workmen
playing cards, enjoying themselves.

And there on that common, humble bed
I had love's body, had those intoxicating lips,
red and sensual,
red lips of such intoxication
that now as I write, after so many years,
in my lonely house, I'm drunk with passion again.

ONE OF THEIR GODS

When one of them moved through the marketplace of Selefkia
just as it was getting dark—
moved like a young man, tall, extremely handsome,
with the joy of being immortal in his eyes,
with his black and perfumed hair—
the people going by would gaze at him,
and one would ask the other if he knew him,
if he was a Greek from Syria, or a stranger.
But some who looked more carefully
would understand and step aside;
and as he disappeared under the arcades,
among the shadows and the evening lights,
going toward the quarter that lives
only at night, with orgies and debauchery,
with every kind of intoxication and desire,
they would wonder which of Them it could be,

and for what suspicious pleasure
he had come down into the streets of Selefkia
from the August Celestial Mansions.

THE GOD ABANDONS ANTONY

When suddenly, at midnight, you hear
an invisible procession going by
with exquisite music, voices,
don't mourn your luck that's failing now,
work gone wrong, your plans
all proving deceptive—don't mourn them uselessly.
As one long prepared, and graced with courage,
say good-bye to her, the Alexandria that is leaving.
Above all, don't fool yourself, don't say
it was a dream, your ears deceived you:
don't degrade yourself with empty hopes like these.
As one long prepared, and graced with courage,
as is right for you who were given this kind of city,
go firmly to the window
and listen with deep emotion, but not
with the whining, the pleas of a coward;
listen—your final delectation—to the voices,
to the exquisite music of that strange procession,
and say good-bye to her, to the Alexandria you are losing.

ITHAKA

As you set out for Ithaka
hope the voyage is a long one,
full of adventure, full of discovery.
Laistrygonians and Cyclops,
angry Poseidon—don't be afraid of them:
you'll never find things like that on your way
as long as you keep your thoughts raised high,
as long as a rare excitement
stirs your spirit and your body.
Laistrygonians and Cyclops,

wild Poseidon—you won't encounter them
unless you bring them along inside your soul,
unless your soul sets them up in front of you.

Hope the voyage is a long one.
May there be many a summer morning when,
with what pleasure, what joy,
you come into harbors seen for the first time;
may you stop at Phoenician trading stations
to buy fine things,
mother of pearl and coral, amber and ebony,
sensual perfume of every kind—
as many sensual perfumes as you can;
and may you visit many Egyptian cities
to gather stores of knowledge from their scholars.

Keep Ithaka always in your mind.
Arriving there is what you are destined for.
But do not hurry the journey at all.
Better if it lasts for years,
so you are old by the time you reach the island,
wealthy with all you have gained on the way,
not expecting Ithaka to make you rich.

Ithaka gave you the marvelous journey.
Without her you would not have set out.
She has nothing left to give you now.

And if you find her poor, Ithaka won't have fooled you.
Wise as you will have become, so full of experience,
you will have understood by then what these Ithakas mean.

FERNANDO PESSOA

Fernando Pessoa (1888–1935) is the greatest poet writing in Portuguese since
Camoens and is increasingly considered to be, with W. B. Yeats and Rainer
Maria Rilke, one of the three most powerful and original modern poets. He
was born in Lisbon but grew up in Natal, South Africa, where he had an

English education. In 1905 he returned to Portugal where he worked until his death as a business correspondent, writing letters for export companies in foreign languages. Very little is known about Pessoa's actual sexual relations; he was, for the most part, a self-confessed "wretched recluse." His work, however, is pervaded by homoeroticism, exemplified by the long, explicitly homosexual poem "Antinous," written in English.

Only a handful of his poems were published in his lifetime; most were discovered, after his death, arranged in piles in a large trunk. Pessoa's startling originality lies in his writing through a variety of "personae"; for each persona he invented a name, horoscope, and distinct literary and philosophical personality. He called these personalities "heteronyms"; the most important are Alberto Caeiro, a Zen-like lover of simplicity, Alvaro de Campos, an anarchist ecstatic, and Ricardo Reis, a classic stoic pessimist. Modern critics such as Octavio Paz have compared Pessoa's brilliantly subtle use of different—and clashing—"voices" to Buddhist notions of the "emptiness" of "created" identity. Pessoa was fascinated all his life by mystical and esoteric literature; his own work celebrates the mystery of the unknowable, infinitely polymorphous "self" and its often lonely and paradoxical journey into knowledge.

MY GLANCE IS CLEAR LIKE A SUNFLOWER

My glance is clear like a sunflower.
I usually take to the roads,
Looking to my right and to my left,
And now and then looking behind me . . .
And what I see each moment
Is something I'd never seen before,
And I'm good at noticing such things . . .
I know how to feel the same essential wonder
That an infant feels if, on being born,
He could note he'd really been born . . .
I feel that I am being born each moment
Into the eternal newness of the World . . .

I believe in the World as in a daisy
Because I see it. But I don't think about it
Because thinking is not understanding . . .

The World was not made for us to think about
(To think is to be eye-sick)
But for us to look at and be in tune with . . .

I have no philosophy: I have senses . . .
If I speak of Nature, it's not because I know what Nature is,
But because I love it, and that's why I love it,
For a lover never knows what he loves,
Why he loves or what love is . . .

Loving is eternal innocence,
And the only innocence is not to think . . .

Alberto Caeiro

THE STARTLING REALITY OF THINGS

The startling reality of things
Is my discovery every single day.
Every thing is what it is,
And it's hard to explain to anyone how much this delights me
And suffices me.

To be whole, it is enough simply to exist.

I've written a good many poems.
I shall write many more, naturally.
Each of my poems speaks of this,
And yet all my poems are different,
Because each thing that exists is one way of saying this.

Sometimes I start looking at a stone.
I don't start thinking, Does it have feeling?
I don't fuss about calling it my sister.
But I get pleasure out of its being a stone,
Enjoying it because it feels nothing,
Enjoying it because it's not at all related to me.

Occasionally I hear the wind blow,
And I find that just hearing the wind blow makes it worth having
    been born.

I don't know what others reading this will think;
But I find it must be good since it's what I think without effort,
With no idea that other people are listening to me think;
Because I think it without thoughts,
Because I say it as my words say it.

I was once called a materialist poet
And was surprised, because I didn't imagine
I could be called anything at all.
I'm not even a poet: I see.
If what I write has any merit, it's not in me;
The merit is there, in my verses.
All this is absolutely independent of my will.

   Alberto Caiero

You men who raised stone pillars to mark the coasts, you who named
   the capes!
Who first traded with the Negroes!
Who first sold slaves from new lands!
Who gave the astonished Negresses their first European orgasm!
You who brought back gold, glass beads, fragrant woods, arrows,
From hillsides exploding with green vegetation!
You men who plundered peaceful African villages,
Scattering the natives with the roar of your cannon,
You who murdered, robbed, tortured, and grabbed the booty
Of the New, thanks to those who with lowered heads
Crushed the mystery of the newfound seas! Hey, hey, hey!
To all of you together, to all of you as though you were one,
To all of you bloody, violent, hated, feared, revered,
I salute you, I salute you, I salute you!
Hey, hey, hey! Hey, hey, hey! Hey, hey, hey!
Hello there, hello there, hello, he . . . lloo . . . ooo!

I want to take off with you, I want to go away with you,
With all of you at once.
To every place you went!
I want to meet the dangers you knew face to face,

To feel across my cheeks the winds that wrinkled yours,
To spit from my lips the salt sea that kissed your lips,
To pitch in with you as you work, to share the storms with you,
To reach like you, at last, extraordinary ports!
To flee with you from civilization!
To lose with you all moral sense!
To feel my humanity change in the far distances!
To drink with you in southern seas
New savageries, new tumults of soul,
New central fires in my volcanic spirit! .. . .

My sedentary, static, orderly, all-too-familiar life! . . .

Yes, yes, yes . . . Nail me to your sea ventures
And my shoulders will love the weight of the cross!
Bind me to each voyage as to a stake
And the pressure of the stake will pierce my spine
And will feel it in one great passive orgasm!
Do what you want with me, so long as it's done at sea,
On deck, to the sound of the waves.
Wound me, kill me, tear me apart!
What I'd like is to bring to Death
A soul spilling over with the Sea,
Dead drunk on everything having to do with the sea,
With sailors as with anchors and capes,
With faraway coasts as with wind sounds,
With the Distant as with the Dock, with shipwrecks
As with run-of-the-mill shipping,
With masts as with waves . . .

 Alvaro de Campos, from Maritime Ode

SALUTATION TO WALT WHITMAN

Infinite Portugal, June eleventh, nineteen hundred and fifteen . . .
A-hoy-hoy-hoy-hoy!

From here in Portugal, with all past ages in my brain,
I salute you, Walt, I salute you, my brother in the Universe,

I, with my monocle and tightly buttoned frock coat,
I am not unworthy of you, Walt, as you well know,
I am not unworthy of you, my greeting is enough to make it
    so . . .
I, so given to indolence, so easily bored,
I am with you, as you well know, and understand you and love you,
And though I never met you, born the same year you died,
I know you loved me too, you knew me, and I am happy.
I know that you knew me, that you considered and explained me,
I know that this is what I am, whether on Brooklyn Ferry ten years
    before I was born
Or strolling up Rua do Ouro thinking about everything that is not
    Rua do Ouro,
And just as you felt everything, so I feel everything, and so here we are
    clasping hands,
Clasping hands, Walt, clasping hands, with the universe doing a
    dance in our soul.

O singer of concrete absolutes, always modern and eternal,
Fiery concubine of the scattered world,
Great pederast brushing up against the diversity of things,
Sexualized by rocks, by trees, by people, by their trades,
Itch for the swiftly passing, for casual encounters, for what's merely
    observed,
My enthusiast for what's inside everything,
My great hero going straight through Death by leaps and bounds,
Roaring, screaming, bellowing greetings to God! . . .

How often do I kiss your picture!
Wherever you are now (I don't know where it is but it is God)
You feel this, I know you feel it, and my kisses are warmer (flesh and
    blood)
And you like it that way, old friend, and you thank me from over
    there—
I know this well, something tells me, some pleasure in my spirit:

Some abstract, slant erection in the depths of my soul . . .

    Alvaro de Campos

TO BE GREAT, BE WHOLE

To be great, be whole
    Nothing, exaggerate nothing that is in you.
Be whole in everything. Put all you are
    Into the smallest thing you do.
The whole moon gleams in every pool,
    It rides so high.

Ricardo Reis

THE VOICE OF GOD

In the night a voice is shining . . .
From inside Outerness I heard it . . .
O Universe, to you I am . . .
Oh the horror of the joy
Of such terror of the torch
Fading, which drives me on!

Ashes of idea and name
In me, and the voice: *O World,*
Seed inside you that I am . . .
Mere echo of me, I'm drowned
In wave on wave of black flame
Where in God I'm swallowed.

Fernando Pessoa, from "Beyond God"

HART CRANE

Hart Crane (1899–1932) was born in Garrettsville, Ohio, the only son of
Grace Hart Crane and C. A. Crane, a hard-driven businessman. His childhood was secure in material ways but emotionally difficult; his whole life
was scarred by an often hysterical relationship with his mentally unstable
mother, whom he adored but could never be with long. From 1916 to 1923
Crane moved between Cleveland and New York, where he had his first
love affairs with men, read voraciously, and wrote many of the lyrics col-

lected in *White Buildings* (1926). In 1923 he moved permanently to New York, where, three years later, he began his major poem, *The Bridge,* which he finished in 1929. His final years were marked by growing alcoholism, inability to find work, and a sadly diminished poetic production. In 1932 he committed suicide by drowning in the Gulf of Mexico.

Although he struggled with his homosexuality all his life, his poetry embraces its revelatory and freeing potential, especially in "Voyages." As Thomas Yingling testifies in his *Hart Crane and the Homosexual Text,* "Crane's generation stood precisely on that historical threshold when homosexuality began to be articulated as an identity through Western cultures, and Crane's is one of the first literary texts to provide literary representations grounded in that articulation."

TO BROOKLYN BRIDGE

How many dawns, chill from his rippling rest
The seagull's wings shall dip and pivot him,
Shedding white rings of tumult, building high
Over the chained bay waters Liberty—

Then, with inviolate curve, forsake our eyes
As apparitional as sails that cross
Some page of figures to be filed away;
—Till elevators drop us from our day . . .

I think of cinemas, panoramic sleights
With multitudes bent toward some flashing scene
Never disclosed, but hastened to again,
Foretold to other eyes on the same screen;

And Thee, across the harbor, silver-paced
As though the sun took step of thee, yet left
Some motion ever unspent in thy stride,—
Implicitly thy freedom staying thee!

Out of some subway scuttle, cell or loft
A bedlamite speeds to thy parapets,
Tilting there momently, shrill shirt ballooning,
A jest falls from the speechless caravan.

Down Wall, from girder into street noon leaks,
A rip-tooth of the sky's acetylene;
All afternoon the cloud-flown derricks turn . . .
Thy cables breathe the North Atlantic still.

And obscure as that heaven of the Jews,
Thy guerdon . . . Accolade thou dost bestow
Of anonymity time cannot raise:
Vibrant reprieve and pardon thou dost show.

O harp and altar, of the fury fused,
(How could mere toil align thy choiring strings!)
Terrific threshold of the prophet's pledge,
Prayer of pariah, and the lover's cry,—

Again the traffic lights that skim thy swift
Unfractioned idiom, immaculate sigh of stars,
Beading thy path—condense eternity:
And we have seen night lifted in thine arms.

Under thy shadow by the piers I waited;
Only in darkness is thy shadow clear.
The City's fiery parcels all undone,
Already snow submerges an iron year . . .

O Sleepless as the river under thee,
Vaulting the sea, the prairies' dreaming sod,
Unto us lowliest sometime sweep, descend
And of the curveship lend a myth to God.

VOYAGES

I

Above the fresh ruffles of the surf
Bright striped urchins flay each other with sand.
They have contrived a conquest for shell shucks,
And their fingers crumble fragments of baked weed
Gaily digging and scattering.

And in answer to their treble interjections
The sun beats lightning on the waves,
The waves fold thunder on the sand;
And could they hear me I would tell them:

O brilliant kids, frisk with your dog,
Fondle your shells and sticks, bleached
By time and the elements; but there is a line
You must not cross nor ever trust beyond it
Spry cordage of your bodies to caresses
Too lichen-faithful from too wide a breast.
The bottom of the sea is cruel.

II

—And yet this great wink of eternity
Of rimless floods, unfettered leewardings,
Samite sheeted and processioned where
Her undinal vast belly moonward bends,
Laughing the wrapt inflections of our love;

Take this Sea, whose diapason knells
On scrolls of silver snowy sentences,
The sceptered terror of whose sessions rends
As her demeanors motion well or ill,
All but the pieties of lovers' hands.

And onward, as bells off San Salvador
Salute the crocus lusters of the stars,
In these poinsettia meadows of her tides,—
Adagios of islands, O my Prodigal,
Complete the dark confessions her veins spell.

Mark how her turning shoulders wind the hours,
And hasten while her penniless rich palms
Pass superscription of bent foam and wave,—
Hasten, while they are true,—sleep, death, desire,
Close round one instant in one floating flower.

Bind us in time, O Seasons clear, and awe.
O minstrel galleons of Carib fire,
Bequeath us to no earthly shore until
Is answered in the vortex of our grave
The seal's wide spindrift gaze toward paradise.

FEDERICO GARCÍA LORCA

Federico García Lorca (1889–1936) is generally considered the greatest Spanish poet and playwright of the century. He was born in Fuente Vaqueros, an Andalusian village to the west of Granada; his mother worked briefly as a schoolteacher and his father was a landowner whose fortunes rose with the boom of the sugar industry. When Federico was eleven, the family moved to Granada but continued to spend summer vacations in the country. Lorca often insisted on the importance of his rural upbringing. "I love the land," he wrote. "All my emotions tie me to it." In 1919 he moved to Madrid where he met many of the leading artists and intellectuals of his generation, including the painter Salvador Dalí (with whom he may have had a brief affair) and the film director Luis Buñuel. In 1929 Lorca moved to New York, where he wrote the anguished and apocalyptic *Poet in New York*. On his return to Spain a year later, Lorca continued to pour out poems and plays; when the Spanish Civil War broke out, his leftist sympathies drove him to espouse the rebel cause. He was murdered in 1936, executed in the countryside outside Granada by order of one of Franco's generals.

Lorca's homosexuality was well known by his personal friends and directly inspired some of his greatest visionary poems—most notably *The Divan at Tamarit* (1931–34), in which he pays distant homage to the love poetry of the Arabs, *Sonnets of Dark Love,* inspired by Rafael Rapun, a young engineering student he fell in love with in 1933, and the sublime "Ode to Walt Whitman," in which Lorca gives us unforgettably the full range of his mystical and radical vision of homosexual love.

GHAZAL OF LOVE UNFORESEEN

No one understood the perfume, ever:
the dark magnolia of your belly.

No one ever knew you martyred
love's hummingbird between your teeth.

A thousand Persian ponies fell asleep
in the moonlit plaza of your brow,
while four nights through I bound
your waist, the enemy of snow.

Between plaster and jasmine
your glance, pale branch of seed.
I searched my breast to give you
the ivory letters saying: Ever.

Ever, ever, my agony's garden,
your elusive form forever:
blood of your veins in my mouth,
your mouth now lightless for my death.

From The Divan at Tamarit

WOUNDS OF LOVE

This light, this fire that devours,
this gray landscape that surrounds me,
this pain that comes from one idea,
this anguish of the sky, the earth, the hour,

and this lament of blood that decorates
a pulseless lyre, a lascivious torch,
this burden of the sea that beats upon me,
this scorpion that dwells within my breast

are all a wreath of love, bed of one wounded,
where, sleepless, I dream of your presence
amid the ruins of my fallen breast.

And though I seek the summit of discretion,
your heart gives me a valley spread below
with hemlock and passion of bitter wisdom.

From Sonnets of Dark Love

THE POET ASKS HIS LOVE TO WRITE HIM

O love of my heart, living death,
in vain I await your written word,
and think, with the withered flower: if I
must live without myself, I wish to lose you.

Air is immortal. The lifeless stone
can neither know the shadow nor avoid it.
And the inner heart doesn't need
the frozen honey flowing from the moon.

But I suffered you, tore open my veins,
tiger and dove on your waist,
caught in a duel of lilies and bites.

Fill, then, with words my madness,
or let me live in the serene,
eternal dark night of the soul.

ODE TO WALT WHITMAN

By the East River and the Bronx
boys were singing, exposing their waists,
with the wheel, with oil, leather, and the hammer.
Ninety thousand miners taking silver from the rocks
and children drawing stairs and perspectives.

But none of them could sleep,
none of them wanted to be the river,
none of them loved the huge leaves
or the shoreline's blue tongue.

By the East River and the Queensboro
boys were battling with industry
and the Jews sold to the river faun
the rose of circumcision,
and over bridges and rooftops, the mouth of the sky emptied
herds of bison driven by the wind.

But none of them paused,
none of them wanted to be a cloud,

none of them looked for ferns
or the yellow wheel of the tambourine.

As soon as the moon rises
the pulleys will spin to alter the sky;
a border of needles will besiege memory
and the coffins will bear away those who don't work.

New York, mire,
New York, wire and death.
What angel is hidden in your cheek?
Whose perfect voice will sing the truths of wheat?
Who, the terrible dream of your bruised anemones?

Not for a moment, Walt Whitman, lovely old man,
have I failed to see your beard full of butterflies,
nor your corduroy trousers frayed by the moon,
nor your thighs as pure as Apollo's,
nor your voice like a column of ash;
old man, beautiful as the mist,
you moaned like a bird
with its sex pierced by a needle.
Enemy of the satyr,
enemy of the vine,
and lover of bodies beneath rough cloth . . .

Not for a moment, virile beauty,
who among mountains of coal, billboards, and railroads,
dreamed of becoming a river and sleeping like a river
with that comrade who would place in your breast
the small ache of an ignorant leopard.

Not for a moment, Adam of blood, Macho,
man alone at sea, Walt Whitman, lovely old man,
because on penthouse roofs,
gathered at bars,
emerging in bunches from the sewers,
trembling between the legs of chauffeurs,
or spinning on dance floors wet with absinthe,
the faggots, Walt Whitman, point you out.

He's one, too! That's right! And they land
on your luminous chaste beard,
blonds from the north, blacks from the sands,
crowds of howls and gestures,
like cats or like snakes,
the faggots, Walt Whitman, the faggots,
clouded with tears, flesh for the whip,
the boot, or the teeth of the lion tamers.

He's one, too! That's right! Stained fingers
point to the shore of your dream
when a friend eats your apple
with a slight taste of gasoline
and the sun sings in the navels
of boys who play under bridges.

But you didn't look for scratched eyes,
nor the darkest swamp where someone submerges children,
nor frozen saliva,
nor the curves slit open like a toad's belly
that the faggots wear in cars and on terraces
while the moon lashes them on the street corners of terror.

You looked for a naked body like a river.
Bull and dream who would join wheel with seaweed,
father of your agony, camellia of your death,
who would groan in the blaze of your hidden equator.

Because it's all right if a man doesn't look for his delight
in tomorrow morning's jungle of blood.
The sky has shores where life is avoided
and there are bodies that shouldn't repeat themselves in the dawn.

Agony, agony, dream, ferment, and dream.
This is the world, my friend, agony, agony.
Bodies decompose beneath the city clocks,
war passes by in tears, followed by a million gray rats,
the rich give their mistresses
small illuminated dying things,
and life is neither noble, nor good, nor sacred.

Man is able, if he wishes, to guide his desire
through a vein of coral or a heavenly naked body.
Tomorrow, loves will become stones, and Time
a breeze that drowses in the branches.

That's why I don't raise my voice, old Walt Whitman,
against the little boy who writes
the name of a girl on his pillow,
nor against the boy who dresses as a bride
in the darkness of the wardrobe,
nor against the solitary men in casinos
who drink prostitution's water with revulsion,
nor against the men with that green look in their eyes
who love other men and burn their lips in silence.

But yes against you, urban faggots,
tumescent flesh and unclean thoughts.
Mothers of mud. Harpies. Sleepless enemies
of the love that bestows crowns of joy.

Always against you, who give boys
drops of foul death with bitter poison.
Always against you,
Fairies of North America,
Pájaros of Havana,
Jotos of Mexico,
Sarasas of Cádiz,
Apios of Seville,
Cancos of Madrid,
Floras of Alicante,
Adelaidas of Portugal.

Faggots of the world, murderers of doves!
Slaves of women. Their bedroom bitches.
Opening in public squares like feverish fans
or ambushed in rigid hemlock landscapes.

No quarter given! Death
spills from your eyes
and gathers gray flowers at the mire's edge.

No quarter given! Attention!
Let the confused, the pure,
the classical, the celebrated, the supplicants
close the doors of the bacchanal to you.

And you, lovely Walt Whitman, stay asleep on the Hudson's banks
with your beard toward the pole, open-handed.
Soft clay or snow, your tongue calls for
comrades to keep watch over your unbodied gazelle.

Sleep on, nothing remains.
Dancing walls stir the prairies
and America drowns itself in machinery and lament.
I want the powerful air from the deepest night
to blow away flowers and inscriptions from the arch where you sleep,
and a black child to inform the gold-craving whites
that the kingdom of grain has arrived.

MAX JACOB

Max Jacob (1876–1944), a Breton Jew, went to Paris for his studies in
1894. Around 1903 Jacob joined Pablo Picasso, Guillaume Apollinaire,
and André Salmon to form the core of the Cubist group at the Bateau
Lavoir. After a mystical vision, Jacob converted to Roman Catholicism
and was baptized in 1915 with Picasso as his godfather. From 1921 to 1928
he lived in retreat at the Benedictine monastery of Saint Benoît-sur-
Loire, where he continued to write poetry and fiction and to paint the
gouaches he sold for a living. He died of pneumonia (from exposure and
ill treatment) at the Nazi camp at Drancy on March 5, 1944.

CHRIST AT THE MOVIES

"When you're eating fruit, child, spit the seeds out,
Or in your little belly a whole tree will sprout,"
They said in my house when I was a boy.
That set me on the wrong track for sure:

Branches in the navel mean fruit all the more.
A tree all my own which no one takes away,
Whose fruit, no sooner eaten, grows back every day!

I have my tree today: my tree is the Cross;
Faith is its gift to my greediness.
Dryad of the gallows, when I summon you, come:
Rescue my life from its cruel humdrum.
Dryad of the gallows, descend like yesterday
Evening at the movies when you sat by me
So close. Your hand! Put your hand upon mine
And your so-human warmth and your breath divine.
Oh! I was sick and tired from thinking too much.
Let my body fold upon yours at the touch.
And you! You deigned, as your shoulder hid my eyes,
To describe the movie and sort out the lines.
We had the cheapest seats, at ninety-five centimes;
You spoke of charity before those murky crimes
The Parisian wants every night for dessert.
Today, I'm alone. Lord, groping at my side
My eager fingers feel only the void.
Without you, my God, the world is blank, inert.
The eyes of my spirit sketch your body still,
But it's mere imagination, an act of the will.
—When I go lug my spleen through Montparnasse
Do you want me to save a place in the cafés
For this body you give so generously
To the humblest, most useless, of servants: to me?
That idiot movie!
Now I find it blessed.
Since you deigned, so my faith would be redressed,
To sit at my side amidst your people there.
A movie seat held you! It is a holy chair!

They call me crazy! Yes! I hear the reader now—
Or blasphemous, you scold with furrowed brow.
Madmen yourselves, if truth can make you laugh.
The Lord is everywhere, and with the worst riffraff.

To feel God in oneself, to hear Him, to reply,
Whether at the movies, in the street, at a café,
This common miracle shouldn't start a fuss:
Outside of church, God's everywhere, and speaks with us.
My madness, if I'm mad, is of a different brand.
Listen: I've seen Him! Twice, close at hand:
It was October seven, Rue Ravignan, in my room—
No! I wasn't drunk, nor in delirium—
In the year nineteen-oh-nine, October seven;
I take you as witness, Lord, who put new leaven
Into me sinning lump of filthiness;
You know what sins had seized me in their fists,
What hell I lived in, what a squalid mess,
What resolutions you raised up like yeast
In this Christian whom, thanks to you and the good priests,
I've become, endowed with sense and reason.
So, the first time, you appeared in my room.
And the second time, it was at a film.
"You go to the movies, then?" with dumbfounded air
Demanded my confessor.—"Yes, Father,
What if I did? Didn't Our Lord go there?"

"The Gang in the Black Suits," thriller by Paul Féval;
The plot's in my heart and not on the screen.
The cops and mounties close round and corral
A thief in dire straits: a sudden sheen
Spreads over the crowd, my eyes fill with tears!
The sheen is a halo, in its light, God appears.
To me, this gift! Why did you choose to meet
Me here? In this movie on a little side street
The drapes of a taper-white mantle enfold
My concierge's four urchins you once told
Me to care for. Can the human soul
Hide no scrap from your eyes, must it be seen whole?
Is there for your vision no mystery in our heart?
Do you penetrate all beings in every part?
Then why? Why this grace
If you know my life in all its ugliness?

If you know my faults and my weaknesses too?
What in me, oh Lord, could interest you?

WILLA CATHER

Willa Cather (1873–1947) was born the eldest of seven children in Black
Creek, Virginia. When she was nine her family moved to the prairie country of Nebraska, whose settlement Cather would immortalize in her novels *O Pioneers* (1913) and *My Ántonia* (1918). At the age of twenty-one, she
graduated from the University of Nebraska, then spent the next few years
doing newspaper work and teaching high school in Pittsburgh. In 1903
Cather's first book, *April Twilights,* a collection of poems, was published,
followed by *The Troll Garden* (1905), a collection of stories. After the publication of her first novel, *Alexander's Bridge,* in 1912, Cather devoted herself full time to writing. Over the years she completed eleven more novels
(including *The Professor's House* and her masterpiece, *Death Comes for the
Archbishop*), four collections of short stories, and two volumes of essays.
Cather won the Pulitzer Prize for her first world war novel, *One of Ours,*
in 1923; when she died in 1947 she was considered by many to be among
the greatest novelists of the twentieth century, the equal of William
Faulkner and Ernest Hemingway.

Cather took great pains to conceal her lesbianism; in her last years she
commanded her friends to destroy all of her correspondence so her pri-
vacy could be protected. Yet between the ages of ten and fourteen, she
had masqueraded as "William Cather," dressing in men's clothing and
wearing her hair in a crew cut; her greatest relationships were all with
women; and her "passionate friendship" with Isabelle McClung seems to
have been an authentic and nourishing love affair. All of Willa Cather's
work is informed by a subtle and profoundly religious vision of human
dignity and potential.

A NIGHT ON THE MESA

I'll never forget the night I got back. I crossed the river an hour before
sunset and hobbled my horse in the wide bottom of Cow Canyon.

The moon was up, though the sun hadn't set, and it had that glittering silveriness the early stars have in high altitudes. The heavenly bodies look so much more remote from the bottom of a deep canyon than they do from the level. The climb of the walls helps out the eye, somehow. I lay down on a solitary rock that was like an island in the bottom of the valley, and looked up. The grey sage-brush and the blue-grey rock around me were already in shadow, but high above me the canyon walls were dyed flame-color with the sunset, and the Cliff City lay in a gold haze against its dark cavern. In a few minutes it, too, was grey, and only the rim rock at the top held the red light. When that was gone, I could still see the copper glow in the pinons along the edge of the top ledges. The arc of sky over the canyon was silvery blue, with its pale yellow moon, and presently stars shivered into it, like crystals dropped into perfectly clear water.

I remember these things, because, in a sense, that was the first night I was ever really on the mesa at all—the first night that all of me was there. This was the first time I ever saw it whole. It all came together in my understanding, as a series of experiments do when you begin to see where they are leading. Something had happened in me that made it possible for me to coordinate and simplify, and that process, going on in my mind, brought with it great happiness. It was possession. The excitement of my first discovery was a very pale feeling compared to this one. For me the mesa was no longer an adventure, but a religious emotion.

From Tom Outland's story in The Professor's House

THE ARCHBISHOP AND THE OLD MEXICAN WOMAN

The court was white with snow, and the shadows of walls and buildings stood out sharply in the faint light from the moon muffled in vapor. In the deep doorway of the sacristy he saw a crouching figure— a woman, he made out, and she was weeping bitterly. He raised her up and took her inside. As soon as he had lit a candle, he recognized her, and could have guessed her errand.

It was an old Mexican woman, called Sada, who was a slave in an American family. They were Protestants, very hostile to the Roman Church, and they did not allow her to go to Mass or to receive the visits of a priest. She was carefully watched at home—but in winter, when the heated rooms of the house were desirable to the family, she was put to sleep in a woodshed. Tonight, unable to sleep for the cold, she had gathered courage for this heroic action, had slipped out through the stable door and come running up an alley-way to the House of God to pray. Finding the front doors of the church fastened, she had made her way into the Bishop's garden and come round to the sacristy, only to find that, too, shut against her.

The Bishop stood holding the candle and watching her face while she spoke her few words; a dark brown peon face, worn thin and sharp by life and sorrow. It seemed to him that he had never seen pure goodness shine out of a human countenance as it did from hers. He saw that she had no stockings under her shoes—the cast-off rawhides of her master—and beneath her frayed black shawl was only a thin calico dress, covered with patches. Her teeth struck together as she stood trying to control her shivering. With one movement of his free hand the Bishop took the furred cloak from his shoulders and put it about her. This frightened her. She cowered under it, murmuring, "Ah, no, no, Padre!"

"You must obey your Padre, my daughter. Draw that cloak about you, and we will go into the church to pray."

The church was utterly black except for the red spark of the sanctuary lamp before the high altar. Taking her hand, and holding the candle before him, he led her across the choir to the Lady Chapel. There he began to light the tapers before the Virgin. Old Sada fell on her knees and kissed the floor. She kissed the feet of the Holy Mother, the pedestal on which they stood, crying all the while. But from the working of her face, from the beautiful tremors which passed over it, he knew they were tears of ecstasy.

"Nineteen years, Father; nineteen years since I have seen the holy things of the altar!"

"All that is passed, Sada. You have remembered the holy things in your heart. We will pray together."

The Bishop knelt beside her, and they began, *O Holy Mary, Queen of Virgins. . .*

When they rose from their knees, Father Latour told Sada he was glad to know that she remembered her prayers so well.

"Ah, Padre, every night I say my Rosary to my Holy Mother, no matter where I sleep!" declared the old creature passionately, looking up into his face and pressing her knotted hands against her breast. . . .

Never, as he afterward told Father Vaillant, had it been permitted him to behold such deep experience of the holy joy of religion as on that pale December night. He was able to feel, kneeling beside her, the preciousness of the thighs of the altar to her who was without possessions; the tapers, the image of the Virgin, the figures of the saints, the Cross that took away indignity from suffering and made pain and poverty a means of fellowship with Christ. Kneeling beside the much enduring bond-woman, he experienced those holy mysteries as he had done in his young manhood. He seemed able to feel all it meant to her to know that there was a Kind Woman in Heaven, though there were such cruel ones on earth. Old people, who have felt blows and toil and known the world's hard hand, need, even more than children do, a woman's tenderness. Only a Woman, divine, could know all that a woman can suffer.

Not often, indeed, had Jean Marie Latour come so near to the Fountain of all Pity as in the Lady Chapel that night; the pity that no man born of woman could ever utterly cut himself off from; that was for the murderer on the scaffold, as it was for the dying soldier or the martyr on the rack. The beautiful concept of Mary pierced the priest's heart like a sword.

From Death Comes for the Archbishop

D. H. LAWRENCE

David Herbert Lawrence was born at Eastwood, Nottinghamshire, in 1885, fourth of the five children of a miner and his middle-class wife. He attended Nottingham High School and University College, Nottingham. After completing his studies in 1908, Lawrence taught for a few years at a boys' school. His career as a schoolteacher was ended in 1911 by an illness that was ultimately diagnosed as tuberculosis. That year also saw the publication of his first novel, *The White Peacock*.

In 1912 Lawrence eloped to Germany with Frieda Weekley, the German wife of his former modern languages tutor. They were married on their return to England in 1914. Lawrence was now living, precariously, by his writing. His greatest novels, *The Rainbow* and *Women in Love,* were completed in 1915 and 1916. The former was suppressed and he could not find a publisher for the latter.

After the war Lawrence began what he called his "savage pilgrimage" in search of a richer way of life than industrial Western civilization could offer. This took him to Sicily, Ceylon, Australia, and finally New Mexico. The Lawrences returned to Europe in 1925. Lawrence's last novel, *Lady Chatterley's Lover,* was banned in 1928 and his paintings were confiscated in 1929. He died in southern France in 1930 at the age of forty-four.

All of Lawrence's greatest work is inspired by an unconventional but passionately sincere quest for a whole and holy way of living. A fearless explorer of sexuality, Lawrence was himself bisexual; in *Women in Love* particularly, he explores what he calls the "hunger in every man" for an eternal bond with another man. He himself had a homosexual affair while writing the book with a young Cornish farmer named Henry Harding. After his death, his wife, Frieda, wrote: "What he had seen and felt and known he gave in his writing to his fellow men, the splendor of living, the hope of more and more life . . . a heroic and immeasurable gift."

"Well then," said Gerald; "shall we strip and begin? Will you have a drink first?"

"No, I don't want one."

"Neither do I."

Gerald fastened the door and pushed the furniture aside. The room was large, there was plenty of space, it was thickly carpeted. Then he quickly threw off his clothes and waited for Birkin . . .

So the two men entwined and wrestled with each other, working nearer and nearer. Both were white and clear, but Gerald flushed smart red where he was touched, and Birkin remained white and tense. He seemed to penetrate into Gerald's more solid, more diffuse bulk, to interfuse his body through the body of the other, as if to bring it subtly into subjection, always seizing with some rapid necromantic foreknowledge every motion of the other flesh, converting and counteracting it, playing upon the limbs and trunk of Gerald like some hard wind. It was as if Birkin's whole physical intelligence interpenetrated into Gerald's body, as if his fine, sublimated energy entered into the flesh of the fuller man, like some potency, casting a fine net, a prison, through the muscles into the very depths of Gerald's physical being.

So they wrestled swiftly, rapturously, intent and mindless at last, two essential white figures working into a tighter, closer oneness of struggle, with a strange, octopus-like knotting and flashing of limbs in the subdued light of the room; a tense white knot of flesh gripped in silence between the walls of old brown books. Now and again came a sharp gasp of breath, or a sound like a sigh, then the rapid thudding of movement on the thickly-carpeted floor, then the strange sound of flesh escaping under flesh. Often, in the white interlaced knot of violent living being that swayed silently, there was no head to be seen, only the swift, tight limbs, the solid white backs, the physical junction of two bodies clinched into oneness. Then would appear the gleaming, ruffled head of Gerald, as the struggle changed, then for a moment the dun-colored, shadow-like head of the other man would lift up from the conflict, the eyes wide and dreadful and sightless.

At length Gerald lay back inert on the carpet, his breast rising in great slow panting, whilst Birkin kneeled over him, almost unconscious. Birkin was much more exhausted. He caught little, short breaths, he could scarcely breathe any more. The earth seemed to tilt and sway, and a complete darkness was coming over his mind. He did not know what happened. He slid forward quite unconscious over Gerald, and Gerald did not notice. Then he was half conscious again, aware only of the strange tilting and sliding of the world. The world was sliding, everything was sliding off into the darkness. And he was sliding, endlessly, endlessly away. . . .

From Women in Love

RESURRECTION

So the children lived the year of Christianity, the epic of the soul of mankind. Year by year the inner, unknown drama went on in them, their hearts were born and came to fullness, suffered on the cross, gave up the ghost, and rose again to unnumbered days, untired, having at least this rhythm of eternity in a ragged, inconsequential life.

But it was becoming a mechanical action now, this drama: birth at Christmas for death at Good Friday. On Easter Sunday the life-drama was as good as finished. For the Resurrection was shadowy and overcome by the shadow of death. . . .

Alas, that a risen Christ has no place with us! Alas, that the memory of the passion of Sorrow and Death and the Grave holds triumph over the pale fact of Resurrection!

But why? Why shall I not rise with my body whole and perfect, shining with strong life? Why, when Mary says: Rabboni, shall I not take her in my arms and kiss her and hold her to my breast? Why is the risen body deadly, and abhorrent with wounds?

The Resurrection is to life, not to death. Shall I not see those who have risen again walk here among men perfect in body and spirit, whole and glad in the flesh, living in the flesh, loving in the flesh, begetting children in the flesh, arrived at last to wholeness, perfect without scar or blemish, healthy without fear of ill-health? Is this not the period of manhood and of joy and fulfillment, after the Resurrection? Who shall be shadowed by Death and the Cross, being risen, and who shall fear the mystic, perfect flesh that belongs to heaven?

Can I not, then, walk this earth in gladness, being risen from sorrow? Can I not eat with my brother happily, and with joy kiss my beloved, after my resurrection, celebrate my marriage in the flesh with feastings, go about my business eagerly, in the joy of my fellows? Is heaven impatient for me, and bitter against this earth, that I should hurry off, or that I should linger pale and untouched? Is the flesh which was crucified become as poison to the crowds in the street, or is it as strong gladness and hope to them, as the first flower blossoming out of the earth's humus?

From The Rainbow

TERRA INCOGNITA

There are vast realms of consciousness still undreamed of
vast ranges of experience, like the humming of unseen harps,

we know nothing of, within us.
Oh, when man has escaped from the barbed-wire entanglement
of his own ideas and his own mechanical devices
there is a marvelous rich world of contact and sheer fluid beauty
and fearless face-to-face awareness of now-naked life
and me, and you, and other men and women,
and grapes, and ghouls, and ghosts and green moonlight
and ruddy-orange limbs stirring the limbo
of the unknown air, and eyes so soft
softer than the space between the stars,
and all things, and nothing, and being and not-being
alternately palpitant,
when at last we escape the barbed-wire enclosure
of *Know Thyself*, knowing we can never know,
we can but touch, and wonder, and ponder, and make our effort
and dangle in a last fastidious fine delight
as the fuchsia does, dangling her reckless drop
of purple after so much putting forth
and slow mounting marvel of a little tree.

WHAT ARE THE GODS?

What are the gods, then, what are the gods?

The gods are nameless and imageless
yet looking in a great full lime-tree of summer
I suddenly saw deep into the eyes of a god:
it is enough.

THE HANDS OF GOD

It is a fearful thing to fall into the hands of the living God.
But it is a much more fearful thing to fall out of them.

Did Lucifer fall through knowledge?
Oh then, pity him, pity him that plunge!

Save me, O God, from falling into the ungodly knowledge
of myself as I am without God.
Let me never know, O God
let me never know what I am or should be
when I have fallen out of your hands, the hands of the living God.

That awful and sickening endless sinking, sinking
through the slow, corruptive levels of disintegrative knowledge
when the self has fallen from the hands of God,
and sinks, seething and sinking, corrupt
and sinking still, in depth after depth of disintegrative consciousness
sinking in the endless undoing, the awful katabolism into the abyss!
even of the soul, fallen from the hands of God!

Save me from that, O God!
Let me never know myself apart from the living God!

PAX

All that matters is to be at one with the living God
to be a creature in the house of the God of Life.

Like a cat asleep on a chair
at peace, in peace
and at one with the master of the house, with the mistress,
at home, at home in the house of the living,
sleeping on the hearth, and yawning before the fire.

Sleeping on the hearth of the living world
yawning at home before the fire of life
feeling the presence of the living God
like a great reassurance
a deep calm in the heart
a presence
as of the master sitting at the board
in his own and greater being,
in the house of life.

Virginia Woolf was born on January 25, 1882, in Hyde Park Gate, London, the daughter of Leslie Stephen, a man of letters, and Julia Duckworth. Virginia's mother's first marriage ended with the death of her husband, leaving her with three children, one of whom, Gerald Duckworth, is known to have sexually molested Woolf as an adolescent. In addition to this trauma, her adolescence was marked by a series of deaths and the first attack of a mental illness that would haunt her for the rest of her life. Her mother died in 1895; her half sister Stella in 1897; her father in 1904; and her beloved brother Thoby in 1906. She suffered her first mental breakdown after her mother's death, and her final one culminated with her own suicide—she walked into the river Ouse on March 28, 1941.

Despite her fragility, Virginia Woolf quickly established herself as one of the leading luminaries of the Bloomsbury movement, and in a series of brilliantly original, visionary novels—notably *Mrs. Dalloway* (1925), *The Waves* (1931), *To the Lighthouse* (1927), and *Between the Acts* (1941)—became a pioneer of modernism.

Virginia married Leonard Woolf in 1912 and remained with him serenely until her death, but her deepest relationships were with women. Virginia's first passionate friendship was with Madge Vaughan, the daughter of John Addington Symonds, whom Woolf met at the age of sixteen and who served as a model for Sally Seton in *Mrs. Dalloway*. Perhaps her greatest love was Vita Sackville-West, whom she met in 1922 and immortalized in all her vigor and sexual omnivorousness in *Orlando* (1928).

Woolf was not in any way "formally" religious, but her worldview is suffused by a visionary light and ecstasy. At her greatest, she, like a Zen mystic, sees the "ordinary" world as a constant unbroken flow of miracle.

The strange thing, on looking back, was the purity, the integrity, of her feeling for Sally. It was not like one's feeling for a man. It was completely disinterested, and besides, it had a quality which could only exist between women, between women just grown up. It was protective, on her side; sprang from a sense of being in league together, a presentiment of something that was bound to part them (they spoke of marriage always as a catastrophe), which led to this chivalry, this protective feeling which was much more on her side than Sally's. For in those days she was completely reckless; did the most idiotic things out of bravado; bicycled round the parapet on the terrace; smoked cigars. Absurd, she was—very absurd. But the charm was overpowering, to her at least, so that she could remember standing in her bedroom at the top of the house holding the hot-water can in her hands and saying aloud, "She is beneath this roof . . . she is beneath this roof!"

No, the words meant absolutely nothing to her now. She could not even get an echo of her old emotion. But she could remember going cold with excitement, and doing her hair in a kind of ecstasy (now the old feeling began to come back to her, as she took out her hairpins, laid them on the dressing-table, began to do her hair), with the rooks flaunting up and down in the pink evening light, and dressing, and going downstairs, and feeling as she crossed the hall "if it were now to die 'twere now to be most happy." That was her feeling—Othello's feeling, and she felt it, she was convinced, as strongly as Shakespeare meant Othello to feel it, all because she was coming down to dinner in a white frock to meet Sally Seton!

She was wearing pink gauze—was that possible? She *seemed*, anyhow, all light, glowing, like some bird or air ball that has flown in, attached itself for a moment to a bramble. But nothing is so strange when one is in love (and what was this except being in love?) as the complete indifference of other people. Aunt Helena just wandered off after dinner; Papa read the paper. . . .

All this was only a background for Sally. She stood by the fireplace talking, in that beautiful voice which made everything she said sound like a caress, to Papa, who had begun to be attracted rather against his will (he never got over lending her one of his books and finding it soaked on the terrace), when suddenly she said, "What a shame to sit indoors!" and they all went out on the terrace and walked up and down. . . . She and Sally fell a little behind. Then came the most exquisite moment of her whole life passing a stone urn with flowers on it. Sally stopped; picked a flower; kissed her on the lips. The whole world might have turned upside down! The others disappeared; there she was alone with Sally. And she felt that she had been given a present, wrapped up, and told just to keep it, not to look at it—a diamond, something infinitely precious, wrapped up, which, as they walked (up and down, up and down), she uncovered, or the radiance burnt through, the revelation, the religious feeling! . . .

From Mrs. Dalloway

The sound of the trumpets died away and Orlando stood stark naked. No human being, since the world began, has ever looked more ravishing. His form combined in one the strength of a man and a woman's grace. As he stood there, the silver trumpets prolonged their note, as if reluctant to leave the lovely sight which their blast had called forth; and Chastity, Purity, and Modesty, inspired, no doubt, by Curiosity, peeped in at the door and threw a garment like a towel at the naked form which, unfortunately, fell short by several inches. Orlando looked himself up and down in a long looking-glass, without showing any signs of discomposure, and went, presumably, to his bath.

We may take advantage of this pause in the narrative to make certain statements. Orlando had become a woman—there is no denying it. But in every other respect, Orlando remained precisely as he had been. The change of sex, though it altered their future, did nothing whatever to alter their identity. Their faces remained, as their portraits prove, practically the same. His memory—but in future we must, for convention's sake, say "her" for "his," and "she" for "he"—her memory then, went back through all the events of her past life without encountering any obstacle. Some slight haziness there may have been, as if a few dark drops had fallen into the clear pool of memory; certain things had become a little dimmed; but that was all. . . .

"Praise God that I'm a woman!" she cried, and was about to run into the extreme folly—than which none is more distressing in woman or man either—of being proud of her sex, when she paused over the singular word which, for all we can do to put it in its place, has crept in at the end of the last sentence; Love. "Love," said Orlando. Instantly—such is its impetuosity—love took a human shape—such is its pride. For where other thoughts are content to remain abstract nothing will satisfy this one but to put on flesh and blood, mantilla and petticoats, hose and jerkin. And as all Orlando's loves had been women, now, through the culpable laggardry of the human frame to adapt itself to convention, though she herself was a woman, it was still a woman she loved; and if the consciousness of being the same sex had any effect at all, it was to quicken and deepen those feelings which she had had as a man. For now a thousand hints and mysteries became plain to her that were then dark. Now, the obscurity, which divides the sexes and lets linger innumerable impurities in its gloom, was removed, and if there is anything in what the poet says about truth and beauty, this affection gained in beauty what it lost in falsity. At last, she cried, she knew Sasha as she was, and in the ardor of this discovery, and in the pursuit of all those treasures which were now revealed, she was so rapt and enchanted that it was as if a cannon ball had exploded at her ear. . . .

From Orlando

THE EMPTY HOUSE

So with the house empty and the doors locked and the mattresses rolled round, those stray airs, advance guards of great armies, blustered in, brushed bare boards, nibbled and fanned, met nothing in bedroom or drawing-room that wholly resisted them but only hangings that flapped, wood that creaked, the bare legs of tables, saucepans and china already furred, tarnished, cracked. What people had shed and left—a pair of shoes, a shooting cap, some faded skirts and coats in wardrobes—those alone kept the human shape and in the emptiness indicated how once they were filled and animated; how hands were busy with hooks and buttons; how once the looking-glass had held a face; had held a world hollowed out in which a figure turned, a hand flashed, the door opened, in came children rushing and tumbling; and went out again. Now, day after day, light turned, like a flower reflected in water, its sharp image on the wall opposite. Only the shadows of the trees, flourishing in the wind, made obeisance on the wall, and for a moment darkened the pool in which light reflected itself; or birds, flying, made a soft spot flutter slowly across the bedroom floor.

So loveliness reigned and stillness, and together made the shape of loveliness itself, a form from which life had parted; solitary like a pool at evening, far distant, seen from a train window, vanishing so quickly that the pool, pale in the evening, is scarcely robbed of its solitude, though once seen. Loveliness and stillness clasped hands in the bedroom, and among the shrouded jugs and sheeted chairs even the prying of the wind, and the soft nose of the clammy sea airs, rubbing, snuffling, iterating, and reiterating their questions—"Will you fade? Will you perish?" scarcely disturbed the peace, the indifference, the air of pure integrity, as if the question they asked scarcely needed that they should answer: we remain.

From To the Lighthouse

THE VISION

"He must have reached it," said Lily Briscoe aloud, feeling suddenly completely tired out. For the Lighthouse had become almost invisible, had melted away into a blue haze, and the effort of looking at it and the effort of thinking of him landing there, which both seemed to be one and the same effort, had stretched her body and mind to the utmost. Ah, but she was relieved. Whatever she had wanted to give him, when he left her that morning, she had given him at last.

"He has landed," she said aloud. "It is finished." Then, surging up, puffing slightly, old Mr. Carmichael stood beside her, looking like an old pagan god, shaggy, with weeds in his hair and the trident (it was only a French novel) in his hand. He stood by her on the edge of the lawn, swaying a little in his bulk and said, shading his eyes with his hand: "They will have landed," and she felt that she had been right. They had not needed to speak. They had been thinking the same things and he had answered her without her asking him anything. He stood there as if he were spreading his hands over all the weakness and suffering of mankind; she thought he was surveying, tolerantly and compassionately, their final destiny. Now he has crowned the occasion, she thought, when his hand slowly fell, as if she had seen him let fall from his great height a wreath of violets and asphodels which, fluttering slowly, lay at length upon the earth.

Quickly, as if she were recalled by something over there, she turned to her canvas. There it was—her picture. Yes, with all its greens and blues, its lines running up and across, its attempt at something. It would be hung in the attics, she thought; it would be destroyed. But what did that matter? she asked herself, taking up her brush again. She looked at the steps; they were empty; she looked at her canvas; it was blurred. With a sudden intensity, as if she saw it clear for a second, she drew a line there, in the center. It was done; it was finished. Yes, she thought, laying down her brush in extreme fatigue, I have had my vision.

From To the Lighthouse

COLETTE

Sidonie-Gabrielle Colette was born on January 28, 1873, in the Burgundian village of Saint Sauveur-en-Puisaye. The house and garden, field and forests she grew up in, presided over by the major figure in her life, her mother, Sido, reappear in her work as a kind of earthly paradise that many of Colette's adult female characters long to regain. At the age of twenty, she married the famous Paris critic Henri Gauthier-Villars (known as Willy), who made her write a series of novels (the "Claudine" series) and signed them himself. Marriage to Willy was painful and tumultuous; Colette left him in 1906 and began to write under her own name. A stream of marvelous novels, essays, and criticism followed for nearly fifty years; when she died in 1954 at age eighty-one, she was revered as the "grande Dame of French literature."

Colette married three times, but was openly bisexual. She had a long off-and-on affair with the Marquise de Morny—who was a cross-dresser. There are lesbian references throughout the Claudine series and in *Tendrils of the Vine* (1908). In 1932 (revised in 1941) Colette wrote a brilliant study of lesbian and homosexual mores in Paris in *The Pure and the Impure.* Four of the nine chapters deal exclusively with lesbians and one with male homosexuals.

Colette was refused a religious burial because of the alleged "immorality" of her life, but there is an unmistakable mystical fervor to her love of nature and her celebration of human sensuality that places her among the great "hidden" religious writers of the century.

THE BED

O our bed, completely bare! A dazzling lamp, slanted above it, denudes it even more. We do not find there, at twilight, the well-devised shade of a lace canopy or the rosy shell-like glow of a night lamp. Fixed star, never rising or setting, our bed never ceases to gleam except when submerged in the velvety depths of night.

Rigid and white, like the body of a dear departed, it is haloed with a perfume, a complicated scent that astounds, that one inhales attentively, in an effort to distinguish the blond essence of your favorite tobacco from the still lighter aroma of your extraordinarily white skin, and the scent of sandalwood that I give off; but that wild odor of crushed grasses, who can tell if it is mine or thine?

Receive us tonight, O our bed, and let your fresh valley deepen a little more beneath the feverish torpor caused by a thrilling spring day spent in the garden and in the woods.

From Sleepless Nights

THE PINK CACTUS

Sir,

You ask me to come and spend a week with you, which means I would be near my daughter, whom I adore. You who live with her know how rarely I see her, how much her presence delights me, and I'm touched that you should ask me to come and see her. All the same I'm not going to accept your kind invitation, for the time being at any rate. The reason is that my pink cactus is probably going to flower. It's a very rare plant I've been given, and I'm told that in our climate it flowers only once every four years. Now, I am already a very old woman, and if I went away when my pink cactus is about to flower, I am certain I shouldn't see it flower again.

So I beg you, Sir, to accept my sincere thanks and my regrets, together with my kind regards.

This note, signed "Sidonie Colette, née Landoy," was written by my mother to one of my husbands, the second. A year later she died, at the age of seventy-seven.

Whenever I feel myself inferior to everything about me, threatened by my own mediocrity, frightened by the discovery that a muscle is losing its strength, a desire its power or a pain the keen edge of its bite, I can still hold up my head and say to myself: "I am the daughter of the woman who wrote that letter—that letter and so many more that I have kept. This one tells me in ten lines that at the age of seventy-six she was planning journeys and undertaking them, but that waiting for the possible bursting into bloom of a tropical flower held everything up and silenced even her heart, made for love. I am the daughter of a woman who, in a mean, close-fisted, confined little place, opened her village home to stray cats, tramps and pregnant servant-girls. I am the daughter of a woman who many a time, when she was in despair at not having enough money for others, ran through the wind-whipped snow to cry from door to door, at the houses of the rich, that a child had just been born in a poverty-stricken home to parents whose feeble, empty hands had no swaddling clothes for it. Let me not forget that I am the daughter of a woman who bent her head, trembling, between the blades of a cactus, her wrinkled face full of ecstasy over the promise of a flower, a woman who herself never ceased to flower, untiringly, during three quarters of a century.

From The Break of Day

PROVENCE

A little wing of light is beating between the two shutters, touching with irregular pulsations the wall or the long heavy table where we write or read or play, that eternal table that has come back from Brittany, as I have come back. Sometimes the wing of light is on the pink-washed wall, and sometimes blue on the blue cotton Moroccan rug. Dressers stacked with books, armchairs and chests of drawers have made a roundabout journey with me over fifteen years, through two or three French provinces. Elegant armchairs with tapering arms, countrified like peasant girls with delicate limbs, yellow plates that sing like bells when you rub them with your finger, dishes of thick white glaze—we are all astonished to find ourselves back in a country that is our own. For is it not the house of my father and my grandparents on the Mourillon, fifty miles from here? It is true that other regions have cradled me, and some of them roughly. A woman lays claim to as many native lands as she has had happy loves. She is born, too, under every sky where she has recovered from the pain of loving. By that reckoning this blue salt shore, bright with tomatoes and pimentos, is doubly mine. How rich it is, and what a lot of time I've spent not knowing of it! The air is light, the grapes ripen so quickly that they are dried and wrinkled on the vine by the sun, the garlic is highly flavored. That noble bareness that thirst sometimes confers on the soil, the refined idleness that one learns from a frugal people—for me these are late-discovered riches. But let me not complain. My maturity is the right time for them. My angular youth would have bled at the touch of the striated, mica-spangled rocks, the forked pine-needles, the agave, the spines of the sea-urchin, the bitter, sticky cistus and the fig tree, the underside of whose every leaf is a wild beast's tongue. What a country! The invader endows it with villas and garages, with motor-cars and dance-halls built to look like *Mas.* The barbarians from the north parcel out the land, speculate and deforest, and that is certainly a great pity. But during the course of the centuries how many ravishers have not fallen in love with such a captive? They arrive plotting to ruin her, stop suddenly and listen to her breathing in her sleep, and then, turning silent and respectful, they softly shut the gate in the fence. Submissive to your wishes, Provence, they fasten on your vine-leaf crown again, replant the pine tree and the fig, sow the variegated melon and have no other desire, Beauty, than to serve you and enjoy it.

The others will inevitably abandon you. Once upon a time they would have dishonored you. But one horde more or less doesn't matter to you. Those who have come on the strength of a casino, a hotel or a post-card will leave you. They will flee, burnt and bitten by your wind white with dust. Keep your lovers, who drink water from the pitcher and the dry wine that ripens in the sand; keep those who pour oil religiously and turn away their heads when they pass in front of dead animals; keep those who rise early and lull themselves asleep in bed in the evening to the faint chugging of the pleasure-boats in the bay. Keep me . . .

From The Break of Day

CHAPTER NINE

DRINK UP THE HEART

LATER TWENTIETH CENTURY

LEWIS THOMPSON

Lewis Thompson is one of the greatest, and least known, mystical writers of the twentieth century. Born in London in 1909, he became a wanderer in his early twenties, traveling in France and Germany, haunted by Rimbaud's vision and by visions of great cities. The London and Paris of Cocteau, Picasso, and Diaghilev in the 1920s made an unforgettable impression on him. At one time he thought of becoming a pianist and was a sensitive interpreter of Bach and Debussy throughout his life.

Thompson lived in India for the last sixteen years of his life and was, for several years, the librarian at the Rajghat school in Benares. He lived with Hindu simplicity, indifferent to the British raj and its lifestyle, and devoted himself completely to an exhilarating, agonizing, and profound spiritual search that took him to ashrams all over India. For a while he had a guru in South India, Sri Atmananda, but a terrible quarrel separated them; later he was to write very savage things about the guru system. Thompson neglected his health and died suddenly in Benares in 1949 at the age of forty, before he had time to prepare his recently completed work for publication. A collection of his aphorisms, *Mirror to the Light,* was edited and published by Richard Lannoy in 1984; the great majority of his unique poetry remains unpublished.

Though Thompson lived his life largely alone, his homosexuality is alluded to in his musings on sexuality in *Mirror to the Light* and is explicitly revealed in his unpublished diaries. No other writer in English in the twentieth century, I believe, writes of mystical experience and discovery with such a fine, ruthless, searing precision and so devastating (and devastated) a candor. Lawrence Durrell emphasized that *Mirror to the Light* was "a book of the highest distinction; self-scrutiny pushed to the point of anguish and described in poetic aphorisms of great density and beauty." Edith Sitwell proclaimed Thompson a genius and his poem "Black Angel" (published for the first time in this anthology) one of the greatest modern poems. Thompson's work prefigures a great deal of radical modern spiritual writing: the time for the discovery of his voice and the celebration of his genius has now, at last, arrived.

TRUTHFULNESS

Christ, Supreme Poet, lived truth so passionately that every gesture of his, at once pure Act and perfect Symbol, embodies the Transcendent.

Baffling like blinding light is this command of form . . .

No act or event can ever be right—clear, transparent, true, economical, happy, luminous, resonant—that is not based in the deepest, simplest truth of the heart. The Heart is central: only when it is true, unquestionable, can every other faculty, perception, response, act and event be perfect, illuminated with love.

Without simplicity, fundamental, bedrock simplicity, there is no freedom of energy: all is knotted, self-complicated, self-obstructing, self-poisoning, self-destroying.

Complication is mental; complexity is organic. The rose is simple and complex. Every artificial rose is complicated—neither simple nor complex.

One looks toward the Heart, itself prior even to Truth, one focuses toward it all one's means of seeing in perfect clarity only by desiring, by worshiping, at every moment, in every occasion, Truth—deeply, with love, humility, true humor.

All problem, all contingency, is resolved by this, for one desires nothing other than what is unimportant—one's individuality, one's appearance in the mind of Others, every kind of perpetuating recognition of the world as such, the common hell of fear, weakness, ignorance, impurity, should be of no account. How can there be, in Love, any happiness but fidelity? This fidelity is a vertical pillar: it is with the utmost humility, honesty, sincerity, that we stand before the face of God.

From Mirror to the Light

THE CHILD

It is Horus and not Osiris who inherits from the Mother, who shares her secrets. The ever-new magical universe is continually reborn in the Child.

Only the grown-up was banished from Eden. The Child eats of the Tree of Life: for him the laws of the universe are magical.

This Childhood and this Magic the Christ restores . . .

The subtlety and ingenuity necessary to sustain and complete the delicacy and complexity of childhood is exasperated—is cast into deserts of perversity, abysses of Ennui—that to be grown-up it is only necessary to be so slow and stupid, so cravenly self-deceptive and self-satisfied.

Till by long alchemy—mercury solidified into the stone that discovers gold in everything—this repressed lyricism and generosity reaches its ultimate in Love.

The Christ's is the triumphant love of the Child absorbing the whole grown-up universe. It regains the pure self-exalting passion and delight of Childhood. It completes the circle into miracle, recovers Eden, "the truth of imagination," all effective names.

From Mirror to the Light

BLACK ANGEL

I

One day that black and shining angel who
Haunted my nights in Arles and at Ajmeer,

Monster of beauty loud with cruel gems,
I shall encounter in some lane at noon
Where painted demons have struck dumb the walls.

Perhaps a glance absorbs, unriddles him;
Or he, or I, will follow to such home
As then I seem to have, and (if his height
Or presence do not shatter it roof and floor,
Leaving me dark in a new wilderness
Acrid with blowing smoke, horizonless),
He will have entered in. And though my garland
Shrivel upon his lightning beauty, I have decked him.

Black Peacock harsh with plumes, our somber legends
Buried you with the Yezidees, or we have mocked you
With the ecstatic irony of red-hot swords.
Now take from me the last shell of my words,
The empty skull, and show me a true body.

2

Mute, inexhaustible music, sweet and mad appalling-lyre,
Machine of destiny, enigma, Sphinx!
Hand, lip, life, limb wander your lunar fire
Lost in impenetrable gleaming subtlety.
Your breast—an echoing cithern of black glass;
A holdless precipice, a ladder without rungs
For suffocating rapture—sheer
Vertical cords Apollo's brazen touch
Alone can find: none other wakes
That diamond music. Avid, raving Sun,
Lewd, leonine,
Beat into adamant your meteor dark.
That obstinate anvil, equally, refracts
The cruel, deft and delicate hammer-pulse
To Vulcan clangor—rings
All song to dust. Or else,
Abyss of silence, orchestrates
All bare and bleeding hells.

The dahlia's crisp and somber
Sun and bitter scent,
Black blood and serpentine
Of leaf and stem—the
Dark marriage, Pluto, Proserpina.

O tongueless terror, solitary bell,
Devouring mouth, unborn, undying Youth,
Time you devour—have ever undermined
The last, lean, anguished, agonistic ground
On which Odysseus, Theseus, Herakles,
Faust, Apollonius, every monster or mage,
In desperate, sick and self-exhausting pride
Might stand and still contrive
Against your cheating magic irony—
You the undoing before it can begin,
The never of all their nightmare, all the absurd,
Blind and baroque, laborious suicide
For which, with wonderful tokens, they were born.

Firm be your sight
Ever before my eyes:
You are the Eye that sees
Yourself by your own light.

The drenching gaze of god, of marigold eyes,
All calm and all caprice, Edenic wantonness,
Empties to piercing void in whom they light upon
All thought, all faculty. The tawny mane
Of raveling hair, like gold, like camphor, shakes
A pollen of fresh iridescences
Over the lintel of nervate, warm obsidian,
The shoulders' sweet and solemn, brute and tender span.

Your back is like the secretive lapse and pull
Of wide and sinewy waters. And the firm,
Heavy, elusive loins, mute bell,
Girt with a chain of iron, a shield of polished iron.
The svelte and lusty body subtly bloomed

As if (white-hot) with ash; that silk astringency
Stained at a vine of hair with maddening ichor—
A subtle serpent, tender, gleaming, harsh
With the deep rut of lilt and lightning fire.

A bolt of thunder rises from beneath
The earth, root of the underworld,
Glittering with rigid and relentless bane,
Volcanic, venomous, wielded by Death's
Cold, all-reversing flame—
Satin with freshness like a young and hard blue rose.

Those doors, those vulcan mouths,
Orpheus, dumb horror-stricken harp, affront: Eurydice
(Springtime Proserpina, Ceres) you seek in vain
Beneath the sun or looking back to see
A scatheless image of immortality:
This judgment only if it weigh, bow down the soul
Drenched in the scorching black roke of the bull
Inherits heaven's unfading flowers, the flowering earth.

Terrible luxury, that dour and dark divide:
Black rose, indigo noose, blue satin brazier
Of subterranean fire—the serpent cave
Pulsing and glittering:
Too close and monster-sweet simplicity.

The dizzying maelstrom's void and valsing walls,
Magnetic drag and drive of spinning steel,
Rock, reel, climb, comb, tower and overtower:
Whelming and overwhelming, floorless deeps
Mine, undermine, breath, speech, mind, memory.

What sorrows dumb from the beginning of the world
And dumb for ever, knife always buried first
And hidden in our own heart—
Unfrontiered tenderness and crime
Here, here in the fathomless heart,
Cry (nectar, venom, Angel, Demon), laugh
So terribly out loud!

3

Wordless: skull, rose;
Bull, meteor;
The singing bone.

A thousand lions
Roar like a sun.
The thunderbolt,
His blinding laugh.

A cup of blood
Drinks and drinks up the heart.

ACROBAT

His mind broods a black diagram,
Pungent like marigold,
Silken like calcined bone,
Blooming with iron and velvet, dumb
Magic, eyeless thorns.

Who dares the calm machine?
So calm, its knives not open not even smiles,
No Cupid-lip of wound;
But blossoming staves and naves,
Leap to a pyramid of expert joys,
Inverted, inside out and back to front,
Static, ecstatic, deft and elegant.

Here flowers the timeless angel, laughing,
Laughing like the Sun.

H.D. (HILDA DOOLITTLE)

Hilda Doolittle (1886–1961) was born and raised in the Moravian town
of Bethlehem, Pennsylvania. She attended Bryn Mawr, where she met
Marianne Moore, William Carlos Williams, and Ezra Pound. Both

Williams and Pound became close friends; H.D. and Pound were briefly engaged. Pound remained her friend and mentor after the engagement ended; and his encouragement that H.D. study the poetry, myths, and culture of the past (especially of the Greek, Roman, and Christian past) became a crucial factor in her later writing, which draws richly (and with great intellectual and spiritual integrity) on ancient religious traditions and archetypes.

In 1911 H.D. left America for England, where she married the poet Richard Aldington and gave birth to a daughter (who was not his); the marriage ended in 1919. H.D.'s lifelong lesbian companion after that was Bryher (Winifred Ellerman), her great love; Bryher adopted H.D.'s daughter, Perdita, and they eventually moved to Switzerland. H.D.'s many books—increasingly celebrated by feminists all over the world—include poetry, translations, a novel, some mystic epigrams on consciousness and transformation, and a play. Jane Hirshfield writes eloquently of H.D. in her anthology *Women in Praise of the Sacred,* stating that the task she set for herself was "finding a way to make of the smoking ruined walls (of modern civilization) a temple open to the spiritual energies of past and present."

THE MYSTERIES

Renaissance Choros

Dark
days are past
and darker days draw near;
darkness on this side,
over there
threatens the spirit
like massed hosts
a sheer
handful
of thrice-doomed spearsmen;
enemy this side,
enemy a part
of hill
and mountain-crest

and under-hill;
nothing before of mystery,
nothing past,
only the emptiness,
pitfall of death,
terror,
the flood,
the earthquake,
stormy ill;
then voice within the turmoil,
that slight breath
that tells as one flower may
of winter past
(that kills
with Pythian bow,
the Delphic pest;)
one flower,
slight voice,
reveals
all holiness
with
"peace
be still."

    from The Mysteries

Amen,
only just now,

my heart-shell
breaks open,

though long ago, the phoenix,
your *bennu* bird

dropped a grain,
as of scalding wax;

there was fragrance, burnt incense,
myrtle, aloes, cedar;

the Kingdom is a Tree
whose roots bind the heart-husk

to earth,
after the ultimate grain,

lodged in the heart-core,
has taken its nourishment.

From "The Walls Do Not Fall"

TRIBUTE TO THE ANGELS

[29]

We have seen her
the world over,
Our Lady of the Goldfinch,
Our Lady of the Candelabra,

Our Lady of the Pomegranate,
Our Lady of the Chair;

we have seen her, an empress,
magnificent in pomp and grace,

and we have seen her
with a single flower

or a cluster of garden-pinks
in a glass beside her;

we have seen her snood
drawn over her hair,

or her face set in profile
with the blue hood and stars;

we have seen her head bowed down
with the weight of a domed crown,

or we have seen her, a wisp of a girl
trapped in a golden halo;

we have seen her with arrow, with doves
and a heart like a valentine;

we have seen her in fine silks imported
from all over the Levant,

and hung with pearls brought
from the city of Constantine;

we have seen her sleeve
of every imaginable shade

of damask and figured brocade;
it is true,

the painters did very well by her;
it is true, they never missed a line

of the suave turn of the head
or subtle shade of lowered eye-lid

or eye-lids half-raised; you find
her everywhere (or did find),

in cathedral, museum, cloister,
at the turn of the palace stair.

[35]
So she must have been pleased with us,
who did not forego our heritage

at the grave-edge;
she must have been pleased

with the straggling company of the brush and quill
who did not deny their birthright;

she must have been pleased with us,
for she looked so kindly at us

under her drift of veils,
and she carried a book.

[36]
Ah (you say), this is Holy Wisdom,
Santa Sophia, the SS of the *Sanctus Spiritus,*

so by facile reasoning, logically
the incarnate symbol of the Holy Ghost;

your Holy Ghost was an apple-tree
smouldering—or rather now burgeoning

with flowers; the fruit of the Tree?
this is the new Eve who comes

clearly to return, to retrieve
what she lost the race,

given over to sin, to death;
she brings the Book of Life, obviously.

[37]
This is a symbol of beauty (you continue),
she is Our Lady universally,

I see her as you project her,
not out of place

flanked by Corinthian capitals,
or in a Coptic nave,

or frozen above the center door
of a Gothic cathedral;

you have done very well by her
(to repeat your own phrase),

you have carved her tall and unmistakable,
a hieratic figure, the veiled Goddess,

whether of the seven delights,
whether of the seven spear-points.

[38]

O yes—you understand, I say,
this is all most satisfactory,

but she wasn't hieratic, she wasn't frozen,
she wasn't very tall;

she is the Vestal
from the days of Numa,

she carries over the cult
of the *Bona Dea*,

she carries a book but it is not
the tome of the ancient wisdom,

the pages, I imagine, are the blank pages
of the unwritten volume of the new;

all you say, is implicit,
all that and much more;

but she is not shut up in a cave
like a Sibyl; she is not

imprisoned in leaden bars
in a colored window;

she is Psyche, the butterfly,
out of the cocoon.

[39]

But nearer than Guardian Angel
or good Daemon,

she is the counter-coin-side
of primitive terror;

she is not-fear, she is not-war,
but she is no symbolic figure

of peace, charity, chastity, goodness,
faith, hope, reward;

she is not Justice with eyes
blindfolded like Love's;

I grant you the dove's symbolic purity,
I grant you her face was innocent

and immaculate and her veils
like the Lamb's Bride,

but the Lamb was not with her,
either as Bridegroom or Child;

her attention is undivided,
we are her bridegroom and lamb;

her book is our book; written
or unwritten, its pages will reveal

a tale of a Fisherman,
a tale of a jar or jars,

the same—different—the same attributes,
different yet the same as before.

DAG HAMMARSKJÖLD

Dag Hammarskjöld was born in Jönköping, Sweden, in 1905 and died near Ndola, Northern Rhodesia, on September 18, 1961, in an airplane crash while flying to negotiate a cease-fire between United Nations and Katanga forces.

The son of the Swedish prime minister during World War I, Hammarskjöld studied law and economics at the universities of Uppsala and Stockholm. He was the undersecretary of the Swedish department of finance from 1936 to 1945. In 1946 he entered the foreign ministry as financial adviser; in 1951 he was elected the vice chairman of the Swedish delegation to the United Nations; and in 1953 he was elected secretary general of the United Nations, a post he held with immense integrity and distinction until his death.

Widely read in poetry and religious philosophy of many kinds, Hammarskjöld translated the poetry of St. John Perse into Swedish. The book *Markings,* which made his spiritual reputation and established him as one of the few authentic mystics in modern times to have also served in public life, was left behind in manuscript and published only after his death. He described it as a "sort of white book concerning my negotiations with myself and with God." His homosexuality was a well-known "secret" and occasions some of his most moving meditations on the nature of divine-human love. *Markings,* from which the following excerpts are taken, is characterized throughout by unsentimental honesty, passion for the Absolute, and an unwavering commitment to serve God in everyday life.

Two old inklings, the far-reaching significance of which I have only recently perceived.

> Through the senses,
> But beyond them.
> Near,
> Even though far off.
> The look a shy caress,
> As their eyes met in complete understanding.

And:
The Lover desires the perfection of the Beloved—which requires, among other things, the liberation of the Beloved from the Lover.

. . .

When you have reached the point where you no longer expect a response, you will at last be able to give in such a way that the other is able to receive, and be grateful. When Love has matured and, through a dissolution of the self into light, become a radiance, then shall the Lover be liberated from dependence upon the Beloved, and the Beloved also made perfect by being liberated from the Lover.

10.5.58

> Fading beeches, bright against
> a dark storm-cloud.
> Wind rips up the forest-pond's

steel-gray water.
On the earth between bloodstains
the tracks of deer.

Silence shatters to pieces
the mind's armor,
leaving it naked before
Autumn's clear eye.

4.10.58

In the faith which is "God's marriage to the soul," you are *one* in
    God, and
God is wholly in you,
just as, for you, He is wholly in all you meet.
With this faith, in prayer you descend into yourself to meet the
    Other,
in the steadfastness and light of this union,
see that all things stand, like yourself, alone before God.
and that each of your acts is an act of creation, conscious, because
    you are a human being with human responsibilities, but governed,
    nevertheless, by the power beyond human consciousness which
    has created man.
You are liberated from things, but you encounter in them an
    experience which has the purity and clarity of revelation.
In the faith which is "God's marriage to the soul," *everything,*
    therefore, has a meaning.
So live, then, that you may use what has been put into your
    hand. . . .

7.29.59

Humility is just as much the opposite of self-abasement as it is of
self-exaltation. To be humble is *not to make comparisons.* Secure in its
reality, the self is neither better nor worse, bigger nor smaller, than
anything else in the universe. It *is*—is nothing, yet at the same time
one with everything. It is in this sense that humility is absolute self-
effacement.

To be nothing in the self-effacement of humility, yet, for the sake of the task, to embody *its* whole weight and importance in your bearing, as the one who has been called to undertake it. To give to people, works, poetry, art, what the self can contribute, and to take, simply and freely, what belongs to it by reason of its identity. Praise and blame, the winds of success and adversity, blow over such a life without leaving a trace or upsetting its balance.

Toward this, so help me, God—

8.4.59

To have humility is to experience reality, not *in relation to ourselves,* but in its sacred independence. It is to see, judge, and act from the point of rest in ourselves. Then, how much disappears, and all that remains falls into place.

In the point of rest at the center of our being, we encounter a world where all things are at rest in the same way. Then a tree becomes a mystery, a cloud a revelation, each man a cosmos of whose riches we can only catch glimpses. The life of simplicity is simple, but it opens to us a book in which we never get beyond the first syllable.

12.25.55

In a dream I walked with God through the deep places of creation; past walls that receded and gates that opened, through hall after hall of silence, darkness and refreshment—the dwelling place of souls acquainted with light and warmth—until, around me, was an infinity into which we all flowed together and lived anew, like the rings made by raindrops falling upon wide expanses of calm dark waters.

MARGUERITE YOURCENAR

Marguerite Yourcenar (1903–87) was one of the most distinguished French writers of the century. On March 6, 1891, Yourcenar took her place in literary history when she became the first female "immortal" admitted to the French Academy since its founding in 1635.

Yourcenar was born Marguerite de Crayencour on June 8, 1903. Her mother died shortly after her birth and Yourcenar spent her childhood traveling with her wealthy father. While still in her teens she published two books privately—*The Gardens of Chimeras* and *The Gods Are Not Dead*—and chose Yourcenar, an anagram of her birth name, as her pen name.

In 1929 she published her first major work, *Alexis,* in which a homosexual married man writes to his wife about why he must leave her and their child and pursue the truth of his identity. In the 1930s Yourcenar came to terms with her own lesbianism. In 1937 she met Grace Frick, an American college professor, who remained her lifelong collaborator and translator until Frick's death in 1979. A series of magnificent mature works followed from the emotional and material security that Grace Frick provided her—*Oriental Studies* (1938), *Coup de Grace* (1939), and her masterpieces *Memoirs of Hadrian* (1951), *The Abyss* (1968), and *What Eternity* (1988, published after her death).

Yourcenar's mind and spirit were ceaselessly curious about mystical reality; in her last years she took the bodhisattva vows of Mahayana Buddhism. In her extraordinary impersonation of the hedonistic mystic Emperor Hadrian, she has left us an unforgettable portrait of a homosexual intelligence that hungers to know and experience everything without mask or evasion, while being open to the noblest forms of love and all levels of mystery. The following excerpts are all from *Memoirs of Hadrian.*

FREEDOM AND SUBMISSION

There is but one thing in which I feel superior to most men: I am freer, and at the same time more compliant, than they dare to be. Nearly all of them fail to recognize their due liberty, and likewise their true servitude. They curse their fetters, but seem sometimes to find them matter for pride. Yet they pass their days in vain license, and do not know how to fashion for themselves the lightest yoke. For my part, I have sought liberty more than power, and power only because it can lead to freedom. What interested me was not a philosophy of the free man (all who try that have proved tiresome), but a technique: I hoped to discover the hinge where our will meets and moves with destiny, and where discipline strengthens, instead of restraining, our nature. Understand clearly that here is no question of harsh Stoic will, which you value too high, nor of some mere abstract choice or refusal, which grossly affronts the conditions of our universe, this solid whole, compounded as it is of objects and bodies. No, I have dreamed of a more secret acquiescence, or of a more supple response. Life was to me a horse to whose motion one yields, but only after having trained the animal to the utmost. Since everything is finally a decision of the mind, however slowly and imperceptibly made, and involves also the body's assent, I strove to attain by degrees to that state of liberty, or of submission, which is almost pure. In this effort gymnastics helped, and dialectics aided me, too. . . .

But it was to the liberty of submission, the most difficult of all, that I applied myself most strenuously. I determined to make the best of whatever situation I was in; during my years of dependence my subjection lost its portion of bitterness, and even ignominy, if I learned to accept it as a useful exercise. Whatever I had I chose to have, obliging myself only to possess it totally, and to taste the experience to the full. Thus the most dreary tasks were accomplished with ease as long as I was willing to give myself to them. Whenever an object repelled me, I made it a subject of study, ingeniously compelling myself to extract from it a motive for enjoyment. If faced with something unforeseen or near cause for despair, like an ambush or a storm at sea, after all measures for the safety of others had been taken, I strove to welcome this hazard, to rejoice in whatever it brought me of the new and unexpected, and thus without shock the ambush or the tempest was incorporated into my plans, or my thoughts. Even in the throes of my worst disaster, I have seen a moment when sheer exhaustion reduced some part of the horror of the experience, and when I made the defeat a thing of my own in being willing to accept it. If ever I am to undergo torture (and illness will doubtless see to that) I cannot be sure of maintaining the impassiveness of a Thrasea, but I shall at least have the resource of resigning myself to my cries. And it is in such a way, with a mixture of reserve and of daring, of submission and revolt carefully concerted, of extreme demand and prudent concession, that I have finally learned to accept myself.

AFTER ANTINOUS'S SUICIDE

I have done all they say to do. I have waited, and sometimes I have prayed. *Audivi voces divinas* [I have heard divine voices]. . . . The light-headed Julia Balbilla believed that she heard the mysterious voice of Memnon at dawn; I have listened for the night's faintest sounds. I have used the unctions of oil and essence of roses which attract the shades; I have set out the bowl of milk, the handful of salt, the drop of blood, supports of their former existence. I have lain down on the marble pavement of the small sanctuary; the light of the stars made its way through the openings of the wall, producing reflections here and there, strange, pale gleams. I have recalled to myself the orders whispered by the priests in the ear of the dead, and the itinerary written on the tomb: *And he will recognize the way. . . . And the guardians of the threshold will let him pass. . . . And he will come and go around those who love him for millions of days. . . .* Sometimes, after long intervals, I have thought to feel the slight stir of an approach, a touch as light as the contact of eyelashes and warm as the hollow of a hand. *And the shade of Patroclus appears at Achilles' side. . . .* I shall never know if that warmth, that sweetness, did not emanate simply from deep within me, the last efforts of a man struggling against solitude and the cold of night. But the question, which arises also in the presence of our living loves, has ceased to interest me now; it matters little to me whether the phantoms whom I evoke come from the limbo of my memory or from that of another world. My soul, if I possess one, is made of the same substance as are these specters; this body with swollen hands and livid nails, this sorry mass almost half dissolved, this sack of ills, of desires and dreams, is hardly more solid or consistent than a shade. I differ from the dead only in my faculty to suffocate some moments longer; in one sense their existence seems to me more assured than my own. Antinous and Plotina are at least as real as myself.

Meditation upon death does not teach one how to die; it does not make the departure more easy, but ease is no longer what I seek. Beloved boy, so willful and brooding, your sacrifice will have enriched not my life but my death. Death's approach reestablishes between us a kind of close complicity: the living beings who surround me, my devoted if sometimes importunate servitors, will never know how little the world interests the two of us now. . . .

I try now to observe my own ending: So far the modifications are as external as those to which time and inclement weather subject any edifice, leaving its architecture and basic material unaltered; I sometimes think that through the crevices I see and touch upon the indestructible foundation, the rock eternal. I am what I always was; I am dying without essential change. At first view the robust child of the gardens in Spain and the ambitious officer regaining his tent and shaking the snowflakes from his shoulders seem both as thoroughly obliterated as I shall be when I shall have gone through the funeral fire; but they are still there; I am inseparable from those parts of myself. The man who howled his grief upon a dead body has not ceased to wail in some corner of my being, in spite of the superhuman, or perhaps subhuman calm into which I am entering already; the voyager immured within the ever sedentary invalid is curious about death because it spells departure. That force which once was I seems still capable of actuating several more lives, or of raising up whole worlds. If by miracle some centuries were suddenly to be added to the few days now left to me I would do the same things over again, even to committing the same errors; I would frequent the same Olympian heights and even the same Infernos. Such a conclusion is an excellent argument in favor of the utility of death, but at the same time it inspires certain doubts as to death's total efficacity.

GOD BECAME MAN

One evening in Osroes' tent, during a feast given in my honor, I observed among the women and long-eyelashed pages a naked, emaciated man who sat utterly motionless. His eyes were wide open, but he seemed to see nothing of that confusion of acrobats and dancers, or those dishes laden with viands. I addressed him through my interpreter but he deigned no reply, for this was indeed a sage. His disciples, however, were more loquacious; these pious beggars came from India, and their master belonged to the powerful caste of Brahmans. I gathered that his meditations led him to believe that the whole universe is only a tissue of illusion and error; for him self-denial, renunciation, death were the sole means of escape from this changing flood of forms whereon, on the contrary, our Heraclitus had willingly been borne along. Beyond the world of the senses he hoped to rejoin the sphere of the purely divine, that unmoving firmament of which Plato, too, had dreamed.

I got some inkling, therefore, in spite of the bungling of my inter-preters, of conceptions not unlike those of certain of our philoso-phers, but expressed by this Indian with more absolute finality. He had reached the state where nothing was left, except his body, to separate him from intangible deity, without substance or form, and with which he would unite; he had resolved to burn himself alive that next morning. Osroes invited me to the solemnity. A pyre of fragrant woods was prepared; the man leaped into it and disappeared without one cry. His disciples gave no sign of sorrow; for them it was not a funeral ceremony.

I pondered these things far into the night which followed. There I lay on a carpet of finest wool on the floor of a tent hung with gleam-ing brocades. A page massaged my feet. From without came the few sounds of that Asiatic night: the whispering of slaves at my door; the soft rustle of a palm, and Opramoas' snores behind a curtain; the stamp of a horse's hoof; from farther away, in the women's quarters, the melancholy murmur of a song. All of that had left the Brahman unmoved. In his veritable passion of refusal he had given himself to the flames as a lover to a bed. He had cast off everything and every-one, and finally himself, like so many garments which served to con-ceal from him that unique presence, the invisible void which was his all.

I felt myself to be different, and ready for wider choice. Austerity, renunciation, negation were not wholly new to me; I had been drawn to them young (as is almost always the case), at the age of twenty. I was even younger when a friend in Rome took me to see the aged Epictetus in his hovel in the Suburra, shortly before Domit-ian ordered his exile. As in his slave days, when a brutal master failed to extract from him even one cry, though the beating broke his leg, so now grown old and frail he was patiently bearing the slow torments of gravel; yet he seemed to me to enjoy a liberty which was almost divine. His crutches, his pallet, the earthenware lamp and wooden spoon in its vessel of clay were objects of admiration to me, the simple tools of a pure life.

But Epictetus gave up too many things, and I had been quick to observe that nothing was more dangerously easy for me than mere re-nunciation. This Indian, more logically, was rejecting life itself. There was much to learn from such pure-hearted fanatics, but on the condition of turning the lesson from the meaning originally intended. These sages were trying to rediscover their god above and beyond the ocean of forms, and to reduce him to that quality of the unique, intangible, and incorporeal which he had foregone in the very act of becoming universal. I perceived differently my relations with the divine. I could see myself as seconding the deity in his effort to give form and order to a world, to develop and multiply its convolutions, extensions, and complexities. I was one of the segments of the wheel, an aspect of that unique force caught up in the multiplicity of things; I was eagle and bull, man and swan, phallus and brain all together, a Proteus who is also a Jupiter.

And it was at about this time that I began to feel myself divine. Don't misunderstand me: I was still, and more than ever, the same man, fed by the fruits and flesh of earth, and giving back to the soil their unconsumed residue, surrendering to sleep with each revolution of the stars, and nearly beside myself when too long deprived of the warming presence of love. My strength and agility, both of mind and of body, had been carefully maintained by purely human disciplines. What more can I say except that all that was lived as godlike experience? The dangerous experiments of youth were over, and its haste to seize the passing hour. At forty-eight I felt free of impatience, assured of myself, and as near perfection as my nature would permit, in fact, eternal. Please realize that all this was wholly on the plane of the intellect; the delirium, if I must use the term, came later on. I was god, to put it simply, because I was man.

ELSA GIDLOW

Elsa Gidlow (1898–1986), like Lewis Thompson, is one of the great unknown—or relatively unknown—modern gay mystics. Born in Yorkshire, England, she emigrated with her family to Canada in her childhood. Later, she moved to the United States, where she worked as a freelance journalist. In 1921 she edited *Pearson's Magazine* in New York. In the 1920s she moved to San Francisco, where she later created her famous home, Druid Heights, on the top of Mount Tamalpais among the majestic redwoods overlooking the Pacific. She lived the latter part of her life with Alan and

Jano Watts, cofounders of the Society for Comparative Philosophy. Elsa wrote poetry for over seventy years, a selection of which is available in *Sapphic Songs: The Love Poetry of Elsa Gidlow (Naiad).* She also wrote *Ask No Man's Pardon: The Philosophical Significance of Being Lesbian, Making for Meditation, Shattering the Mirror,* and shortly before her death in 1986 the completed autobiography *Elsa, I Come with My Songs* (all published by Booklegger).

Like Whitman, Elsa Gidlow sings "the body electric"; drawing on her own increasingly ecstatic and holy experience of sexual passion, and she has written some of the most explosive "tantric" poems in any language. For many modern seekers, she is a radical pioneer of a whole new adventure of sexual spiritual freedom, in the name and with the empowering grace of the Divine Mother.

HYMN TO A MYSTERY

Your Woman Flower blooms
To my touch
     opens
To Probing kiss; I, bee
To its honey, plunge
To being's core.

Warm, convolute,
What marvel of function;
Sepal, petal; part
Them, find stamen
Stigma stiff to finger,
The cryptic ovary
Secreting nectar.

Phoenix flesh that
Living, dies,
And dies
To live again
In ecstasy.

Warm Woman Flower
Apotheosis

Of all life's cooler blooms,
On what altar with
What mass shall I
Celebrate
Your mystery?

REGION OF NO BIRDS

Where earth groans with earthquake,
I know you.
Where the waters boil black
And the dragons are,
You are immersed in me.
Beyond pleasure, where terror is kissed
And the small I's die,
In that region of no birds,
One does not speak prettily of love.

IN THE BLAZE OF LOVE

In the blaze of love it is known:
We are particles each of each
We are cells of the Mother of all
We cannot be cast off
From sister cells or from Her.

Her breath is the breath of our lungs
Her heartbeat times our own;
Where She is winged we fly,
We swim with Her dolphins; wind
through rocks with Her jeweled snakes;
We bloom in Her million flowers;
We grow in Her ancient trees
And die in a night with Her moths.

In rock we wait for Her
Dreaming of fin or flesh,
Of the awful miracle
Of human heart and mind.

In the blaze of love it is known,
No being, no life is born,
Exists, or dies alone.

ORGASM

Two in collusion
Plotting—simply—pleasure—
A playing together.

We could not know it for the time
The loin's explosion would beget
Volcanoes.

So still the dawn
Quivering on the rim of day;
Your waking touch invading
Dreams.

Sleep: co-conspirator—
No sentry at love's
Gate.

Gentle, gentle
The double kiss:
Mouth vulva open.

In mutual bliss
Each into each
Merging.

Dawn's furnace reddens;
The blood's drums mutter.
Enthused
No longer self-possessing,
As Maenads of Bacchus, we,
Possessed.

Enter, O, enter
The inmost Holy Place;
At the altar, self-anointing

And anointed, dance
Your dance.

Till flesh, transfused
With burning breath becomes
Veil of the Goddess; and
Earth heaves.

The fiery lava floods;
We whirl with the stars,
No cell of self un-
exploded.

LOVE IN AGE

All bliss known on earth I have found
In you, Woman, Lover-Beloved;
Beyond reason loved; beyond care
Of self or safety in the passionate years
When youth must find—cost no matter—
Haven or Heaven.
      And now
        in age
Your being mirrors the Divinity.

You have taken me beyond transport
To nether worlds where no man,
Though brave, travels willing (but, quaking,
To regain wife or life)
      shown me
The fury figure of Kali death—dancing on
My ravished hopes;
      yet, from them,
from their silt and muck
      reborn
What nourishes the soul.

Woman, so gentle in my arms
Loving, you have opened to me
Fierce, my own dark heart

And found therein and to me reflected
My source of light.

Here on this bed holding you
In passion-shattered wonder, lip to lip
Limb twined with limb
In oblivion of Thee and Me,
Breathing our mingled sweat,
Juices spilled out
        mutually anointing

Here on this bed, holding you
So human in your need
        (and knowing mine)
Miraculous, the human veil is rent.

Lover-beloved, Woman
Small and strong in my arms
        I know in you
The Goddess
        Mystery
            fecund Emptiness
From which all fullness comes
And universes flower.

WHAT IF?—

(THE MILLION-AND-FIRST MEDITATION AND THE LAST)

What if we smashed the mirrors
And saw our true face?
What if we left the Sacred Books to the worms
And found our True Mind?
What if we burned the wooden Buddhas?
Gave the stone Buddhas back to the mountains?
Dispersed the gurus with a great laugh
And discovered the path we had always been on?
What if we told the Saviors
We were saved from our first breath
And the healers—If you could heal yourselves

All would be healed?
What if we washed clean of Authority's ordure
And smelled the fresh smell of our own bodies?
What if, as Eve eating the Fruit of the Tree of Knowledge,
We knew the "Patriarchal Curse" a mere natural thunder
Bringing Eden a cleansing rain?
What if, in the lightning's flash
We saw there were

NO

Mirrors
Sacred Books
Buddhas
Gurus
Saviors
Healers
Authority
And Knowledge was standing stark under the sky
Feet naked to earth
Eyes there for whatever light falls.

What if—?

A CREED FOR FREE WOMEN*

*AND SUCH MEN AS FEEL HAPPY WITH IT.

I am.
I am from and of The Mother.
I am as I am.
Willfully harming none, none may question me.

As no free-growing tree serves another or requires to be served.
As no lion or lamb or mouse is bound or binds,
No plant or blade of grass nor ocean fish,
So I am not here to serve or be served.

I am Child of every Mother,
Mother of each daughter,
Sister of every woman,
And lover of whom I choose or chooses me.

Together or alone we dance Her Dance,
We do the work of The Mother.

She we have called Goddess for human comprehension.
She, the Source, never-to-be-grasped Mystery,
Terrible Cauldron, Womb,
Spinning out of her the unimaginably small
And the immeasurably vast—
Galaxies, worlds, flaming suns—
And our Earth, fertile with her beneficence,
Here, offering tenderest flowers.
(Yet flowers whose roots may split rock.)

I, we, Mothers, Sisters, Lovers,
Infinitely small out of her vastness,
Yet our roots too may split rock,
Rock of the rigid, the oppressive
In human affairs.

Thus is She
And being of Her
Thus am I.
Powered by Her,
As she gives, I may give,
Even of my blood and breath:
But none may require it;
And none may question me.

I am.
I am That I am.

AUDRE LORDE

Audre Lorde was born in New York in 1934, graduated from Hunter College, where she later became an English professor, and received her M.L.S. from Columbia. A poet, prose writer, and activist, Lorde was openly lesbian and throughout her work stressed the need for women everywhere to unite and heighten awareness of the sexual, political, and racial issues that confronted them. In *Zami: A New Spelling of My Name* (1982) Lorde expanded the definition of lesbianism to include women who center their lives emotionally around other women as well as women who share sexual intimacy with each other. In her collections of poetry, notably *Coal* (1976), *The Black Unicorn* (1978), and *Our Dead Behind Us* (1986), and in her great essay "Uses of the Erotic: The Erotic as Power," Audre Lorde affirms and celebrates her identity as a lesbian black woman, empowered by her sexuality and racial past and by the Divine Mother to stand for the denied and menaced inner richness of all exploited beings everywhere, and to praise the liberated human divine body, free at last from all prisons of patriarchal shame. The courage and emotional splendor of her work has inspired feminists everywhere. After her early death from cancer in 1992, her reputation and the sacred importance of her work continue to grow.

WOMAN FOREVER

I have always wanted to be both man and woman, to incorporate the strongest and richest parts of my mother and father within/into me—to share valleys and mountains upon my body the way the earth does in hills and peaks.

I would like to enter a woman the way any man can, and to be entered—to leave and to be left—to be hot and hard and soft all at the same time in the cause of our loving. I would like to drive forward and at other times to rest or be driven. When I sit and play in the waters of my bath I love to feel the deep inside parts of me, sliding and folded and tender and deep. Other times I like to fantasize the core of it, my pearl, a protruding part of me, hard and sensitive and vulnerable in a different way.

I have felt the age-old triangle of mother father child, with the "I" at its eternal core, elongate and flatten out into the elegantly strong triad of grandmother mother daughter, with the "I" moving back and forth flowing in either or both directions as needed.

Woman forever. My body, a living representation of other life older longer wiser. The mountains and valleys, trees, rocks. Sand and flowers and water and stone. Made in earth.

Speak earth and bless me with what is richest
make sky flow honey out of my hips
rigid as mountains
spread over a valley
carved out by the mouth of rain.

And I knew when I entered her I was
high wind in her forests hollow
fingers whispering sound
honey flowed
from the split cup
impaled on a lance of tongues
on the tips of her breasts on her navel
and my breath
howling into her entrances
through lungs of pain.

Greedy as herring-gulls
or a child
I swing out over the earth
over and over
again.

From "New York Head Shop and Museum"

THE EROTIC

The erotic functions for me in several ways, and the first is in the
power which comes from sharing deeply any pursuit with another
person. The sharing of joy, whether physical, emotional, psychic or intellectual, forms a bridge between the sharers which can be the basis
for understanding much of what is not shared between them, and
lessens the threat of their difference.

Another important way in which the erotic connection functions is
the open and fearless underlining of my capacity for joy. In the way
my body stretches to music and opens into response, hearkening to its
deepest rhythms, so every level upon which I sense also opens to the
erotically satisfying experience, whether it is dancing, building a
bookcase, writing a poem, examining an idea.

That self-connection shared is a measure of the joy which I know myself to be capable of feeling, a reminder of my capacity for feeling. And that deep and irreplaceable knowledge of my capacity for joy comes to demand from all of my life that it be lived within the knowledge that such satisfaction is possible, and does not have to be called marriage, nor god, nor an afterlife.

This is one reason why the erotic is so feared, and so often relegated to the bedroom alone, when it is recognized at all. For once we begin to feel deeply all the aspects of our lives, we begin to demand from ourselves and from our lives pursuits that they feel in accordance with that joy which we know ourselves to be capable of. Our erotic knowledge empowers us, becomes a lens through which we scrutinize all aspects of our existence, forcing ourselves to evaluate those aspects honestly in terms of their relative meaning within our lives. And this is a grave responsibility, projected from within each of us, not to settle for the convenient, the shoddy, the conventionally expected, nor the merely safe.

From "Uses of the Erotic: The Erotic as Power"

CALL

Holy ghost woman
stolen out of your name
Rainbow Serpent
whose faces have been forgotten
Mother loosen my tongue or adorn me
with a lighter burden
Aido Hwedo* is coming.

On worn kitchen stools and tables
we are piecing our weapons together
scraps of different histories
do not let us shatter
any altar
she who scrubs the capitol toilets, listening
is our sister's youngest daughter

Aido Hwedo: The Rainbow Serpent; also a representation of all ancient divinities who must be worshiped but whose names and faces have been lost in time.

gnarled Harriet's anointed
you have not been without honor
even the young guerrilla has chosen
yells as she fires into the thicket
Aido Hwedo is coming.

I have written your names on my cheekbone
dreamed your eyes   flesh my epiphany
most ancient goddesses   hear me
enter
I have not forgotten your worship
nor my sisters
nor the sons of my daughters
my children watch for your print
in their labors
and they say Aido Hwedo is coming.

I am a Black woman   turning
mouthing your name as a password
through seductions   self-slaughter
and I believe in the holy ghost
mother
in your flames beyond our vision
blown light through the fingers of women
enduring   warring
sometimes outside your name
we do not choose all our rituals
Thandi Modise   winged girl of Soweto
brought fire back home in the snout of a mortar
and passes the word from her prison cell whispering
Aido Hwedo is coming.

Rainbow Serpent who must not go
unspoken
I have offered up the safety of separations
sung the spirals of power
and what fills the spaces
before power unfolds or flounders

in desirable nonessentials
I am a Black woman   stripped down
and praying
my whole life has been an altar
worth its ending
and I say Aido Hwedo is coming.

I may be a weed in the garden
of women I have loved
who are still
trapped in their season
but even they shriek
as they rip burning gold from their skins
Aido Hwedo is coming.

We are learning by heart
what has never been taught
you are my given   fire-tongued
Oya   Seboulisa   Mawu   Afrekete
and now we are mourning our sisters
lost to the false hush of sorrow
to hardness and hatchets and childbirth
and we are shouting

Rosa Parks and Fannie Lou Hamer
Assata Shakur and Yaa Asantewa
my mother and Winnie Mandela are singing
in my throat
the holy ghosts' linguist
one iron silence broken
Aido Hwedo is calling
calling
your daughters are named
and conceiving
Mother loosen my tongue
or adorn me
with a lighter burden
Aido Hwedo is coming.

Aido Hwedo is coming.

Aido Hwedo is coming.

HILDEGARD ELSBERG

Hildegard Elsberg was born in Germany in 1906 and died in early February 1997. Active in Loheland gymnastics as a child, she took majors in language and performing arts, focusing on Laban movement and modern dance with Kurt Joos. Later, she earned a degree in physiotherapy and found her understanding of the body and its role in human transformation dramatically influenced by the intuitive approach of inquiry at the Elsa Gindler school.

In 1937, Hildegard Elsberg left Hitler's Germany for India, where she taught dance and music in Catholic schools in South India and spent several summers at the feet of Ramana Maharshi in his ashram at Tiruvanamalai. In 1947 she emigrated to the United States, where she quickly established a practice integrating Eastern and Western principles of psychospiritual awareness through the body. During the next decades, she taught with Alan Watts, cooperated with Fritz Kunkel at his Institute in Los Angeles, and worked with Jungians Helen Luke and Robert Johnson, and the Guild for Psychological Studies.

Elsberg's extraordinarily pure, fierce, clairvoyant mystic poetry has been published only in very limited private editions; the great majority of it was written during a decade of almost total retreat from the world (1975–85) and has the seared authority of authentic spiritual solitude. Elsberg wrote of herself, "My life is a sacred road to which I pay a natural reverence. I have been born with the genes of self-inquiry . . . and strangely life or God has answered me in this vein. It is a mystery to be born just as it is a mystery to die and between these two mysteries life itself is a mystery, life itself is sacred."

MATER

Mother, mère, from your source
you come floating
on your mother-of-pearl ship

offering
your ample moon-breast, you,
mother-lode,
la mer, your
mother, our tides,
periods of blood, milk and
father-admission, material
womb, sprung-silk-well, matrix.

Mothers enter the earth,
walk the earth, plant the earth,
are earth planted. You
become what you plant,
wheat, corn, rice, you
anciently nourish, you
become rivers of milk for
us, your children. You
sit, at each life-station
centrally planted, the tentpole.

Mater, in your skirts blossom
child-buds, sons, daughters,
your skirts rustle
with sobs and laughter.
Your hair is wet with
death-tracing tears, your face
radiates gifts of birth.
Your bud-children harvest
fruits of their initiations,
you too, Mutter, ripen, become
all in one: food, nimbus, Madonna.

THE ALTAR

At what altar, I Am, am I bidden to sacrifice?

Here, on the earth, until today an anvil
on which you forged, at my command, your form,
and also in this world a foothold for your coined work.

Begin by weeping into the sacrificial mold libations of
your tears, at having to surrender the
just accomplished shape you knew yourself to be,
and by which too, awhile, you were known of a few men.

Strew grains, more generous than those garnered in
the fields of this wide earth.
Pour precious oil of patience upon the altar slab;
put forth your hand, like Milarepa that mountainous sage
and suffer that to be torn down again
and once again, which you built up
while serving life.

Is your peremptory demand, I Am, that I must offer
on the earth-stone form and anchor, grain and oil,
so that my person should permit a wider space for
your wise counsel to fulfill itself?

Your faithful brick I alone know where to fit
into the infinite temple-wall, somewhere between
the base, where all the crushed reside, and those
who have eaten earth for a long time—and
the dirges and the psalms, the Misereres and
light-emitting Hallelujahs.
I place the color of your chip in mine own mosaic,
the fragile thread spun forth from your frail life,
I know to weave in tapestry magnificent.

Your part is: trust and let and be assured.

SONG OF ANGELS III

Sword-carrier of justice
wings frosted by cold air of divine detachment,
before your implacable presence
our passionate life-blood is stayed,
our ardent pulse numb with terror.

Celestial strider, rider in glory,
pouring out vials, wisdom-filled;

parched fields of our comprehension ravaged gardens bereft,
their fruits of knowledge fallen, gnawed by the worm,
stretch wide beneath your dew.

You, planter of the heart-tree,
ruby on your holy forehead, perpetually plummeting
charity from your infinite perspectives,
by your fire melt, you, our floes,
grip, you, formidable, in piercing pity, those roots.

Angel of the great Turning,
meet at crossroads the voyager,
step in the way of a mountaineer, flung into spiraling descent,
who wring from themselves lonely return;
your glowing joy is their viaticum.

Majestic messenger from the land beyond the river,
you, of fierce mercy, by our hair,
from the bowels of our yearning, pull us across.
Blow on your resounding trumpet
splendor of sunrise in a new land.

BIBLIOGRAPHY

Boswell, John. *Christianity, Social Tolerance, and Homosexuality.* Chicago: Univ. of Chicago Press, 1976.

Carpenter, Edward. *Intermediate Types Among Primitive Folk: A Study in Social Revolution (1919).* New York: Arno Press, 1975.

Conner, Randolph P. *Blossom of Bone: Reclaiming the Connections Between Homoeroticism and the Sacred.* San Francisco: HarperSanFrancisco, 1993.

Conner, Randy P., David Sparks, and Mariya Sparks. *Cassell's Encyclopedia of Queer Myth, Symbol, and Spirit.* London: Cassell, 1997.

Downing, Christine. *Myths and Mysteries of Same-Sex Love.* New York: Continuum, 1989.

Eisler, Riane. *The Chalice and the Blade: Our History, Our Future.* San Francisco: Harper & Row, 1987.

———. *Sacred Pleasure.* San Francisco: HarperSanFrancisco, 1995.

Faderman, Lillian, ed. *Chloe Plus Olivia: An Anthology of Lesbian Literature from the 17th Century to the Present.* New York: Viking Penguin, 1994.

Hay, Harry. "Neither Boy Nor Girl: Reclaiming Our Ancient Gay Cultural and Spiritual Legitimacy; Third Gender." *RFD: A Country Journal for Gay Men Everywhere* 74 (1993).

Hopcke, Robert H. *Jung, Jungians, and Homosexuality.* Boston: Shambhala, 1989.

Hopcke, Robert H., K. L. Carrington, and S. Wirth, eds. *Same-Sex Love and the Path to Wholeness.* Boston: Shambhala, 1993.

Mariechild, Diane (with Marcelina Martin). *Lesbian Sacred Sexuality.* Oakland, CA: Wingbow Press, 1995.

Roscoe, Will. *The Zuni Man-Woman.* Albuquerque: University of New Mexico Press, 1991.

Roscoe, Will, ed. *Living the Spirit: A Gay American Anthology.* New York: St. Martin's Press, 1988.

Summers, Claude J., ed. *The Gay and Lesbian Literary Heritage: The Reader's Companion to the Writers and Their Works, from Antiquity to the Present.* New York: Henry Holt, 1995.

Thompson, Mark, ed. *Gay Spirit: Myth and Meaning.* New York: St. Martin's Press, 1987.

———. *Gay Soul: Finding the Heart of Gay Spirit and Nature.* San Francisco: HarperSanFrancisco, 1994.

Walker, Mitch. *Visionary Love: A Spirit of Gay Mythology.* San Francisco: Tree-roots Press, 1980.